An
Extravagant
HUNGER

ANNE ZIMMERMAN

An Extravagant HUNGER

THE PASSIONATE YEARS OF
M.F.K. FISHER

COUNTERPOINT
BERKELEY

Library of Congress Cataloging-in-Publication Data

Zimmerman, Anne, 1977-
An extravagant hunger : the passionate years of M.F.K. Fisher / Anne Zimmerman.
p. cm.
ISBN-13: 978-1-58243-804-7
ISBN-10: 1-58243-804-8
1. Fisher, M. F. K. (Mary Frances Kennedy), 1908-1992. 2. Authors, American—20th century—Biography. 3. Food writers—United States—Biography. I. Title.
PS3511.I7428Z99 2011
641'.092—dc22
[B]
2010030883

Jacket design by Gerilyn Attebery
Jacket art by Laura Parker
Interior design by Megan Jones Design
Printed in the United States of America

COUNTERPOINT
1919 Fifth Street
Berkeley, CA 94710

www.counterpointpress.com

Distributed by Publishers Group West

10 9 8 7 6 5 4 3 2 1

 ROBERT LESCHER

"We write to taste life twice, in the moment, and in retrospection."
—ANAÏS NIN

Contents

FOREWORD: Honeymoon

MARY FRANCES KENNEDY and Al Fisher boarded the RMS *Berengaria* in late September 1929, towing stacks of suitcases and wedding gifts: ribboned baskets of exotic fruits, gourmet chocolates, and flowers. The display, so ripe and fragrant, seemed especially extravagant amid the third-class steerage cabin and its hard sleeping berths.

Their cargo raised the suspicions of the passengers and crew. After the steward determined that Mary Frances and Al weren't famous—not writers or actors in disguise—he laughed, christening them "the honeymoon couple." Indeed, they were merely students, moving to France so that Al, twenty-seven, could begin working toward an advanced degree in literature. Mary Frances, twenty-one, had given little thought to what she would do so far from home. She certainly didn't know that in France she would launch an entirely different journey and begin to pen the rich, finely tuned prose that would help define modern food writing—and, decades later, still make taste buds tingle. For now, she was just another newlywed.

What had begun as a casual summer romance morphed into a quick engagement. After marrying in an Episcopal church in the Southern California town of San Gabriel, the couple's first extended days and nights were spent traveling by train from Los Angeles to New York. Their new life was all adventure and excitement, especially their stop in Dodge City, Kansas, where a boy strolled the platform calling, "Telegram for Mrs. Alfred Young Fisher!" Upon arriving in Manhattan, Mary Frances's final brush with familiarity was an afternoon of shopping and dinner with her aunt and cousin. Soon she was boarding the ship, standing with Al as the New York City skyline faded into oblivion.

As the *Berengaria* left the harbor, Mary Frances and Al knew only that France was a daring starting point. World War I had ended just a decade before, and the country had yet to recover economically or socially. What's more, the couple had a limited income and no place to live, and neither spoke much French. They couldn't anticipate how a life abroad would test their fledgling marriage.

She was pretty, tall and slim, with a round face, big eyes, and full lips. Her dark hair was frequently pulled back, perhaps because she wanted to appear older—and more sophisticated. Yet at a time when few women attended college, Mary Frances had been to three. She had almost always performed poorly: not because she wasn't intelligent but because she had never really tried. During a year at Occidental College shortly before she married, Mary Frances had flaunted her affinity for dances and parties.

Despite her love for fun, however, she never drank the bathtub gin that was poured, lukewarm, from fraternity boys' hip flasks. No, she wanted wine: "good chilled wines," she would later write. She was allowed to drink them occasionally at home, and she required them from her dates, even though she'd been warned that no boys would take her out if she continued to be so demanding.

She didn't care if the boys (or anyone at Occidental) liked her. She'd already set her sights on one man: a spindly poet with an angular face, timid smile, and light, wavy hair. Al Fisher's gangly arms and legs made him resemble an adolescent animal, but his dark poetry signaled an intensity and intellectualism that she found intriguing. And Al was wild about Mary Frances, pursuing her heatedly until he was confident she was his.

Uninspired by her education and desperate to avoid her parents' dutiful and restricted household, she took a calculated risk with Al. Did she love him? She thought she did. And she knew he would take her to France. Their shipboard accommodations, no matter how spare, heightened the drama. Mary Frances described third class as the "exciting, adventurous and smart thing to do . . . Part of the whole perfect scheme of things."

Many of their shipmates were emigrants. In a letter to her father, Rex Kennedy, the editor and publisher of the Whittier, California, *News,* Mary Frances reported "lots of Jews and Germans, and a few French, Serbian, Polish, two Hindus, and about five Americans" in their area of the vessel. There were rabbis, fan dancers, and a buxom Swedish woman who propositioned Al at the beginning of the trip, slipping him a piece of paper inscribed with her cabin number.

On the massive *Berengaria,* four thousand passengers could mingle, misbehave, eat, and find entertainment in the hundreds of rooms. Mary Frances and Al were tempted by movies, gambling, and a library stuffed with seemingly countless tomes. But she spent a large portion of the journey writing home to her family. The letters—two to three per day— were composed on creamy stationery embossed, in a deep royal blue, with CUNARD LINE. And they begin to trace the personality that would mold and steer Mary Frances as she developed into the premier chronicler of how and why we eat.

Some days she wrote to every family member: Rex, her mother Edith, and three siblings, all younger: Anne, Norah, and David. The Kennedy family was close. They were wealthy Midwesterners transplanted to California, and then to Whittier's conservative, largely Quaker enclave. Her letters to them were cheerful and descriptive. She told her family everything about the ship, how she and Al passed their time, whom they met, what they ate.

"The second day out was rough, really rough," she wrote. "[P]eople who didn't have sense enough to disappear hovered disconsolately near the rail. By wearing a hat over my ears and keeping my eyes on . . . [my] latest books, I retained my composure." Her descriptions of the ship's food, however, were vibrant and colorful: "The food is really very good," she told her family. "[N]ot scrumptious, but simply gobs of it." Following the lead of her parents, who had often described their dining out in great detail to their children, Mary Frances regaled her family with tales of a breakfast spread that included coffee, oranges, and a buffet of large muffins. There were kidney omelets and Yarmouth bloaters made from smoked and salted broiled herring. It's clear she wanted her family to picture the boundless buffet, just as she had pictured every restaurant dish her parents had described to her as a young girl.

At lunch, there was always a buffet to marvel over or a long sit-down meal of six or more courses. Cocktails were served before a multicourse dinner, followed by a fountain of liquors that helped them digest everything in their slowly expanding stomachs. She declared to her father that she and Al ate and drank with a "perfectly revolting relish."

They had come of age during the years of Prohibition. Although the consumption of alcohol was illegal in the United States, Mary Frances's father kept bottles of wine and sherry at home. While on the ship, Mary Frances relished not only drinking but boasting about it in her letters. To

Rex she wrote, "[W]e have drunk, gambled, and caroused . . . Instead of having only a cocktail, we've had that and liquor later and sometimes wine."

Though the couple kept to themselves during the early part of the day, they often gathered with shipmates for meals and entertainment in the afternoons and evenings. Mary Frances described one of their dining mates as a "fat, funny little old Englishwoman, wife of a sailor" that she and Al liked immensely. They were less fond of a "suspiciously well bred and languid" English woman and her daughter, who were embarrassed about traveling in third class. They were alternately entertained by, and weary of, a trio of rowdy young men from New York, and a "queer tall, beaked Englishman" named Major Baker, who was "like something out of a novel and a most perfect storyteller."

She recommended that the family gather to read her letters, explaining, "I simply can't tell every thing to each one of you, and I'm bulging at the sides with this and that—everything is so awfully new." She signed her letters "Dote," affectionate family shorthand for "Daughter."

Mary Frances had ached to escape California and her family, yet many of her letters offer meticulous information about how they could visit her in France. She told her mother, "[I]f I were you I would come Second [class] . . . for the trouble with Third would be the awfully steep and numerous flights of steps and the awful planks they quaintly call berths." The notes to Anne concerned clothes and accessories. "[B]ring lots of sweaters and skirts and coats to go over dresses and stay-on hats and warm stockings and low heeled shoes," for long days on the ship, Mary Frances instructed.

IN ALL OF the letters, Al is barely mentioned. He is a sidekick—next to her at dinner or the gambling table, or lounging dreamily beside her on deck. There are only occasional gushes of the love and romantic passion one might expect from a new bride. "We've had one argument," she wrote home, "about his not kneeling in church." The letter finishes with a confession that she and Al were "counting the days till next June," when her family might visit. Already, it seems, the two longed for familiar personalities to stoke their conversation—and adoration.

Al's letters were only slightly more forthcoming about the couple's early days of marriage. In a letter to Rex and Edith, Al said that Mary Frances did little but "read, rest, and write a few letters—and eat." He thought her "bounding appetite" was healthy, but remarked that "I've not been a husband long enough to know what is just right."

He was loath to proclaim too much happiness with his new bride: "It doesn't seem that two people are any happier than we are," he wrote, tempering his enthusiasm by adding, "but I guess this has happened to many people in the world over a period of years, and that they have always felt just the same." Did the realities of marriage differ from what he had expected?

The *Berengaria* had promised a romantic retreat, but despite their private room, the newly married couple's intimate moments had not been as frequent or as satisfying as she had hoped. A friend of Al's later claimed that Mary Frances had, turned out to be "not what [Al] wanted in bed at all." He had longed for Mary Frances. Once he had her as his bride, disinterest grew.

Still, Mary Frances wrote her mother that they were "bounding with vim and vigor" and that she "loved Al more every minute." It was the first of many sweeping statements Mary Frances would pen to mask the hurts Al would heap on her over the coming years. Her optimism was a healing tactic, and she hoped it would convince her family (and herself) that she was as happy as any newlywed should be.

As their days at sea drew to a close, Mary Frances wrote one last time to her mother. "I'm sorry it's the last day out," she wrote. The couple's arrival in Cherbourg, France, the next morning would bring new challenges and further travel: onward to Dijon, where Al would begin his studies. In Dijon, Mary Frances's life would change in many of the ways she had hoped—and many she had not. During her years in the country, Mary Frances would flourish, drinking coveted wines and eating epic meals ranging from the rustic to decadent.

Yet a careful study of numerous unpublished personal accounts and private papers, whose contents have helped shape this book, reveals that her writing about everyday culinary delights—whether in letters, journals, or in her various books—became a way to codify an occasionally lonely existence. By her thirty-sixth birthday, she would be divorced and widowed. She would experience the Great Depression and World War II from both sides of the ocean, and become an unwed mother who delighted in the mystery surrounding her daughter's parentage.

She would also create a literary persona, writing under the name M.F.K. Fisher. Her essays and books—such as *Serve It Forth, Consider the Oyster, How to Cook a Wolf, and The Gastronomical Me*—sprang from a voracious appetite that the *Berengaria* merely whetted.

Her writing would bind food, love, sex, the pleasure of eating well and reveling in the senses. Yet behind the beautiful descriptions of memorable meals there would be hardship and catastrophe. This understanding of life's inherent pleasures and agonies are the reason her work endured. And it all began in her childhood kitchen, amid boiling strawberry jam.

A Growing Appetite

M.F.K. FISHER BELIEVED that she could remember the first thing she tasted—not the first flavor of her life, but the bite that transformed her from a mere consumer of food to a connoisseur of tastes. "The first thing I remember tasting and then wanting to taste again," she wrote in *The Gastronomical Me*, "is the grayish-pink fuzz my grandmother skimmed from a spitting kettle of strawberry jam."

She was about four years old, and canning and preserving summer fruit was a ritual in the Kennedys' Southern California household. Her grandmother, Mary Frances Oliver Holbrook, who had moved in with the family, said children didn't belong in the kitchen. But she sometimes let Mary Frances and her sister Anne pull the stems off cherries before they were pitted. Mary Frances still wasn't old enough, though, to stir the molten fruit with a wooden spoon.

For now, she was content to watch the ripe fruit that sat rotting in crates on the porch before it was processed. She smelled the wafting sweetness of combined fruit and sugar as it cooked on the stove. Every so often she would enter the kitchen where her grandmother stood over the pot, "a sacrificial priestess in the steam." With deft hands, she'd skim bubbling froth from the jam into a white saucer near the stove. And then, if Mary Frances was especially lucky, she was allowed to put her fingers into the cooling froth. Then she would lick her small hands clean. The jam, she would later recall, was "warm and sweet and odorous. I loved it."

As an adult, Mary Frances expressed her profound delight in eating and drinking. And though it was likely innate, it was honed by her childhood experiences. The Kennedy kitchen, like the Kennedy family, was ruled by opposing ideals of repression and desire. Grandmother Holbrook's scalding strawberry froth fueled one of Mary Frances's first and most delicious food memories. Yet her grandmother also preached repression, and disdain for the pleasures of eating.

The contrast between her grandmother's ascetic regime and the looser, more enjoyable meals that graced the table when she was away, baffled Mary Frances. It forced her, even as a child, to decide what she liked. Her taste fled from dull and bland. That jam for instance, was sweet, full of texture and temperature, and undeniably delicious. It was one of many tastes that created a girl—and then a woman—ruled by hungers large and small.

BEFORE SHE WAS M.F.K. Fisher, the sophisticated writer and traveler, she was Mary Frances Kennedy, born on July 3, 1908 in Albion, Michigan, a small town near the Kalamazoo River. M.F.K. Fisher wrote a lot about her childhood, most notably in the memoir *Among Friends*. She describes herself as leaping forth "only a few minutes before midnight, in a supreme effort from my mother, whose husband had assured her that I would be named Indepencia if I arrived on the fourth." Instead she was named after her grandmother.

But her childhood recollections, many told again and again throughout her life with few varying details, should be taken with a liberal sprinkling of salt. As she admitted, "I may have stretched things a tiny bit, here and there, but I have never said that people were there who weren't." In spite of potential exaggerations and dramatic leaps of faith, M.F.K. Fisher's childhood stories are distinctly hers: the colorful descriptions illuminating her origins and subsequent journeys.

Hers was a childhood filled with "Sunday strips"—pieces of toast prepared by her father, Rex, on Sunday mornings and topped with a variety of honeys and jams. But young Mary Frances and Anne craved and created their own taste sensations, picking clumps of fresh black tar off the hot street in front of their house and chewing the sticky pieces as if they were gum. After long days at school and afternoons spent reading, the food on the dinner table was so reliably bad that she would recall, often in great detail, the occasional heavenly dish.

HER PARENTS, REX and Edith Oliver Holbrook Kennedy, seemed mismatched. Rex loomed over six feet tall and had dark hair and piercing eyes. He was dashing, intelligent, and had a taste for travel and adventure. Edith, with her round, soft face was quieter, more refined, and so aloof that at times she appeared snobbish. The two met in 1902. Rex, who was working for a newspaper in Onalla, Iowa, was introduced to Edith by her brother, Evans Holbrook. They fell immediately in love, though it's hard to imagine what an extroverted, thrill-seeking Rex found intriguing about the shy, proud Edith.

Rex had been born into the newspaper business. His family owned a collection of weekly papers in the Midwest, but he secretly hoped he might avoid a career that tied him to a boring small town. Edith's parents didn't like Rex; they believed that their daughter, who had been educated at boarding schools and a ladies' seminary, deserved someone wealthier and more educated. They shipped her off to Dresden, Germany, hoping, as Mary Frances would recall, that Edith would forget the "gawky young journalist that she was determined to marry." But Edith's eighteen months abroad only intensified her feelings for Rex. The two married in 1904.

Soon afterward, Rex and Edith moved to Albion, where Rex joined his brother Walter in running the Albion *Evening Recorder*. The Kennedys stayed in Albion until shortly after Anne's birth, in 1910. A weak baby, she suffered from digestive problems—and Edith began to wonder if Michigan's Midwestern climate contributed to the child's poor health. Rex, full of wanderlust, was only too happy to move. He readily sold his share in the *Recorder* to Walter, and the family was free.

Mary Frances later considered her family the "first beatniks of the far west—unwittingly of course." They traveled by train toward Washington's Puget Sound, where Edith's uncle owned a small island outside Seattle. But Rex, wanting distance from Edith's family, settled his family in a deserted cabin across the bay.

Their small cabin was stately but dingy—the Kennedy family was roughing it, much to Edith's dismay. In a very early memory, Mary Frances, at most three years old, recalled watching baby Anne roll on a blanket on a rocky beach while she played at the bottom of a beached rowboat, carefully scooping cupful after cupful of dirty water from the bottom of the boat.

While living in the cabin, Rex spent his days collecting and selling scrap teak and mahogany and pondering where to settle his family permanently. He was committed to doing something, anything, different from what his family history dictated. So when his scavenging venture failed, the family headed south, where Rex could try ranching.

In Ventura County, California, the family lived one hundred feet from the foggy beach. Rex began planting a grove of oranges on an inland property he hoped to buy. Mary Frances's memories of this time are shadowy: "An orange tree was an orange tree, and grass was grass, and those are the first two growing things I remember clearly, although somewhere in my dimmest consciousness are the rows of tall eucalyptus trees bending and creaking in a sea wind, in Ventura where we stayed for a few unfortunate months . . . Wind, fog, cold . . . But the beautiful trees are my own, somewhere far back."

Rex soon discovered, however, that the planting ground in Ventura was solid hardpan. Still desperate to avoid a newspaper job, he toyed with becoming a geologist. But there were children to feed, and Rex was broke. He returned to the publishing world, working briefly as the city editor for a large San Diego daily. Then, with help from his recently widowed mother-in-law, Grandmother Holbrook, Rex bought the *Whittier News* in 1912.

Whittier, a sleepy town south of Los Angeles with a cloistered reputation, had been established as a Quaker settlement at the end of the nineteenth century. When Rex bought the paper, Whittier had only about five thousand residents, most of them Quakers, or "Friends." As Episcopals, the Kennedy family was considered an intruder in the enclave; nobody in town thought they would stay long.

Instead, Rex would own the paper—and the Kennedys would live in Whittier—for decades. His decision, influenced by his domineering mother-in-law and unhappy wife, would stabilize his nomadic family. The choice, however, would also be stifling: At times, all of the Kennedys would feel suffocated by the cliquish, deeply religious locals.

Mary Frances, in particular, always felt different from her Quaker classmates and friends. This feeling of personal isolation, coupled with a deep urge to escape her surroundings, was something she learned from her withdrawn mother and vagabond father. But the trait was honed in Whittier. As a child, Mary Frances never felt accepted. She may have contrived that perception, but it was one that she would carry with her through numerous schools, travels at sea, and an adult life abroad.

Yet her childhood environment also made her excel at being alone. Mary Frances loved her books, and escaped often into her head. Growing up in Whittier created a self-reliant, determined young girl, who, from a very young age, longed to experience something vastly bigger and more sophisticated.

Perhaps this is why so many of her early childhood memories center on food. The daily living (and eating) in Whittier was uninspiring. But trips with her parents to Los Angeles, punctuated by excursions to colorful ice cream parlors and dimly lit restaurants with exotic menus, were thrilling. So were the humble moments—road trips with Rex where Mary Frances and her sister ate peach pie, warmed by the sun as they drove in an open-topped car through the California desert. Each trip made her hungry for more.

ONCE SETTLED IN Whittier, in an elegant home bought by Grandmother Holbrook, the differences between Rex and Edith's personalities became more pronounced. Rex worked hard. His schedule often left little time for home and family, which irked Edith. But even when Rex did have free time, he often chose to spend it away from his wife, daughters, and opinionated mother-in-law, who lived with them until her death, when Mary Frances was twelve. After sending the paper to press each night, Rex would wander to the poor parts of town to chat with the hobos that traveled through Whittier by foot or train. Rex enjoyed these free-spirited men, whose lives lacked structure and responsibility, qualities to which he'd long aspired. Often he provided them with work or money or even a place to stay, much to his wife's chagrin.

The family's most memorable visitor was a Scottish drifter named Charles Somerville, who lived briefly in the Kennedy family garage, and worked as a handyman, babysitter, and storyteller. When Mary Frances was six and Anne was four, they helped Charles make butterscotch candy in the family kitchen.

The small girls perched on stools and watched Charles. "At exactly the right moment he tipped out the pale brown syrup onto buttered cookie sheets, to let it spread evenly, magically, like glass, and he cut a knife across it to make little squares. Then we had to wait . . . Finally it was time for him to crack off a sliver of the glass . . . Deftly he picked up the panes of colored crystal, and broke them into neat patties along the knife marks, and placed them in fancy pyramids on two or three plates . . . Just as deftly he washed off every sign that we had spent a good afternoon in the kitchen, and he went out the back door." Edith proclaimed the candy, divinely buttery, the best she had ever eaten.

Charles then moved on to lollipops. He brought home dozens of candy sticks and made whorls of caramel on buttered cookie sheets before placing a plain stick firmly in the center of each round. Mary Frances loved the pops. The sticks never loosened, and the sweetness was addictive. But soon Charles's technique was discovered. He would not only stick his spit-moistened thumb into the boiling pot of butterscotch to test for readiness—he would gather the sticks he needed from the schoolyard and dirty sidewalks.

Edith and Grandmother Holbrook were horrified. Rex, in Charles's defense, insisted that boiling the sticks had destroyed any germs they might have carried. But his wife and mother-in-law prevailed, and Charles was booted from the garage.

In *Among Friends*, Mary Frances suggested that her father befriended men like Charles Somerville because Rex "plainly drew some vicarious satisfaction from being able to talk with them . . . [and] send them stumbling along again on the paths he secretly dreamed of treading." But Mary Frances was clearly intrigued by them, too. And her own wanderlust was likely born from a desire to fulfill the dreams of travel that her father could not.

As Rex and Grandmother Holbrook struggled for power over the home, Edith would retreat to her room. Upon arriving in Whittier, Edith had begun volunteer work and regularly attended the Episcopal church. But no matter how hard she tried to be social, she made few friends in town—she preferred solitude to the company of the religious locals. Within months, Edith had abandoned the role of wife to a prominent Whittier businessman, a role she had coveted during her family's traveling days. Rex was a visible presence in the Whittier community, but Edith rarely left the house. She attended church and the library, and occasionally she and Rex ventured to the theatre or dined out.

Edith loved her vast library of books, and spent most afternoons in her room, reclining in her favorite chair, surrounded by piles of novels. But soon her desire for solitude began to border on the pathological. Mary Frances recalled her mother spending most of her time in bed with what her daughter described as a "Sick Headache." In later life, Mary Frances theorized the condition could have been a migraine, hormonal imbalance, or Edith's reaction to her "life as a middle-class woman" in an isolated small town. Whatever the reason, the headaches were an escape, and to Mary Frances, her mother was often unavailable.

As a child, Mary Frances didn't understand her mother's urge to retreat. But Edith's actions were influential. As she grew, Mary Frances would continue to invest minimally in new situations, preferring instead to escape to environments she could control—her writing room, a library, a café, or the kitchen.

Edith spent a good portion of Mary Frances's childhood pregnant or recovering from childbirth. In 1917, when Mary Frances was nine and Anne was seven, another sister, Norah, was born. Three years later, in 1920, Edith gave birth to a boy, David.

As they grew the Kennedy children were often teased "indirectly for being non-Quaker and directly for being of foreign descent." It was assumed, for instance, that because Kennedy was an Irish surname that their father was a rowdy drinker and that their mother belonged in somebody else's kitchen. Mary Frances remembered the teasing this way:

"'What does your big fat Irish mother do?'"

"'My mother takes care of us,' [she] would call back, disdaining to reply to any of the adjectives."

"'Oh no she doesn't! She's the cook. All Irish women are cooks.'"

Her family was vastly more interesting than her classmates could ever have imagined, and Mary Frances longed to protect them. She was plucky and capable of delivering spiteful tongue-lashings to her classmates, yet she never succeeded in changing their misconceptions.

Even if she could convince them that her parents were educated and well behaved, the reality of her world was still vastly different from the rowdy environment they imagined. Mary Frances never spoke of the teasing at home, preferring instead to build a tough and occasionally aloof exterior that she hoped would protect her from life's snobbery and cruelty.

Yet these taunts did not make Mary Frances detest the kitchen. Neither did her grandmother's severe belief that food was for sustenance only; nor he mother's ambivalence about cooking. Mary Frances was bright enough to realize that whoever controlled the kitchen ran the house, and she was keen to befriend whoever happened to stand on the other side of the swinging door.

Her perceptions of food and of eating were greatly influenced by the routines of food preparation and consumption that she observed at home. In the early twentieth century, women, food, and love were pervasively bound. Women were responsible for household management, cooking, and child-rearing. A mother's cooking was considered emblematic of the love she felt for the family. Most women learned about cooking and other domestic pursuits from their mothers. Daughters stood by their mother's side as they cooked and cleaned. They learned domestic routines early and they practiced their skills often. Cooking and cleaning were chores that would make them better women, and someday, better wives.

But the fine-born Edith disliked the daily responsibilities of cooking. She did, however, enjoy eating. So she sought out the best hired help. "Kitchen wenches," as Edith called them, would occasionally prep recipes plucked from a cookbook. Then, if Edith desired, she could come to the kitchen in the late afternoon to finish executing the dish. Among the help, turnover was high. Edith's erratic behavior and exacting standards, along with the dominating personalities of the two other adults in the home, four young children, and numerous dietary preferences and restrictions, created a rarely satisfied crew.

Edith was forever at war with herself over how much control she wanted over domestic issues and child-rearing. She was torn between the duty associated with being a wife and mother and her desire for solitary activities. She disliked the responsibility of daily menu planning and meal execution, but enjoyed, when not feeling pressured, to exert her creativity. On a whim, she would make her way to the kitchen, pull out the fresh butter and eggs, and begin mixing a cake.

When she was in the mood to bake, Edith's cakes, piled with swaths of rich icing and stuffed with chopped nuts and dried fruits, were devoured by her children and Rex—but never by Grandmother Holbrook, who despised sweets. Trapped in the dueling roles of mother, wife, and daughter, it was impossible for Edith to please everyone.

Mary Frances felt closer to her mother in the kitchen than she did in Edith's dim bedroom. And though Mary Frances claimed she couldn't remember ever learning anything directly related to cooking from her mother, certain images never left her, such as Edith's preparing to fry croquettes: "She had lovely arms, and the name of the little balls was exotic, and I knew that they would be delectable." Mary Frances was, she would recall, "somewhat in awe of [Edith's] powers over me," later writing, "I am sure that I have lived this long because of the things she taught me about eating and drinking and even behaving."

She became attuned to how her mother's personality shifted when she escaped the confines of home and could cook for sheer pleasure. Edith's most ambitious accomplishments came at the family's summer cottage on Laguna Beach, about thirty-five miles from Whittier. Calmed by the ocean waters and miles of blonde sand, Edith relaxed. She became, as her daughter described her, "a happy young woman, with her small town laces loosened."

The solitary woman who, in Whittier, "seldom felt psychologically sturdy enough to . . . invite even two people to the house to eat" planned lively dinner parties. As Mary Frances described it, her mother "sailed through messy noisy delicious meals."

The contrast was sharp—and rattling. At home, Edith stayed out of the kitchen as much as possible. In Laguna, glad to avoid staff and the pressure of bowing to her mother's sensual strictures, she looked forward to simple, enjoyable meals. Mary Frances remembered her standing for hours, frying countless batches of oysters for partygoers to enjoy. For dessert they'd feast on Edith's specialty, a monumental cake, baked and decorated to perfection. Edith's distinction between cooking for fun and cooking for necessity would influence Mary Frances's lifelong view of the kitchen.

MARY FRANCES COULD have become a picky eater under her grandmother's influence. Instead, in rebellion, she began to value pleasure over repression; she would seek out abundance in food, and in life, again and again.

Nevertheless, Grandmother Holbrook's stern demeanor and plump pocketbook flattened the Kennedy family's dinners and lives. Born in Ireland, she had come to America by boat during the potato famine. Mary Frances later declared that the sturdy, wrinkled woman "disbelieved in everything pleasurable . . . except what was directly connected to Christian life." Grandmother Holbrook demanded bland, underseasoned and overcooked foods: boiled potatoes, turnips, and carrots dressed in a gloppy white sauce. She believed that the plainer a dish was, the better it was for you, and the more you must suffer while eating it as a way to prove your "innate worth as a Christian."

Once or twice a year Grandmother Holbrook traveled the long distance to Battle Creek, Michigan, to relax. The curative waters, rest, exercise, healthy vegetarian diet, and cleansing enema treatments administered at the health resort run by Dr. John Harvey Kellogg (of the Kellogg cereal dynasty) were intended to counteract devotees' stressful lives, balancing the stimulant effects of spicy and flavorful foods. Grandmother Holbrook was already committed to Kellogg's daily regime, and didn't require many of the treatments other, more occasionally hedonistic visitors, demanded. Still, she relished the chance to escape and spend time with people similarly enthusiastic about good health.

When Grandmother was away, the Kennedys played. They gorged on "gastronomic sprees," eating all the foods that she could not or would not tolerate. Mary Frances described the vacations from Grandmother Holbrook as joyous. "Nothing made us happier than to be told that next week she would leave for Battle Creek . . . It made our mouths water. No more pale bland overcooked under seasoned barely palatable food adapted to her gastric requirements . . . No more Boiled Dressing on watery lettuce!"

Edith, in particular, seemed to relish the respite from her mother's eye and tongue. She shed her worries and came out of her room, eager to interact with her husband and children. She ate what she pleased and was easygoing and full of laughter at the table. Rex opened bottles of sherry and served a local wine he called "red ink." The family dined on treats of grilled sweetbreads, rare roast beef, cream-of-mushroom soup, skewered kidneys served with a dash of sherry, puff pastry, and hot chocolate with marshmallows.

Mary Frances could not understand her grandmother's overbearing rules, or why "anything that made us all so gay and contented could be forbidden by God." Nor could she understand why Edith and Rex didn't defend their right to eat as they wanted: decadently and well.

The battle for the dinner table forced Mary Frances to become increasingly observant, mentally cataloging meals both somber and sublime. Regardless of what was on the table, her early dining experiences were formative, linking food with joy. Food was power; food was passion. In Grandmother Holbrook's case, food was religion and restraint. But then someone arrived in Mary Frances's life who taught her that food could also be love.

The family called her Aunt Gwen, though she wasn't a relation. Edith had met her, the daughter of English missionaries, at an Episcopal service shortly after the Kennedys arrived in Whittier. The bond among Gwen, Mary Frances, and Anne was immediate, and Rex and Edith were happy to let their girls spend time with the caring and capable woman.

Gwen was at the helm of the Kennedy's Laguna Beach cottage, watching the children during the week while Rex and Edith appeared only on weekends. She moved seamlessly between the two Kennedy worlds: the refined quiet of the Painter Street home and the wild of the beach. She became a companion and surrogate mother to the girls— "the core of our lives."

Gwen was a big woman: tall, adventurous, with dark unruly hair, ruddy cheeks, and coarse skin from the days she spent in the sun. She spoke with a strange accent that reflected her missionary upbringing: part British, part Japanese, part New Zealand outback. She'd been married briefly to an Englishman, a soldier who had died in Europe shortly after their wedding.

Mary Frances called Aunt Gwen a "gusty river bringing food and excitement and adventure" into their lives. She was strong, both physically and emotionally, "loving but no nonsense . . . She possessed an enormous energy in her strong body, and gave it eagerly to anyone who would accept it."

Aunt Gwen was attentive to the girls in a way that their parents were not. She took Mary Frances and Anne to the beach for long stretches of the summer and taught them how to steam mussels, roast kelp leaves, and skin eels. They hiked the desert as she identified the flora and fauna. Whatever the trip, they packed pockets full of fried egg sandwiches—one to eat when they'd reached their destination and another to squirrel away, ponder, and eat if their stomachs insisted on it. These greasy but nourishing treats became an integral part of Mary Frances's food memory. She recalled with fondness the taste and texture of the sandwiches, wrapped in wax paper and stuck into a pocket while still warm.

Meals like this taught Mary Frances that food was nurturing and could be loved simply and declaratively. This was not what she had learned from the women in her life so far: Grandmother Holbrook's blandness and Edith's erratic, frenzied, episodic baking taught Mary Frances that the kitchen was fraught with expectation and emotion. But Gwen's meals were flavorful, colorful, and filled with love. They were simple, but they made her feel profoundly cared for.

Later Mary Frances would remark that she could easily write a recipe for a fried egg sandwich similar to the one she enjoyed as a child. But what was more important than the ingredients and method used to make the sandwich was the memory of the crisp-yolky-salty food and what it said about how Aunt Gwen had helped feed her young body and her soul.

Together Gwen, Mary Frances, and Anne plucked fruit from knotty old trees found in their neighborhood. They ate their fruit fresh and ripe, sometimes still warm from the sun. Gwen taught them how to peel peaches and oranges, pit cherries, and to peel and slice bananas and eat them daintily, as a lady would. This reverence for fresh fruit and vegetables flouted the doctrine of stewed plums that ruled the Kennedy home for most of the girls' childhood. Finally, Mary Frances understood where her food came from and had the freedom to enjoy eating.

Gwen loved rustic, peasant-style cooking done over an open flame. Rex built her a three-stone hearth just outside the door of the Kennedys' summer beach shack. Gwen used her spare setup to boil water, make toast for breakfast, fry fish, make egg sandwiches, caramelize bananas, and steam mussels fresh from the ocean waters just beyond the back door. Someone, often Gwen or Rex, would swim at low tide to a large rock that was covered with barnacles and mollusks. Using a bucket tossed from the shore, they'd gather dozens of mussels, carefully prying them from the rock with a dull piece of metal. Next began the task of maneuvering back to shore with a bucketful of fresh mollusks. The waters swirled all around; more than once, the treasures were lost.

A fire was started early in the afternoon on mussel-hunting days, and by the time the swimmer appeared with the catch, coals were glowing and hot. Next came the artful layering of seaweed, wet sea grasses, cleaned mussels and several folded wet flour sacks. Finally the top was placed on the impromptu cooker: a blackened can. The mussels steamed while hungry family members and friends gathered in anticipation. At just the right moment Rex would put out the fire and pry the can open. The mussels were heaped into bowls and doused with butter and lemon juice. Mary Frances remembered that they were "crisp in the mouth, delicately briny, plump and often bearded." Their fresh-cooked catch were a lovely orange color, occasionally tinged with purple and black.

After a long reprieve from day-to-day parenting while she was pregnant with Norah and David, Edith began to notice the affection and loyalty her older children felt for Aunt Gwen. She didn't like it. Edith arranged Gwen's termination by using her pull as a regular churchgoer and wife of the newspaper publisher to secure a coveted nursing post for Gwen at a church hospital. Later Mary Frances would remark that she was sure that her mother truly hated Gwen and was jealous of the special bond between her and the Kennedy children. Had Gwen not been willing to move on from her job at the Kennedy home, Mary Frances believed, Edith would have found some way to remove her from their lives. But Gwen was willing, though perhaps not happy, to move on. And Edith believed she had banished a maternal competitor from her children's lives.

It was with Aunt Gwen that Mary Frances developed an appreciation for clandestine meals composed of a few sublime ingredients and eaten alone or nearly alone. On notable days, a Sunday or a birthday, days when the "moon and stars were right," Aunt Gwen, Mary Frances, and Anne would retreat to Gwen's kitchen in Whittier or to the small dark kitchen in Laguna Beach. Under the bare hanging bulb or beside a flickering kerosene lamp, Gwen would make cocoa toast for dinner.

The recipe was simple: bread toasted so well it was nearly black, and buttered till it dripped golden. The toast was cut into squares and placed at the bottom of shallow bowls, covered in hot cocoa till the squares bobbed, then sunk under the weight of the warm chocolate mass. On very special days, marshmallows were added.

For the three, this was the sacrament. Like Gwen's mythic fried egg sandwiches, cocoa toast became indelibly etched in Mary Frances's young memory. Cocoa toast was something special that she, Anne, and Aunt Gwen shared in a dark room with no light, hot chocolate seeping into crispy pockets of bread: a formative meal, never forgotten.

Later Mary Frances wrote that it was Aunt Gwen who taught her "the nuances of cooking in relation to him/her who does it, and why." Her food education thus far had been bewildering as she watched the adults in her family spar over philosophies and tastes. She always ate what was put in front of her. But only occasionally, on special days, was the food good enough to ponder and truly enjoy.

Aunt Gwen helped Mary Frances understand that the personality of the cook is imbued in food. Meals tasted different and better when they were fresh, full of life, and made with passion and love. Neither may have realized it at the time, but Aunt Gwen helped Mary Frances grow as an eater and as a person, helping her to discover not only who she was, but who she wanted to be.

After Aunt Gwen left, one of the Kennedy family's most memorable cooks, Ora, taught a nine-year-old Mary Frances another early lesson about the power a cook wields over those she feeds. Ora was a remarkable talent, a "spare grey-haired woman" who did astonishing things with ordinary ingredients.

Mary Frances described Ora's reverence for the kitchen as near ecstatic: "She loved to cook the way some people love to pray or dance or fight." She used fresh herbs as seasonings, garnished homemade pies with cutouts of stars, and cut her meat by hand instead of using a grinder. Once Mary Frances was sent away from the dinner table because she let out an unladylike moan of delight when Ora placed a platter of beef hash topped with golden pastry and garnished with bits of parsley and watercress in front of Rex.

Grandmother Holbrook, of course, hated Ora. She mistrusted the delight Ora took in food and flavors and cursed the enjoyment the Kennedys derived from what she cooked. Grandmother Holbrook claimed to not be able to eat anything that Ora made—it was too exotic, too unknown.

Ora's tenure with the Kennedys would have likely been brief thanks to Grandmother's "nervous stomach" and staunch opinions. But Ora put her own end to things, killing her mother and then herself with her impeccably sharpened French knife on a quiet Sunday morning. The Whittier police reported that Ora used her knife neatly to slice her mother into several pieces. She then used the blade to tear the canvas tent they lived in on the outskirts of town into clean ribbons before deftly slicing her own wrists and throat. The police reported that after the murder and all its carnage, the French knife remained flawless.

Mary Frances was fascinated by the crime—was her Grandmother Holbrook right? Could a flavorful bite inspire terrible, even monstrous, behavior? Mary Frances didn't really think so. But she recognized, somehow, that Ora's passion had helped create both sumptuous meals and unspeakable horror. With Ora gone, Mary Frances sat in a dim dining room, picking at a plainly dressed plate, watching the adults sitting around her at the table. Food was far more than just sustenance. Of that much she was now certain.

As a very young child, Mary Frances was aware that her parents were different depending on who was at the table: "It was plain to me that there was a mysterious connection and I planned to study it." The easiest route was to get into the kitchen, learn to create dishes, and observe what happened when she fed people. As a little girl, she pestered whoever was in the kitchen to let her stand on a pile of dictionaries and stir cake batters, beat eggs, and measure flour and sugar. Craving attention, she "easily fell into the role of cook's helper."

Her interest in food and cooking helped secure her spot in a family that was consumed by idiosyncrasy. "I had to fight for my place on stage," she said. Cooking was "my way to show that I was there too."

By the age of ten Mary Frances claimed that she no longer needed the pile of dictionaries to reach her wooden spoon into her pot on the stove—and that, most importantly, she was a capable cook. She was used to the dank hideaway fondly known as the kitchen, and understood its best and darkest secrets. She could make a sponge cake and knew how to adjust proportions of spices in recipes.

For the rest of her family, the kitchen was a place to be avoided: For Edith it was fraught with the complexities of love and caretaking; for Grandmother Holbrook, it was emblematic of sin, and the devilish pleasure some derived from food. For the hired help the kitchen must have been the equivalent of a modern, dark cubicle with fluorescent light. But for Mary Frances the kitchen was someplace magical, a doorway, not unlike other magic doorways in fables and fiction, to a new and exciting world.

She collected food memories like souvenirs: The bite of chocolate frosted birthday cake might be the only one she had for weeks. Fresh fruits dripping with sun-kissed juices were a snack to remember. The flavors of simple, salty fish pulled fresh from the sea, and grilled only moments later, offered a succulent end to a summer day. Most of all, meals eaten with close friends or family, removed from the watchful eye of rule-bound adults, were savored and treasured. Each exquisite detail was filed away, saved for a time when, as a writer, she would be free to re-create the moment and taste it again and again.

The Art of Knowing Yourself

*I*N 1920, GRANDMOTHER Holbrook died, and the plates served at the Kennedy dinner table became reliably satisfying. The family uttered a happy sigh, glad to be free from the heavy weight of their matriarch's obtrusive values. Edith loosened her grip on the cooks she employed, who began to cook more ambitiously, using fresh, local ingredients. For the first time in a decade, Rex and Edith lived alone with their brood. Free to make decisions about their family's future, they decided to move from their tidy neighborhood home to a small orange-growing ranch a few miles outside town.

Edith was particularly happy with the change and began making more forays into the kitchen. The wide space indulged her reclusive tendencies while liberating her family from the watchful eye of Quaker neighbors who had never welcomed the Episcopal family into their homes. On the ranch they could grow their own food: oranges, blackberries, plums, dates, asparagus, and artichokes. They could raise animals, too: cows, chickens, and other fowl. It seemed a perfect fit for a group who valued both isolation and exploration.

But Mary Frances disliked the confining country atmosphere. She bloomed from a helpful eldest daughter into a disagreeable and capricious teenager. For Mary Frances's first day at her new, rural school, Edith woke early to pack a special lunch for her daughter. Mary Frances later claimed the ladylike spread she unpacked cost her "two weeks of trust and acceptance from my bucolic companions."

Edith had included a "silver knife for spreading the neat packet of bread slices; two small screw top jars which had once held samples of some kind of face cream, now filled with mayonnaise and blackberry jam, salt and pepper in little folds of wax paper which spilled onto my skirt; [and] a ripe sliced tomato which followed them into my lap."

Mary Frances's classmates devoured rustic, heartier foods: "thick pieces of bread with a slab of last night's pot roast stuck between them." Immediately she sensed she didn't fit in. And when she spilled some of her food, she was embarrassed by their laughter. Her peers' dismissive reaction hurt. Leaving Whittier was supposed to help her make friends. Midyear, she transferred to John Muir Junior High, a more urbane school back in Whittier. But that, too, failed to help the overly serious girl who later described herself as "sad and drudging in my pursuit after things."

As a child Mary Frances had loved reading, and her best subject in school was English. She claimed to have begun writing poetry at age five and to have been working on a novel by the time she was nine. But not long after beginning her formal schooling, Mary Frances started searching for reasons to ditch the classroom. Coughs and colds, chickenpox, measles, and general malaise were all used as excuses to skip school, lounge on the couch, and read.

Edith recognized her daughter's symptoms, and diagnosed that she was bored with the classroom's everyday routine and minutiae. And though Edith continually modeled a form of self-education that began and ended with books, she could not support her daughter's dream of educating herself solely from the family library. Mary Frances was promptly sent back to school, but she remained ambivalent about it her entire life, much preferring the knowledge that could be gained outside of a formal education.

Now that she was in junior high, Mary Frances's typically casual approach to her education became more problematic. Her parents urged her to take academic and social responsibilities more seriously, but she balked at a mold that didn't seem to fit her. She felt constantly rejected by her peers, rural and citified alike. Why would she want to conform to their standards?

She also felt inevitable pressure from her parents, pressure she was quick to resist. Though she was tall, like Rex, she didn't long to be head of the class, as he had been. She took piano lessons because Edith had as a girl, but resisted the idea of being sent away to school, as her mother had been, even though she was unhappy in Whittier.

She felt that her creative interests—music, art, and writing—were dismissed by her parents. As a small girl she had been miffed when her parents laughed at her early novel-writing attempts—this was likely just amusement at their precocious daughter. But the idea that her parents didn't support her creativity took hold and grew.

She would describe her adolescent creative ideas as meeting "neither praise nor blame . . . Nothing was ever done to guide or encourage me." Whether this was true or another manifestation of Mary Frances's self-protective aloofness is unclear. What matters is that she believed it was true. Even as an adult, she was convinced that Rex and Edith weren't proud of her published writing.

Mary Frances's youthful perception that her parents were uninterested in her talents and successes irked her. She became increasingly lackadaisical at school, convinced that no matter what she did, she couldn't please her parents. Edith despised her daughter's attitude, remarking that she couldn't stand to have her around the house when she was so "horrible, rude, and surly." It was quickly decided that the next stop for Mary Frances was boarding school.

The summer before Mary Frances and Anne left Whittier for the all-female Bishop's School in La Jolla, California, near San Diego, Rex put his daughters to work. He used them as stringers for the *Whittier News*: Whenever a staffer was sick or absent, one of the girls would take their place. They would write up the weekly social calendar or other brief human-interest stories under professional deadline pressure. Mary Frances sometimes wrote up to fifteen stories a day, all typed on a stubborn old Remington.

Rex must have recognized his daughter's talent, but his praise was minimal. Indeed, he treated her just like the employees she replaced: He was demanding and occasionally gruff. Her competence was rewarded not with thanks or accolades but with the assignment of another story. "I was filled with eagerness, then, partly romantic and partly hereditary, to know more about my father's newspaper office," she wrote later. "He humored me, but only a little: I was a woman, and he wanted to save all that for David."

Nonetheless, Mary Frances looked forward to the time with her father and the opportunity to practice composing and shaping her ideas. A quick writer, she would never read or edit her prose. She believed that she usually got it right the first time—a theory, true or not, that she maintained throughout a lifetime of writing.

Bishop's would be the first of three high schools Mary Frances would attend before graduation. In the fall of 1924, Mary Frances and Anne traveled the short distance south from Whittier to La Jolla. Mary Frances wrote that it felt like "light-miles" from home, describing herself as "euphoric to be away for the first time in my life from younger siblings and Whittier Union High."

Mary Frances and Anne were essentially the local girls at Bishop's, a small school with only seventy boarders and a few dozen day students. Most of their classmates were "out-of-state-children whose families wintered in California, and the daughters of the newly rich . . . Pretension and snobbishness flourished." Yet again, the Kennedy sisters were thrust into an environment where they felt like outsiders.

Never fond of cliques, Mary Frances believed that her time at Bishop's would be different from her experience at previous schools. Arriving for tenth grade, she hoped her classmates would accept her and that she would make friends. But the social skepticism she had been acquiring—and had inherited from her mother—would mar her entry into this setting, too. Though she wanted people to like her, and dreamed of being popular, she was reluctant to share much of herself with her classmates. A growing isolationist, she failed to make close friends, and to many, she appeared aloof and snobbish. And no wonder: Mary Frances believed herself superior to most of the other girls. They bored her.

But the dining hall proved a great equalizer. The Bishop's girls reveled in the splendid meals made for them by the school cook, Mrs. Cheever. They had fresh milk to drink for breakfast—and, for their biscuits, honey collected from bees that swarmed the nearby Torrey Pines. Lunchtime picnics of crisp, hot fried chicken on the beach were accompanied by abundant piles of garden-fresh greens. For Bishop's Christmas party, Mrs. Cheever daringly served fresh oysters on the half shell. It was a bold choice for a girls' dinner dance, and one of Mary Frances's first ventures into the world of formal dining. Though she had begun eating more decadently since Grandmother Holbrook died, she was unaccustomed to the exotic.

The old barn on The Bishop's School property housed a sparkling Christmas tree, dozens of candles, and a scattering of green pine branches and boughs. Place cards dotted the formally set tables, which were arranged in a semicircle so the girls could dance after dinner. They all knew there would be no boys at the party but still wore skirts or pretty dresses, long chiffon scarves, and flowers in their hair. Some even wore makeup, a hint of rouge or lipstick, to make their faces glow.

Mary Frances was seated between a "loose lined and dreamy" senior, who went by her last name, Olmsted, and a junior named Inez, notorious for her profanity. Usually Inez took no notice of Mary Frances, but on this night she smiled and looked nearly friendly. For sophomore Mary Frances this seat was a social coup, an experience that stoked her fantasies of being the popular girl.

A line of houseboys deposited a plate of lovely raw oysters in front of each girl. Spellbound, and perhaps a little fearful, the girls waited in anticipation for someone to take a bite. Next to Mary Frances, the experienced Olmsted murmured, "Delicious" after plucking the oyster from its shell and putting it deftly into her mouth. Mary Frances decided she must be confident. She remembered Edith telling her that it was vulgar to do anything with an oyster but swallow it quickly and alive.

"Oh, I love Blue Points!" she exclaimed.

Slightly bemused and aware that she was being watched, Mary Frances decided to swallow the oyster, just as Olmsted had. With surprising neatness, and with no hint that it was an unfamiliar food, she scooped the briny creature into her mouth and paused a moment before swallowing. Her taste buds, she later recalled, shouted, "Oysters are simply marvelous! More, more!" She felt "light and attractive and daring to know what I had done." The world of parties and fine dining was intoxicating, Mary Frances realized. She hungered for more.

MARY FRANCES'S DESIRE to devour a bigger world was profound enough that after a seemingly happy year and a half at The Bishop's School, she inexplicably withdrew. She opted to finish her junior year at the bigger and more diverse Whittier Union High School. But the following fall, it was back to boarding school. Mary Frances and Anne attended Miss Harker's School for Girls, a preparatory boarding school adjacent to the campus of Stanford University in Palo Alto, California. After graduating in 1927, she spent the summer with her family in Laguna.

During her high school career, she had failed to distinguish herself academically and had made few friends. Yet she seemed unconcerned by her haphazard path. Her relaxed approach to her future was a result of her belief that she was "marking time" and that she "must go through the motions in order to escape."

She knew she wanted to see more of the world and loathed the idea of living at home, unmarried, while she waited for someone or something to happen. That summer she pleaded with her father to help her find a job at a newspaper in a city far away. "Timbuktu, anything, I wanted to travel," she said, "to see something besides Whittier." Yet the job never materialized.

Mary Frances decided she would like to go to college, believing that more schooling was her best bet for escaping Whittier. Rex and Edith begrudgingly agreed. They decided that she should enroll at a school near them—perhaps the University of Southern California—that was close enough for her to commute or, if she joined a sorority, take the bus home and help care for her younger siblings on the weekends.

But Mary Frances didn't share her parents' enthusiasm for attending college in Los Angeles. As the summer days passed, she became moody, full of "undirected energies of a thousand kinds." She prayed that something—anything—would happen to disrupt her parents' plans for her future.

As the summer of 1927 ended, Rex and Edith astonished Mary Frances by suggesting that she leave California to attend Illinois College, about 250 miles south of Chicago, with her cousin Nan. To Mary Frances, the idea of being at a school far from home, with boys and numerous social opportunities, was exhilarating.

Before her departure, her moods vacillated between elation ("Astounding! I am going to Illinois College—have escaped the Ranch! Hurrah!") and terror. She wrote in her journal that she felt a "horrible, sick fullness" whenever she considered leaving her home and family, especially Anne, for nine months. She also wrote of her high expectations for her college experience, resolving not to be "so damn lazy," hoping that the men in Illinois might be more interesting and better-looking than those she'd met that summer in Laguna Beach.

Mary Frances traveled as far as Chicago with her uncle, Evans Holbrook, Edith's brother. She spent most of her time on the observation platform or in the ladies' room, staring at herself in the mirror. She was "horribly self-conscious" on the trip; she wanted everyone to notice her and find her mysterious and fascinating, but said she died a "small hideous death" if anyone stared too hard in her direction.

She met Evans in the dining car for lunch and for dinner. He was a regular traveler and had a deep appreciation for formal dining and was mild mannered yet firm in his conviction that Mary Frances needed to learn more about herself and her tastes.

One day in the dining car, Evans asked Mary Frances if she would prefer an asparagus or a wild mushroom omelet. Mary Frances replied that she didn't care. She was startled when Evans responded, "You should never say that again, dear girl. It is stupid, which you are not. It implies that the attentions of your host are basically wasted on you. So make up your mind before you open your mouth. Let him believe, even if it is a lie, that you would infinitely prefer that exotic wild asparagus to the banal mushrooms, or vice versa. Let him feel that it matters to you . . . and even that he does!"

Mary Frances was speechless, but Evans wasn't done yet. "All this," he continued, "may someday teach you about the art of seduction, as well as the more important art of knowing yourself."

Finished with his lecture, Evans ordered two asparagus omelets. Mary Frances, red-faced and with tears pricking at the corners of her eyes, contemplated running straight to the ladies' room. But she was proud enough to know that what Uncle Evans thought of her depended on her poise and continued presence at the table.

AFTER HER INITIAL excitement, Mary Frances became "lonely and uncomfortable" during her months at Illinois College and considered quitting and returning home almost as soon as she arrived. She was surprised at how much she missed her family and the California climate; but she knew that she couldn't leave, fearing that dropping out of yet another school would prove to Rex and Edith that she was a failure and a coward.

Aside from her cousin Nan, and Nan's roommate Rachel, the students at Illinois College were distant and cold, hardly an improvement from the snobby girls at Bishop's. Her attempts at making friends were met with haughty stares. At a celebratory dinner, Mary Frances offered her dorm mates fresh avocados that Rex had sent across the country. She found the funny-looking fruit an exotic treat, but her classmates turned up their noses. The snub forever irked her, and her resulting attitude toward her classmates certified her reputation as a stuck-up California girl. With little to do and no interest in her classes, Mary Frances centered her life on meals. She later described her time in Illinois as a year of "conscious gourmandize."

The weekends were her reprieve from the terrible food in the college cafeteria. Saturday afternoons were spent at a diner called Coffee and

Waffle, where Mary Frances and Nan could eat four waffles and drink unlimited coffee for 40 cents. Next the girls would head off to the movies, buying bags of candies to tuck into their pockets for the show. Before returning to the dorm they often indulged in another waffle, accompanied by a mug of hot chocolate. They reached home full and relaxed.

Sundays were the same. Dressed in their church clothes, Mary Frances and Nan would trudge across campus to the school cafeteria that served all-you-could-eat cinnamon rolls—a sweet indulgence that compensated for the impassable food served the rest of the week. The girls would munch on the rich rounds of butter, sugar, and cinnamon until they were sick. Then, instead of continuing on to church as they were expected to, they would go back home to their beds. Irritability, indigestion, headaches, and tears to accompany the girls' homesickness often characterized the day.

But there was nothing more indulgent than the secret suppers the girls made and ate in Nan and Rachel's room. They would buy ginger ale, dinner rolls, packages of cream cheese and anchovies, bottles of French dressing and "at least six heads of the most beautiful expensive lettuce we could find." After locking the door, they'd open the ginger ale, pour the amber fizz into their bathroom mugs, and toast themselves. Next, having loosened the belts on their woolen bathrobes, they'd feast on bowl after bowl of torn lettuce, a spread made by mixing cream cheese and anchovies, and the pillowy rolls.

At exam time, Mary Frances paid for the nights she spent pulled up to a candlelit table eating cream cheese, soft bread, and lettuce while listening to the Victrola as it moaned in the dorm room. In her final examination book for her biology test, she wrote that she did not know the answers to any of the questions—and that she did not care. "I am losing five hours of credit," she remarked. "Too bad, isn't it?" She blamed her failure on uninspiring teachers and classes.

She left Illinois College early in 1928, after only one semester. She was glib about her typical departure. "This year has been an amazing adventure in many ways," she wrote in her journal, "but thank God I'm ending this part of it tomorrow. My train leaves for dear old California at noon." She had learned one thing from her brief experience in the Midwest: She hated the cold and bleak grayness of winter, a feeling she would retain for the rest of her life. If she ever again moved from California, she hoped it would be "to the South Seas, maybe, or perhaps Alaska, because there the snow is entire and white." Meanwhile, her future was, once again, uncertain.

AFTER A LINGERING bout with bronchitis left her weak and hacking, Mary Frances, now twenty, enrolled in Whittier College for the spring of 1928. She hoped that a successful semester at home would override her poor academic performance in Illinois and that she could register the following fall as a sophomore at nearby Occidental College. But she lacked too many credits. If she wanted to attend Occidental, she would have to go to summer school. She signed up for classes at the University of California, Los Angeles, (UCLA) and met Al Fisher one day in the library.

The couple's meeting seemed fated: Both Mary Frances and Al found in each the other a desire to experience a larger and more colorful life.

Alfred Young Fisher, then twenty-five, had been born in New York City but raised in Los Angeles, where his father was the pastor of the Third Presbyterian Church. When he met Mary Frances, he was home for the summer from Wyoming, where he was teaching school. Tall, with a light-colored pompadour and kind eyes, he escaped his religious family and hot days in the city by burying his head in books.

He hadn't always been so scholarly. Early in his college career, years before he met Mary Frances, Al had flunked out of UCLA and his family sent him to work in the oilfields as punishment. After a brutally hot summer of manual labor, Al decided to return to school. He gave UCLA one more try, then abandoned its sunny, athletic atmosphere—which would have also required him to enlist in the army corps. Al went first to Princeton Preparatory School and then to Princeton University.

He excelled there, becoming the class poet for his graduating class of 1927, a capable athlete, and made friends for life. He was far more comfortable with its bookish environment, where men went to class dressed, he said, as "carefully and correctly as for a New York speakeasy evening with a deb."

Al immersed himself in literature and theology, two subjects that would influence both his writing and his academic career. He was considered intelligent, but self-conscious and insecure. A friend claimed that Al wrote an impressive seventy-thousand word essay on the function of literary criticism. But after it was criticized, he burned it.

He, too, could be cold and aloof, which made him even more attractive to Mary Frances. He guarded his privacy, buried his emotions, and had few good friends. Bob Spackman, one of his few close mates, later described his friend's life as having "little to do with people. It was lived, like any born writer's, in an endless structuring and articulation of his creativity, the mumble and mutter of the poetic mind."

Mary Frances loved playing the muse. Al fancied himself a poet on the verge of greatness and reveled in her praise. The mere thought of her was often inspiring: One night, Al composed fifty sonnets in his characteristic tight and spindly script. The sonnets had been written, he said, "one after another . . . The night was bitter cold . . . the planets flamed behind the great mountains, and everywhere in the grove there was silence . . . Time and space slipped away from me and only returned with the dawn."

Al was dreadfully afraid of rejection, which fueled his relentless pursuit of Mary Frances. "This girl, this one with burning look and torch," he wrote in a sonnet. "I'd crave destruction so I had her love." But underneath their infatuation, tension brewed. There was a gentle but persistent tug between Mary Frances's desire for Al's attention and his need for space to think and to write. Young and naive, she was blind to his keeping her affections at arm's length, never noticing that he always chose to invest his emotions in his work, not in her.

Later, Mary Frances would realize that part of the reason Al was attracted to her was that she was nice enough to take home to his religious parents, but still daring enough to drink, smoke cigarettes, read obscure literature, and be interested in a life abroad. Mary Frances initially liked Al for the same reasons. She would later admit that when she met Al, he wanted to leave his family and she wanted to leave hers. Al wanted to go to France, and she had "wanted to go anywhere at all. Anywhere. France, anyplace. It didn't matter to me. Away, away."

Al, however, was more capable of orchestrating his own departure. As a man, his ability to flee current circumstances was limited only by imagination and budget. For Mary Frances, to bolt from the confines of home and family would require structure and a plan.

IN LATE AUGUST 1928, Al returned to his teaching job at Valley Ranch Preparatory School in Wyoming, and Mary Frances and Anne traveled from Whittier to Occidental College. Located in the small community of Eagle Rock, a suburb just north of Los Angeles, Occidental was an enclave of wealthy Protestant youth. The blue notes of jazz music ruled at fraternity dances, parties, and local clubs where wealthy co-eds smoked cigarettes and drank bootleg alcohol. But though Mary Frances went to parties, she rarely dated, remarking that she was not interested in seeing new people. She had, she said, an "off-campus romance well into gear."

Anne was a freshman, Mary Frances a sophomore, having worked over the summer to make up the missing credits. But within a few weeks, she slipped back into her cavalier ways. She had described herself as not brilliant, but bright enough that she never had to work too hard at academics. So she breezed through exams and helped classmates cheat on theirs. For fun she honed her writing skills by writing brief articles for the school paper.

She lived in a campus apartment with Anne while waiting, she said, for something big. In anticipation, she spent sunny afternoons working to acquire and maintain the perfect Gertrude Lawrence tan. She lay out on the roof so much, she said, that the sun nearly blinded her. The love letters that a bronzed Mary Frances pulled from the mailbox must have convinced her that Al was worth waiting for. Yet she later claimed that she wasn't sure it was love that she had found with Al—it was, instead, "something." The romantic prose had helped to fill her with deep emotions that, for an inexperienced young woman, must have seemed very much like love.

Then Al proposed marriage and asked Mary Frances to go with him to France. Mary Frances accepted, exhilarated by the opportunity. She had never imagined that the chance to leave California and move abroad would present itself in the form of marriage. But a wedding seemed the best answer to Mary Frances's uncertainties about what to do with the rest of her life. As a young woman in the late 1920s, her career path dictated marriage, children, volunteer work, and housekeeping. Al's career and travel plans allowed her to delay starting a family, which she desired eventually but not anytime soon. Mary Frances compared her feelings about marrying Al and moving to France to that of a savage animal. "I fled family and friends and security like a suddenly freed pigeon, or mole, or wildcat . . . At last I was MYSELF."

As their wedding day, September 5, 1929, approached, Mary Frances awaited their departure with glee. Her parents were excited too. They viewed Al, a proper Presbyterian minister's son, as a solid match.

The frivolity and decadence of the 1920s pulled at the young couple. They would not get rich living in Europe, but they might join in just a bit of the art, color, music, intellectual conversation, and literature of the glittering age.

But what they found harder to acknowledge—to themselves and each other—was a growing concern, even before they were married, that they might not be ready for such a serious commitment. Mary Frances later said that she felt "hopeless" standing at the altar and was fearful of how marriage would change her freewheeling relationship with Al.

Al began to feel suffocatingly tied to his bride and would later say that shortly before marrying Mary Frances he "dallied" with another woman. His willingness to betray the woman he supposedly loved, even on a casual level, should have been an indication of future troubles, he later realized. "Perhaps I should have taken it as some sort of 'sign' about my behavior in the future," he wrote. "For, married or not, a beautiful woman always excites me in the same simple, direct fashion."

Another omen: The wedding date fell only a month and a half before the stock market crash that began the Great Depression. The global aftershocks prescribed that their time in Europe would be vastly different from what they planned.

DESPITE MARY FRANCES'S lack of commentary about the first days of her marriage, there's little doubt that it had been a remarkably quick series of life-changing events. A mere week and a half after standing in front of family and friends and pledging to be Al Fisher's wife, she stood next to him on a boat bound for Cherbourg. Their new life together was about to begin.

3

Ready, At Last, to Live

WHEN THE *BERENGARIA* dropped anchor in France, Mary Frances and Al were met by Bob Spackman and his new wife, Mary Anne. The foursome traveled into Paris by train.

The train car was hot and stuffy, crowded with dirty, tired passengers. The one bright spot: the lunch Mary Frances described as one of the most important meals of her life. Not only was it her first in France; it defined for her the differences between American and French cuisine and culture.

The French bread—the first she had ever tasted—came in large chunks, with a crusty exterior and feathery interior. With just one bite, Mary Frances knew she could never return to the bland loaves of home. The salad was a mix of garden and bitter greens, so fresh that she claimed to see a stray beetle crawling among the leaves. The greens were dressed with simple olive oil and tart vinegar and were flavorful in a way the chopped iceberg salad of childhood had never been.

The quintessentially French setting provided the perfect accompaniment: harried waiters dressed in black and white, carafes of simple wine on each table, neat rolls of butter, and the plate of small apples that made its way around the dining car when everyone had finished. After collecting the lunch plates, waiters served cupfuls of rich, black coffee. It was strong, bitter, and unlike any she'd had before. Mary Frances surveyed the bustling scene, looking out over the stained tablecloth, half-empty wine bottles, and the blank faces of the strangers who surrounded her. "Suddenly I recognized my own possibilities as a person," she would write, "and I was almost stunned by the knowledge that never again would I eat or drink as I had done for my first twenty years, sanely and well but unthinkingly."

From the French, Mary Frances would to learn to eat and drink meaningfully. Her meals would inspire a devout appreciation for fresh meats and produce, fine spices, pungent cheeses, crusty breads, and delicate sweets. Her three years of expatriate living would teach her how to compose multicourse meals and savor each bite.

But the most important lesson M.F.K. Fisher would learn in France was how to articulate the profound importance of nourishment. She had learned about the pleasures of food as a child. As a woman she would learn how to experience that pleasure fully and completely and write about it in ravishing detail.

On the train, however, her mind was squarely on lunch. Indeed, she believed that the past few weeks—her wedding, the train ride east to New York harbor, and the days on the *Berengaria*, had all been preparation leading to "1:43 PM, September 25, 1929, when I picked up a last delicious crust crumb from the table, smiled dazedly at my love, peered incredulously at a great cathedral on the horizon, and recognized myself as a newborn sentient human being, ready at last to live."

PARIS, WHERE THE couple would spend a few days before continuing on to Dijon, was everything she had imagined: "It should always be seen, the first time, with the eyes of childhood or of love," she wrote. "I was almost twenty-one, but much younger than girls are now, I think. And I was wrapped in a passionate mist."

The couple's first night was a whirlwind: After they checked into their hotel, Bob and Mary Anne took Mary Frances and Al to the Ritz for a cocktail and then out to dinner; Mary Frances told her family that it was the most wonderful meal she had ever consumed. This propensity for hyperbole would continue throughout her stay in France. Almost daily, she was transfixed by the vast array of authentic French cuisine, constantly proclaiming the next dish more wonderful and delicious than the last.

Mary Frances and Al knew many people in the city. Most were Al's friends—academics studying at English universities who were on vacations from study. Mary Frances's acquaintances were women, most of them middle-aged and living in Paris on allowances from their American husbands. She described them as "generous, foolish souls who needed several champagne cocktails at the Ritz Bar after their daily shopping."

Her aunt, Elizabeth Holbrook (whom she called Aunt Bess), was also living in Paris that autumn. After dinner with the Spackmans, the couple took a taxi to her pension, where they drank fancy liquors and met dozens of Bess's female friends. The presence of so many excited women eager to question the newlyweds about their future was exhausting, and Mary Frances and Al quickly left for their hotel, eager to rest.

THEY AWOKE TO a city teeming with bohemian culture. The poor French economy had encouraged Americans from all backgrounds to flock to Paris, a sophisticated but inexpensive cultural capital made even more vibrant by the brightest minds in arts and literature. When Mary Frances and Al arrived, frivolity ruled. But the party was squelched soon after by the fall of the American stock market, in October 1929.

The crash occurred at the end of a decade of indulgence, unrestrained materialism, rapidly changing social values, and fast living: bootleg gin, smoking, and blunt sexuality. The twenties also saw the rise of the Jazz Age, flapper culture, and Modernist art and literature, as young people used their creativity to explore life's meaning.

Paris was a particularly beguiling destination for creative expatriates, in part because of such cultural doyennes as Gertrude Stein, Sylvia Beach, and Natalie Barney, who established literary salons, bookstores, and small presses dedicated to the publication of Modernist work.

Stein coined the term the Lost Generation to describe the young artists and writers whose work embodied the era's thriving spirit. Ernest Hemingway, F. Scott Fitzgerald, and Sherwood Anderson were among the most famous writers of the period. Their fiction told the stories of disaffected youth who used alcohol, parties, and indulgence as a salve for the lack of meaning in their lives.

Mary Frances and Al were undoubtedly familiar with the literary and artistic movements in Paris during the 1920s. In particular, it's likely that Al read small press literary magazines that championed Modernist verse in the style of James Joyce, Ezra Pound, and T. S. Eliot. It's also likely that Al believed living in France would inspire and push his writing forward, perhaps even bringing him the great literary acclaim he desperately wanted. Mary Frances, however, despite all her excitement, intelligence, and curiosity, had few personal goals.

The couple moved into the Hotel Quai Voltaire on Paris's Left Bank. It was a stylish part of town with views of the Seine's bookstalls, and the Louvre. The neighborhood was filled with poor American student pilgrims.

Paris awakened her senses: "The hot chocolate and rich croissants were the most delicious things, there in bed with the Seine flowing past me and pigeons wheeling around the grey Palace mansards, that I have ever eaten. They were really the first thing I had tasted since we were married . . . tasted to remember. They were a part of the warmth and excitement of that hotel room, with Paris waiting."

Mary Frances eagerly adopted Parisian habits. She and Al ate breakfast in bed at nine and had lunch around two. In the afternoon, she shopped and wandered the streets, pausing for a cup of tea followed by evening cocktails, dinner, and finally liquor at a café. Days ended around midnight. It was "an awful life for the earnest young student."

One morning the two slept late, ate their *petite déjeuner* in bed, and then walked around the corner to a restaurant called Michaud for a long lunch. By the time they were done with the meal, it was three in the afternoon. When they arrived at their room Mary Frances quickly rushed Al out the door, eager for a few quiet moments alone.

She sat down and composed a letter to her family. "I made Al depart for a stroll along the bookstalls in front of the hotel, while I write letters and wash stockings," she wrote. "So far I've only done this. I'm sitting in the open window—and there's the street, the trees, the little stalls, the Seine, and the Louvre across from me. It's hard to do anything but hang out the window and look at things."

She described the city as "the most wonderful thing I have ever known . . . All France, since the first light, has been a sort of Oz to us—I didn't know everything would be different, even the trees and forks. I love it."

Having studied French in college, Mary Frances was pleased with how quickly she began to communicate with Parisians. Al was not so fortunate. He knew nothing about the language, and struggled to pick up even the most basic phrases. Mary Frances served as translator and communicator: shopping, commandeering taxis, and helping them maneuver their new hometown on foot. She hoped that with more practice she would be even better at ordering lunch, discussing laundry with the washwoman, and artfully directing taxi drivers.

She was taken with French fashion. She loved the boys and men in their berets and shorts and was inspired by the sophistication of French women. She was astounded most by the prices: Everything in France was significantly less expensive. Bottles of bordeaux and chianti could be had for a mere 90 cents; chablis was just 76 cents; a large carafe of good beer was 12 cents. It soon became hard not to stop for a drink. Rather than waste precious time scurrying to see Paris landmarks, Mary Frances was content to sit in a cafe, people-watch, write in her journal, or read.

She claimed she had introductory letters to many of the Paris literati, including Gertrude Stein and Alice Toklas, who held famous literary and artistic gatherings at their home on Paris's Left Bank. Al claimed he had letters that would have connected them with F. Scott Fitzgerald, Colette, and Sylvia Beach.

But the couple was reluctant to call on these connections. Mary Frances said that Al wanted to socialize in the famed expatriate literary circle, but that she did not. She thought the expat crowd was indulgent, petty, and uninterested in an authentic French life: "They knew everybody and gossiped . . . They weren't French at all. They made no effort to be French. They were all Americans-in-Paris. It was not the kind of life I wanted."

Al finally did meet Beach and spend some time at the English-language bookstore Shakespeare and Co. with other American intellectuals. But Mary Frances kept her letters of introduction hidden away. Of the letter that would have introduced her to Gertrude and Alice she said, "I could not bring myself to present it. I could not walk around the corner with the letter in my hand."

BUT STILL, THE most difficult connection to make was the one with her husband. Mary Frances felt discombobulated, as if her marriage to Al was not unfolding as she imagined. In one letter she wrote that she hoped that she and her husband would soon "be more together than either one of us had ever dreamed of being." It was a reference to the couple's emotional and sexual life, still lacking the intensity she'd desired. Of more immediate concern: It was time for Mary Frances and Al to move on to Dijon, a bustling city a few hours southeast. On the day before they left, Mary Frances wrote a letter to her family exclaiming that she felt "blindfolded because I know so little."

Aunt Bess insisted on hiring a car and driving the couple to Dijon before continuing on to vacation in Italy with a friend. The group traveled southeast on the Paris–Lyon highway by Pierce limousine, stopping for lunch at a restaurant in the small town of Avallon. Mary Frances reveled in a simple potato soufflé with a crispy brown crust and piles of cheese and chives. The potatoes, she recalled, were treated with "real respect and admiration." She realized that the French valued even the simplest of foods, and she loudly agreed. She'd never been fond of potatoes, for instance, but had always believed in their potential—that they could be splendid if not mashed or baked—a bland accompaniment to Sunday steak or pot roast. The soufflé confirmed that a humble vegetable could be transformed into something magical by the addition of only a few ingredients: butter, cream, cheese, a handful of chopped bright green chives.

The life Mary Frances was living in France, with all its realizations and epiphanies, hardly seemed related to the one she was used to in America. In her new world, there were moments when she was unsure of exactly who she was and how she was supposed to behave.

But as her days continued, Mary Frances would find a new way of seeing. It was slow process, a deliberate unwrapping of the self, as the young M.F.K. Fisher began to explore exactly who she wanted to be.

4

A Charmed Gastronomic Circle

*P*ARIS HAD BEEN glittering and full of light. Dijon was dark, gray, and ugly. Mary Frances described it as a Grimm's fairytale: There were crooked cobblestone streets and stone houses with mossy roofs. In autumn, the air was ripe with harvested fruit, musky wine cellars, and the putrid smells of humans and animals.

In comparison to the sophistication of Paris, Dijon seemed dowdy and provincial. But it was steeped in history. For more than a hundred years, Dijon had been a center of European power ruled by the Valois dukes. Their reign had ended in 1477, but they left a city of palaces and grand buildings, with colorful Flemish ceramic-tile roofs. There were gothic cathedrals with thin steeples, and more than a dozen bell towers. The city was famous for its Dijon mustard, cassis liquor, and for being the epicenter of one of the finest wine regions in the world: the rolling hills surrounding the city were marked with expansive vineyards.

Dijon would render an undeniable influence over the life and creative trajectory of the young M.F.K. Fisher. "It was there," she said, "that I started to grow up, to study, to make love, to eat and drink, to be me and not what I was expected to be." Her arrival, on September 28, 1929, heralded one of the most exciting, vibrant, and crucial chapters in her life.

AFTER CHECKING INTO the posh Hotel la Cloche, the couple spent two exhausting days viewing run-down rentals. Mary Frances described the one they selected, on the Rue du Petit-Potet, as a "veritable palace after some of the hovels we've climbed through."

The boardinghouse was owned by Monsieur and Madame Ollangier, who often had several rooms for rent. But as Mary Frances and Al unpacked their steamer trunks, they realized they were the only tenants. This was a coup: food was included with the monthly rent, so the Fishers and Ollangiers often enjoyed raucous meals together, giving Mary Frances and Al the perfect opportunity to practice their French and learn the Dijonaise life.

Their living space was two small rooms; there was no kitchen and no private bathroom. Even the larger of the rooms was claustrophobic, with space only for a lumpy bed and armoire. The smaller room, Al's study, held a single bed that doubled as a couch, a slim desk, and a narrow row of bookshelves. A cramped closet held a washbowl, a gas plate, and a kidney-shaped pan on squat legs. The toilet was downstairs by the courtyard.

The Ollangiers refused to start the central heating before December. To brave the chilly mornings of early autumn, Mary Frances wore Al's flannel bathrobe over her clothes. Through their small windows she could see Dijon's crooked chimney pots and high-pitched roofs. It was the landscape she and Al had dreamed of in the months before their departure. Mary Frances wrote that their new home was "so amazing that I can't realize it all."

FOR THEIR ONE-MONTH wedding anniversary, Mary Frances and Al decided to dress up and celebrate. Clutching a handwritten note of recommendation from Madame Ollangier, they made their way toward one of the nicest restaurants in town: Aux Trois Faisans. En route they stopped for a cocktail, ordering martinis, but were instead served a huge tumbler full of vermouth and water, in which a limp lemon piece floated. The drink delivered an "enormous kick," and the couple staggered as they left the bar.

They soon spotted what they thought was the restaurant, on the elegant Place d'Armes. But they were shocked when the inside resembled a low-end saloon, teeming with rowdy drinkers. The restaurant, it turned out, was upstairs. With the help of a bartender, the couple snaked their way through a quiet courtyard, up some rickety stairs, then past the kitchen, pantry, offices, and bathrooms of the restaurant until they entered a small dining room. There they showed their recommendation to the headwaiter and were led to a table for two.

Mary Frances and Al had trouble translating the menu; it didn't help that they were already a little drunk. They ordered two prix fixe meals and were surprised when they were presented with dish after dish, a seemingly endless stream of courses. There was wine, eight kinds of hors d'oeuvres, a creamy soup, courses of fish, meat, cheese, and dessert. Finally they were served fruits, coffee, and as a final sweet bite, tiny little cakes.

Mary Frances said they survived the meal only because of their youth and enthusiasm. They ate with what she called a "steady avid curiosity. Everything that was brought to the table was so new, so wonderfully cooked, that what might have been . . . a gluttonous orgy was, for our fresh ignorance, constant refreshment . . . We were immune, safe in a charmed gastronomic circle." The meal was the biggest and most elaborate the couple had ever eaten together, and the whole bill, including the tip, was $2.84.

Achingly full and wide awake, Mary Frances and Al continued on to a café after dinner, where they listened to music as Al drank sherry and Mary Frances sipped on a café crème. When they finally left for home, they wove a bit as they strolled across Dijon's cobblestones. Intoxicated and giddy, they felt as if they had "seen the far shores of another world. We were drunk with the land breeze that blew from it, and the sure knowledge that it lay waiting for us."

After a childhood wrapped in Grandmother Holbrook's suspicion of food and pleasure, Mary Frances now considered each new meal as something to be discussed endlessly, and written about, in minute detail, in letters home or in the private journals she kept. "It's an art and a religion, this French food," she wrote, "and I'm already an ardent follower of the faith."

She enjoyed dining with the Ollangiers, who were typically French in their approach to the couple: They were friendly and curious yet didn't pry into Mary Frances and Al's private life. Of the Ollangiers, Madame was the dynamic and colorful half. She looked younger than her years and was a tireless worker who oversaw the cooking and marketing, gave piano lessons, and occasionally gave public performances. She told loud jokes that mocked her husband's proper Parisian affectations, and her bawdy behavior could intimidate nearly anyone. She had a gift for scuttling from shop to market, searching for the best deals on foodstuffs that were unripe or a bit past their prime—but, with a little love, still completely edible. Under Madame Ollangier's direction, Mary Frances said even boiled shoe could be made nourishing and full of heavenly flavor.

Mary Frances's meals were prepared by the cooks that Madame Ollangier employed, so Mary Frances had the luxury of experiencing dishes without ever having to plan a menu, buy food, or clean up. She seemed never to tire of eating, though for six months after her arrival, her newly rich diet induced terrible stomachaches.

She was careful to describe her meals in great detail so that her family would understand the nuance of each flavor and texture. She described the small cakes in a pastry shop not by how they looked but by the interplay of their textures and their mingling of sweet and salty flavors. No matter how rich the cakes, there was "always something brittle or salty about them—a shell of hard chocolate or sugar, or ground up peanut stuff or something like that."

What she may not have realized was how paying such great attention to her senses would change her. Knowing she would write home about almost everything she ate and saw, she became increasingly observant. While on vacation she described a soup she ate in Southern France as "bright yellow spaghetti all tangled around several dozen red crabs." This rich and vivid writing was probably a far more effective form of creative practice than the hours she spent tied to the typewriter struggling to turn a phrase, but she didn't know that yet.

Since Mary Frances rarely cooked for herself in Dijon, she only once shared a recipe for a French food she loved: She sent Edith her translation of a recipe for crêpes. She described them as easy to make and having substitutable ingredients—Edith could use cognac, or whiskey, or vanilla as a flavoring. She instructed her mother to eat them rolled up with jam or sprinkled with sugar but advised against dressing them with pancake syrup.

She was also falling in love with wine. She drank mostly table wine or *vin ordinaire*. But she was delighted to discover that many of the wines she had considered common were great—bottles from Burgundian vintages or vineyards that would today be remarkable finds.

In December 1929, the couple took the Christmas-gift money that Al's teetotaling parents had sent and bought a bottle of red wine from the Chambertin vineyard. The vineyard, cultivated by several producers, is still considered one of the finest in the world. Mary Frances and

Al were interested in tasting it because they heard the vineyard, and the wines it produced, were among the best in Burgundy. Despite the prominence of wine in French culture, Mary Frances had to be careful when she mentioned alcohol to Rex and Edith. Soon after their arrival in Dijon, Rex reprimanded her for her letters' many accounts of drinking. Her defense: She thought her parents might be interested in what she and Al drank, since Rex and Edith seemed to enjoy a glass every once in a while. Moreover, she said the French seemed to handle their alcohol well—distinctly better than Americans did. She imagined her sister Anne saw far more drunk people on the Occidental campus than she and Al saw in Dijon. Drinking was "the best thing to do over here," she explained, and "every time we order a new kind we wish you were here."

Not long after settling in Dijon, Mary Frances discovered she could attend free classes at the Beaux Arts, a fine-arts school that was part of the French national system. The classes would help her improve her language skills and utilize some of the creative energy she felt building inside her. Al was relieved when he learned his wife would have something to keep her occupied while he focused on his work.

She began with a two-hour class in modeling and sculpture, and also took courses in drawing and art history. As her classes continued, it became clear that Mary Frances had little flair for art but a huge amount of motivation. She practiced her drawing for hours but was rarely proud of anything she produced. Each sketch started well, but she often got lost somewhere in the middle and ended up with an image that, in her opinion, failed to capture her artistic intent. She hoped that at some point she would be able to draw something with character. If she was never able to achieve this, she worried Al and her family would think her classes at the Beaux Arts were a waste of time.

Meanwhile, the couple's life had developed an easy, if predictable, routine. Both Mary Frances and Al attended classes in the mornings and returned to the Ollangiers for their lunch. The midday meal would last for hours, partly because of the conversations that began around the table. The group often sat around after seven or eight courses smoking cigarettes and engaging in political discussion. It was interesting, if at times a little tiring. After breaking away from the conversation and remnants of the meal, the couple would head upstairs for a bite of something sweet or a nip of liquor before Al returned to the library. Then Mary Frances would "read or write letters or simply sit and look out the window" until the afternoon had passed into evening.

As it grew colder and the heat was finally turned on, she spent much of her time slumped over the radiator. Al returned home around six o'clock and the couple would sit and talk or take a stroll before dinner. Supper was never over before nine, and after the meal the couple would return to their rooms, where Al would study and Mary Frances would read or write letters until they went to bed. She described this routine as the "story of almost every day . . . It may sound rather dull, but it isn't."

She wrote her mother that she was happily lost in what she described as her "newly married state of unconsciousness." To Anne she claimed that her feelings for Al had deepened so much that when she thought of her wedding day she believed, by comparison, that she had "positively hated him when we marched up the aisle."

Mary Frances was feigning contentment, saying that her "whole life, until I met Al, was a kind of searching for what I have now." But it wasn't always easy being married to him, which she realized and feared. "I hope it lasts," she later wrote of her marriage. "I think I'll always love Al, and I think he'll always love me, but I don't know that we'll always love each other."

She often felt "lost soulish" after long days in a foreign city with no one familiar nearby. As in America, she had made few friends. Al was a distracted husband, more concerned with the demands of his schedule than nurturing their young marriage. She was constantly waiting for him—for his arrival home, for him to be done with his work, for him to be in the mood for fun and adventure. Spackman later remarked that Mary Frances was "naturally unable to diagnose . . . the specialized loneliness" of life with Al Fisher.

She found solace in the beauty of her new city and carried her writing and drawing instruments with her everywhere. She ducked into Dijon's old churches to sketch women attending mass in candlelit naves. She ate puffy brioche and drank hot chocolate in local cake shops on cold afternoons. She thought of food "all the time" and remarked that if Al didn't seem just as hungry, she'd be worried about her ravenous appetite.

She began working on a novel, describing it as a "shilling shocker," a piece of pulp fiction that might be worthwhile if she could just figure out how to end it. In her journal she wrote that she believed that "[c]heap novels are about the best I'll ever do, I think. Maybe I can earn some money with them while Al's writing the Real English."

Sure that her writing talent paled in comparison to her husband's, she was determined to write for an hour each day. That's what Al did, and she was sure the dedication powered his creativity. But whenever she sat down to compose, the words wouldn't come. She spent hours looking for the correct letters on the typewriter, fretting over words, and crossing out sentences she didn't like.

One day, wandering the streets of Dijon, she finished some errands, practiced her sketching, and then stopped at a deserted teahouse. She described the solitary meal of tea and toast as "boring and desolate." She walked home slowly, not quite ready to return.

She arrived to find that Al had decided to stop studying so he could surprise her with a late-afternoon walk and the promise of a sweet treat. Mary Frances was furious, cold, and too full of toast to go back out again. She wished that he had told her about his plan to stop studying early and was alternately miffed and flattered by his sudden desire to spend time with her. Al didn't seem to realize that she was developing a life that extended beyond waiting for him; nor did he realize that she would have abandoned it all at the promise of a few hours of time together.

With few other outlets, Mary Frances found it hard to keep Al and his needs from shaping and consuming her days. He set the agenda. "I wish Al would come home now, instead of in half an hour," she wrote in her journal. "Perhaps he will . . . and probably he won't." This constant deferring to Al's schedule, mood, and needs sapped her self-confidence. "All my life that has any reality is connected with him." Everything else in her world sprang from her imagination—and there was only so much drawing, writing, and thinking she could do.

She did her best to revel in Al's intellect and promising writing talent, telling Edith that she wouldn't want to be in France with a husband who was boring or stupid. One evening, after waiting long past the time Al had promised to come and pick her up from the Beaux Arts, she remarked that she knew Al was "in the library and has forgotten me. Everything sweeps before him in the fine fervor of hunting through bibliographies . . . I with the rest. I think I can acknowledge that without jealousy. I knew more or less what I was marrying." She described her relationship with her husband as a mix of "bliss and mild monotony."

Al's rigorous, academic mindset extended to his marriage. Though he fancied himself a true romantic and seemed to savor the overtly adoring duties associated with being a husband—he delivered bouquets of flowers to Mary Frances weekly and regularly took her to dinner or the movies—he failed to invest more than adoring flourishes in their relationship.

He appears to have been particularly ambivalent about physical intimacy. Mary Frances believed that Al was a virgin when they married. But regardless of his sexual experience, Al quickly became uninterested in developing sexual chemistry with his new bride. His attitude was hurtful—she simply couldn't understand why her husband was so uninterested in her.

Later Mary Frances said that Al seemed to be frightened by the physical act of sex; she theorized that he had been influenced by his religious upbringing. Al also told her that he was terrified of contracting a sexually transmitted disease, which he associated with Mary Frances's occasional visits to Dijon's public baths.

The city's plumbing was so inadequate that home bathing required heating and carrying water up several flights of stairs. Bathhouses were clean, safe, and had private rooms. A bath cost only 8 cents, and Mary Frances could soak for an indulgent twenty minutes before an attendant would knock, signaling that it was time to dry off and dress. But Al was horrified at the thought of communal bathing. Mary Frances claimed that he refused to sleep with her for an entire month after her first trip—he wanted to make sure she had not contracted syphilis or crabs.

Rather than working to foster greater intimacy in their marriage, Al retreated. He was exceedingly moody, which had the desired effect of pushing Mary Frances further away. Ever the dominant personality, Al viewed Mary Frances as a wife who could fulfill his sexual desires as needed. Bob Spackman later remarked that his friend treated women as objects, "rather than as a complementary personality." Ultimately he seemed to have little interest in cultivating a rich and well-rounded partnership.

Outwardly, however, Al claimed to take great joy in his marriage and, in particular, in Mary Frances's success as a new bride and home-maker. He wrote detailed letters to Rex and Edith documenting her proficiency at household chores, and recounting how happy being a wife seemed to make her. He described Mary Frances as "perfectly splendid about everything . . . She makes me keep my things in order and even helps me by folding shirts and things. Besides, she mends my socks, sews on buttons and organizes the laundry. She also washes her own stockings and negligee which in my eyes is nothing short of beautiful." He admitted that when he saw her doing household tasks he couldn't help but "look forward to the time when we shall have our own house and our own possessions together all at once."

Mary Frances's own feelings about her household duties were more subdued. She left school around noon each day, planning to do housework. But after completing just enough to look productive, she placed her darning aside to write more letters. She knew she should behave like a good wife and "keep up a pretense of being married and domestic," but it wasn't what she wanted to do. When Al wrote to Rex and Edith that Mary Frances wailed and shrieked when she found a hole in a sock or a shirt with a missing button, one must wonder if he truly understood her exclamations. Was she really shrieking over a sock—or was her frustration much deeper?

She coped by focusing her attention on her artwork, her writing, and on her sister, Anne. She was convinced that Anne should come and live with her and Al in Dijon for the next academic year. Edith and Rex agreed, hoping that a year away would break Anne's poor habits of boys, parties, and lackluster studying. Mary Frances promised to find a three-room apartment so that the trio could live together. She wanted three rooms not for the newlyweds' privacy but for her and for Anne: They wouldn't have to worry about talking loud and disturbing Al's papers. With extra rooms, they would be shielded from Al's muttering and hissing as he studied and worked at home. According to Mary Frances, Al had numerous habits that could drive a person crazy, but she insisted that she was still content being married to her "favourite Lord of Creation." It's hard to know if this nickname for Al was penned in abject adoration, jest, or with just a hint of venom. And despite the attention Mary Frances paid to preparing, she would have to wait nearly a year for Anne's arrival—if she arrived at all.

AFTER A COUPLE of months, Mary Frances became thoroughly frustrated by her isolation in Dijon. She described herself as fussing around all day, with little to show for it. She was particularly worried that her language skills weren't developing more quickly. She only spoke French with the Ollangiers, a few classmates and instructors at the Beaux Arts, and shopkeepers. The rest of the time she was reading, writing, and speaking in English. Still, she begged her sister to continue to send regular letters. "Write to me often, Sis," she pleaded. "I needn't go into the reasons, but you know why."

She was irritated that Al, simply because he was a man, had more opportunities than she for social and linguistic advancement. In a letter to Anne she wrote, "he hears French lectures and reads French books and then is privileged by his sex to talk to anyone . . . he's already met several quite interesting people." A French lieutenant visited several times a week to help Al with his conversation and grammar skills. Mary Frances listened to their conversations through the thin walls of her bedroom, cribbing tips from the private lessons, from which she was forbidden.

She must have done a good job of expressing her frustrations and dissatisfaction about her few French-speaking opportunities to Al, because he soon found her a cadre of female conversation partners. In a letter to Edith, Al described one as looking like a tomato (red in the face), the second like a bean (tall), and the third a Burbank potato (dark and earthy). He found his wife's dedication to her French remarkable. But to her it was less exceptional—the afternoon conversations were her means of survival. Lessons gave her contact with humans who weren't her husband or the Ollangiers. She was also competitive, and hated the idea that Al's proficiency might surpass hers.

Bob and Mary Anne Spackman visited the couple in Dijon and were surprised that Al had dared to bring the "petted daughter of a well-to-do family abroad to a shabby room in the Rue du Petit Potet." He said the couple "lived in near poverty" and that day after day Al left Mary Frances, "pretty much plantée la, while he went off to the café in the Place du Thèatre, and wrote." Bob and Mary Anne were also shocked by the formalities present in the Fishers' daily relationship. Their polite interactions, heavy with "yes dear" and "no thank you dear," seemed to belie a lack of intimacy and a relative lack of understanding about what marriage was truly about.

Spackman also noticed that the Fishers' marriage seemed to lack newlywed passion, while he and his new bride were making love two to three times a day. He observed that "Mary Frances simply was not behaving like a girl in love at all. If what Spackman said was true, Mary Frances hinted at her unhappiness very subtly. Most of the time she was glad to proclaim her love proudly, almost as if it were something that needed to be proven again and again.

FOR THEIR FIRST Christmas as a married couple, Al and Mary Frances traveled to Cassis, a small village on the Mediterranean. Rex and Edith funded the trip, and Monsieur Ollangier helped them plan it, mapping them through Avignon, Arles, and the neighboring port of Marseille. He made a list of all the fine restaurants along the way and the famous dishes they might see on a menu—the trip was just as much a gastro-nomical pilgrimage as it was a holiday. When the couple left Dijon, the first snow of the year was falling as the train slowly left the station. It made the characteristically grim city lighter and more beautiful—there were no footprints in the snow and there was no noise. It was a quiet and lovely start to their holiday.

Cassis was beautiful: Cliffs rose out of the deep-blue water, and there were groves of pine, cypress, and olive trees. On Christmas Eve they walked to a small chapel, redolent with hundreds of candles, for midnight Mass. There they joined the small seaside community as they sang carols and reenacted the Nativity. After the Mass, locals gave Mary Frances and Al glasses of sweet wine and invited them to share a celebratory Christmas feast. They ate and drank into the early hours of the morning before stumbling down the hill to their portside hotel.

The trip was romantic and beautiful, and she hoped they could return to Cassis again and again. But Al rebuffed the idea, saying that he wouldn't want to ruin the good memory of a place by returning to it. He believed, as Mary Frances described it, that "if people knew real happiness anywhere, they must never expect to find it there again." To his wife it was an ominous declaration.

On Christmas Day, Mary Frances and Al toasted Rex and Edith by drinking a bottle of Châteauneuf-du-Pape and eating capon—small roasted larks—that were dark, crumbling, and pungent. The couple couldn't stand the taste, but were proud that their bellies were strong enough to stomach the French delicacy. They were mournful because they had no presents to open, but Mary Frances was pleased with the gifts they'd received before leaving Dijon: books, candy, and a pair of nice gloves for both of them. On the day that they left Cassis, she sent her family a postcard that read "it hurts like everything to leave."

THE SHIFT FROM 1929 into a new decade passed without fanfare. It was bitterly cold in Dijon, and for Mary Frances there was little to do but muse and write. The Ollangiers had unexpectedly announced they were selling their home. They believed Mary Frances and Al could stay on as renters, but they didn't yet know who the new owners would be. The uncertainty about their future made her a little nervous.

There were other things eating at her too, particularly her growing confusion about her wifely duties and how they clashed with her overwhelming creative urges. In a letter to Anne, she described a dinner with Al that ended at one in the morning in a heated conversation about the books Al wanted to write and the books Mary Frances dreamed of writing but "couldn't write if I wanted to."

The couple rarely sparred, partly because they were never deeply engaged enough to argue. But when the topic of creativity arose, Mary Frances was eager to fight for the opportunity to pursue her artistic inclinations. Al, meanwhile, thought Mary Frances's creative interests were charming, but not something that required such devotion. Her primary responsibility was to be his wife. At some point they would return to the United States and her world would be composed of duties associated with housekeeping and child-rearing. Her creative pursuits would be just a fond memory.

So, in late January 1930, she took preemptive action: She decided to return to school full time, at the University of Dijon. She planned to study for a certificate in English literature—a demanding one-year course, taught entirely in French. A few weeks later, she broadened her goal: a diploma that would allow her to teach French in any foreign country. On top of all that, she also toyed with taking two private art lessons a week.

Although she insisted that she was one of the two happiest people on earth—Al, of course, being the other—Mary Frances was clearly unfulfilled. She told Edith, "I used to pride myself on being rather independent, but I've certainly taken a turn in the opposite direction, these last six months." Still unsure of what, precisely, a new marriage should offer, Mary Frances deferred repeatedly to Al, hoping that he would take more interest in her if she were complacent. But Al hardly noticed.

IN AN ATTEMPT to expand their social circle, the couple joined Le Club Alpin. The group took long, rambling walks almost every weekend, and the hikes always ended with a huge meal in a village restaurant. The couple's first excursion was a fifteen-mile trek over small mountains, up cliffs, along canals, and through enormous fields of deep mud and dirt.

Mary Frances had only one complaint: The men and the women who belonged to the club seemed to consider her fragile and inept. The reason couldn't be her physique: Tall, and a bit sturdier due to indulgent French treats, she was hardly birdlike. Mary Frances was irritated by the idea that the club members, robust older French men and women, might find her stupid because of her imperfect French—or dismiss her intellectually because she was an American woman.

Eventually, the group did provide some of the companionship she so desperately needed. More than once Mary Frances attended hikes without Al; she was equally happy to send him off into the woods. One lazy Sunday morning she wrote to tell Edith that Al was gone for the day and that it was "really quite nice for a change, though I wouldn't want it to happen very often. I simply can't work when he's around . . . and neither can he."

The couple's dwindling finances further complicated their time together. At the end of many months, with money running short, they frantically cut corners: Cheap beer was consumed instead of aperitifs; there were no more trips to the movies. Occasionally Al became "morbid about being in debt, not supporting his wife, and so on."

Preferring to ignore the reality, that her family was a crucial source of financial support, Mary Frances laughed off Al's worries. In a letter to her father she shared a more pressing concern: Though Al believed that Mary Frances was a fine wife, he had never eaten anything she'd cooked. She dreaded the day when, their having left France, her culinary skills would have to compete with the meals they'd enjoyed there.

Indeed, Mary Frances seemed wholly unaware of the fiscal crisis in the United States and oblivious of the fact that money might be tight in her family's home, too. Regardless, Rex and Edith, though occasionally pinched, were still trying to provide the funds their daughter needed. At times it must have been aggravating to receive long letters full of stories of raucous dinners with numerous bottles of wine, endless trips to the movies, and train travels to other French towns—all funded from Rex and Edith Kennedy's pocketbook.

The money Rex and Edith sent was intended for their daughter; Al received his own stipend from the American Legion scholarship. But Mary Frances shared almost everything with him. Al was acutely aware of his lack of financial viability and how this might trouble his wife's family and friends. He anxiously searched for additional funding sources to plug the holes in their budget.

In late spring, Anne Kennedy announced that she would not go to France for the following school year. Mary Frances claimed that she always knew her sister wouldn't leave her boyfriend and college social scene. So, still eager for companions, she turned her persuasive powers on Lawrence Clark Powell, an acquaintance from Occidental interested in completing his advanced degree abroad. In a letter she described the many amazing perks of foreign living. She and Al were "leading exactly the kind of life we've always wanted to." Later Larry said it was that letter, with its witty and friendly tone, that lured him overseas.

To quell any sadness or hard feelings that might have followed Anne's decision, Edith and Anne decided to visit England for the summer. Mary Frances would meet them, without Al, for a vacation of sightseeing, museums, and theater. Next they would visit Dijon but only briefly—just long enough to see the city and Mary Frances's home.

Mary Frances claimed she never thought of protesting when Edith suggested she spend the summer away from her new husband. Her mother, ever the isolationist, thought married couples benefited from the occasional long separation or private vacation. Mary Frances looked forward to the vacation but disliked the idea of spending so much time away from Al. So she was hurt by how easily he agreed to her extended trip. Although she said he seemed "broodish" about the possibility of her absence, he was ultimately ambivalent about her travel plans. Secretly, Mary Frances believed Al would be glad to be rid of her, even accusing him of showing overt pleasure when he handed her the train tickets for her journey.

MARY FRANCES, EDITH, and Anne spent the summer of 1930 in fancy hotels and took high tea—an array of savory cold cuts and cheeses, complemented by sweet scones, cakes, and tea—nearly every afternoon. In London, Mary Frances made a side trip to Oxford to visit the Spackmans, and while there, admitted that she often felt lonely and hated living so far away from her family.

Her time away from Al made Mary Frances fully realize just how solitary and unromantic her newlywed life in Dijon had been. Worse, the company of Edith and Anne was not as comforting as she had hoped—even her mother and sister could not fill the void in her life.

There was a new, odd distance in her relationship with her sister. Both Anne and Mary Frances had changed over the course of their year apart: Mary Frances had become worldly and interested in creative and literary pursuits while Anne remained crazy about boys, parties, and clothing. As a result, Mary Frances became increasingly interested in her youngest sister, Norah.

Norah was thirteen, and Mary Frances had lived away from home for much of Norah's childhood; they didn't know each other well. Perhaps Mary Frances saw Norah as young enough to benefit from, and welcome, the influence of a cosmopolitan older sister.

In July 1930, Mary Frances wrote to Norah, offering unabashed creative advice concerning a poem Norah had published in her school paper. She told Norah: "When I was about your age, I saw beautiful things, I tried to make them into words, as you're beginning to do. And when I showed them to people, they were either smiled at kindly or ignored." She encouraged Norah to keep writing and, if she wanted, to send her verses to her sister. "You can trust me with your poems," she told her.

In return, Mary Frances hoped to send a few things that she'd written. But she wanted honest, thorough criticism, not the wandering thoughts of a young schoolgirl. She asked Norah not to mention her letter and her intimate confessions to anyone in their family. "Don't talk about it to anyone else, that's all," she said. "I've showed you a part of a private me."

It's hard to imagine how Norah must have responded to the letter from her older sister that displayed the words FOR PRIVATE READING when folded. She couldn't have understood the letter for what it was: an admission of her eldest sister's creative frustration and loneliness.

AT THE END of the summer, Mary Frances returned to Dijon with Edith and Anne, eager to show off her new home. After a whirlwind tour of the city, punctuated by food-and-wine-fueled dinners with Al, her family left. The quiet and loneliness penetrated her, and her letter and journal writing dwindled as she struggled to regain her position in her home and marriage.

Mary Frances and Al's first wedding anniversary, September 5, 1930, was a "perfect blue day with a hint of autumn when the breeze blows from the lake." The two were vacationing in the small town of Gérardmer, in the Vosges mountains of France, before their fall classes resumed.

The scenery was stunning. There was a lake, "ink-black in the shadow of the mountains, silver blue in the middle." A walking path circled it under "enormous fir trees that grew from the tops of the mountains to the water, like feathers."

After a summer apart the couple went on long walks, rented canoes, played billiards, sat in beer halls, and drank red Alsatian wine. She said that everyone who met them thought they were on their honeymoon, but she knew the truth: that they were already a staid and settled old couple. No longer newlyweds, they were about to begin their second year in France.

The mountains towered above her like the greatest cathedrals in Europe. But there was something foreboding about the vacation. Despite her return from her summer trip, Mary Frances still felt miles away from her husband. Sitting across from him, fingering the stem of a wineglass and watching the dark lake shine, she was desperate to bridge the gap. But Al was so remote, and her romantic advances so often ignored. She was saddened to realize she wasn't quite sure how to make her marriage bloom.

$$\boxed{5}$$

Letters and Loneliness

*D*URING M.F.K. FISHER'S second year in France, fewer letters flew between Dijon and Whittier. After the long summer holiday with her mother and sister, Mary Frances believed that she had exhausted her supply of insights and anecdotes. The letters she did send were almost perfunctory. She had little to say and was tired of the effort it took to write imaginative and newsy reports of her life in France.

Besides, Edith was slow to respond, which disturbed Mary Frances. She hated to find her mailbox empty, insisting that Edith should have much to share: Whittier gossip, family news, and whatever firm opinion she held that day.

Perhaps what truly exasperated Mary Frances was the effort it took to consistently happy and cheerful in her correspondence. After Edith and Anne left Europe, a typical day was comprised of sleeping in, reading, people watching at a café, visiting the library, and an evening spent at the movies or in her bathrobe reading, writing, or listening as Al read aloud. Once she would have reveled in such a lazy existence. But now it felt dull and indulgent. She wished she'd bought a cribbage set when she was in England.

Meanwhile, Larry Powell had arrived from California and moved into an empty room in the Rue du Petit Potet townhouse. He was a handsome twenty-four-year-old with thick brown hair, large brown eyes, and an expansive grin. He was intelligent, talkative, vivacious—the opposite of Al's dreamy intensity. His proximity to Mary Frances and Al's small apartment was ideal, and the three became fast friends.

Al helped Larry organize his thesis material and introduced him to his academic adviser, George Connes. Then, after the university approved Larry's thesis topic, the work of the California poet Robinson Jeffers, Al began to help Larry with his writing. Soon the two were studying together in the library, writing in cafés, and discussing avant-garde authors and literature into the wee hours. Larry helped Al loosen up, teaching him about music and encouraging him to be more relaxed in Dijon.

Larry and Mary Frances also became close friends. Not wanting anyone to think her interest in him was anything other than friendly, she was careful not to say too much about Larry in her letters home. She even told Anne that anything she wrote about Larry was for her ears alone. "I know nothing about him that could shock a flea, and wouldn't tell anyone if I did," she wrote. But "the most significant detail can grow enough to do harm—and our relations here are too pleasant to be spoiled by a third-rate scandal."

Although there's nothing to suggest that Larry and Mary Frances were romantically involved while in Dijon, his presence surely upset the already delicate balance of the Fishers' marriage. Instead of spending time together, as a couple, they now spent time with Larry. Soon, curiosity about Larry's life and exploits threatened to eclipse much of their interest in each other. Both were blind to how the third personality might influence their relationship: Al was happy to have another person to help keep his wife occupied, Mary Frances was glad finally to feel adored. Were Larry's flirtations innocent? If they weren't, Al never seemed to notice.

The three often spent cold evenings dressed in bathrobes over their clothes to keep warm, enjoying wine and intense philosophical discussions. Mary Frances listened intently as her husband and Larry tackled art, literature, and culture and read their poetry aloud. She was discouraged from participating in their conversations, her comments dismissed by the men's chuckles, sighs, and eye rolls. No matter how much she knew, the two—Al in particular—never took her intellect seriously.

To Al and Larry, she appeared the perfect acolyte—quietly listening and knitting as their bantering grew fiercer and drunker. Later Larry wondered just what sort of ideas flew through her mind as she listened to them talk. Was she mentally composing her own lines? Refuting their grandiose theories? Whatever the internal dialogue, she made it seem as if she was basking in admiration, preferring these petite salons to her usual staid evenings.

AL HAD SURVIVED his first stressful year as a student but remained intensely focused on his academic and creative work. He was particularly engrossed in the epic poem he was writing: "The Ghost in the Underblows."

The idea came to him dramatically: "I suddenly found myself with a plan for a poem," he wrote in a preface to a draft. "[I] . . . found myself writing it as though the world and the devil depended on it, for tomorrow I was going to die . . . I wrote The Ghost because I had to; it seized on me as any vision does, and every effort I could make could not keep me always balanced and in control of it."

Al envisioned the poem as spanning sixty-six books, the same number as the Bible's. And he dared to envision that the two works would eventually be read in concert. Al truly believed that the creative and intellectual effort he put into the poem would make him the American equivalent of James Joyce or Percy Bysshe Shelley.

Mary Frances thought her husband was a good writer but that he needed to "emerge from his preconceived ideas of style and his few remaining vestiges of Presbyterian boyhood." She pushed him with gentle criticism that led him to spend long days crafting his poem.

Hopeful that his writing might be critically studied someday, he described himself pretentiously, in the third person, at the end of a draft: "At this time in his life Fisher was well and happy," he wrote. "He was studying ten hours a day, making notes toward the composition of his dissertation . . . France, long the objective of his effort, was joyful for him; life was abundant, and The Ghost was a compelling vision." Already a distracted husband, Al's epic was swallowing all his attention.

Mary Frances was trying to keep busy and help her husband, but it was hard. Some particularly cold mornings, Al opted to stay home from the library and work in their cramped quarters. She struggled to keep quiet, avoiding the typewriter and its loud, clacking keys. But she constantly needed something: an eraser, a book on a shelf over Al's head, or handiwork that lay next to him. "The room's so narrow," she wrote, "no matter how small a move I make, I have to clamber over him."

Occasionally Al's mood shifted so quickly that she seemed to disrupt him without even trying. One journal entry describes the couple's return home after an outing. After stepping away to hang her coat and tidy her hair she returned to find Al sitting on the radiator with a manuscript in his hands. She had been gone only moments but already Al was lost in thought, "quiet as a wraith." She quickly apologized, saying she was "sorry to disturb his muse though there is no excuse for such obvious flippancy as we both know." The abrupt shift in Al's demeanor deflated her, and she felt his emotional distance: "Everything that pressed against my mind had melted like snow on a warm cheek but with no wet tracings, only a realization of its absence."

She became consumed by a sense of "thwarted energy." She was anxious to return to school but had been advised to delay her fall classes at the University of Dijon; she was too far ahead of the other students, who were just beginning their study of English literature. She kept herself occupied by helping Al work on the indexes for his thesis and started several writing projects. Each morning she went to a dusty bookshop run by a Monsieur Venot to dig through stacks and catalogs to research her potential subjects: Leonardo da Vinci and Julien Benda, a French novelist and philosopher. In the afternoon she worked at home, typing her notes until her eyes and fingers ached.

She also returned to the Beaux Arts, taking evening classes in sculpture from an older man named Yencesse. He encouraged her work in clay, and Mary Frances pestered him with a stream of questions about art and technique. She liked her instructor's attention, which she lacked at home, and longed for his reassurance and gentle critiques.

Despite Al and Mary Frances's emotional and physical dissonance, they began two writing projects that they hoped to finish together. The first was another dime-store thriller; the second was a scholarly portrait of the novelist Paul Bourget, a French intellectual and master of the psychological thriller. Both projects were executed in a similar fashion: Al would expound and Mary Frances would write. But though Al hoped that his wife's devotion to their writing projects would springboard him to fame, the effect would be the opposite. Unintentionally, he helped her sharpen her pen.

At home, piles of hole-riddled socks and worn-out collars mounted in the corner, begging to be mended. But Mary Frances's fingers began to "yawn at the thought and turn numb" when she considered her chores. She hardly believed that the secrets to her happiness lay in a sewing basket.

It was becoming harder to find happiness anywhere in her home. After the Ollangiers, her lively French friends, sold the building, they left Dijon, and Mary Frances missed them dearly. The new landlords of the house on Rue du Petit Potet, the Rigulots, were different. Once wealthy, they were now on the brink of ruin. They had purchased the small townhouse in the hope of regaining stability.

But to Mary Frances's surprise, she found that Madame Rigulot was "one of the most unreservedly sensual people" she had ever met. Despite the woman's financial woes, she sought only the best for her kitchen— pure butter, fine cooking wines, perfect produce. Their meals, though not exactly haute cuisine, were beautifully prepared. Dishes were simple and hearty, made delicious by sharp technique and the purest ingredients. Everyone ate well and drank fine wine even on weekdays—Mary Frances was sure she and Al ate much more than they paid for every month.

The Rigulots' food was some of the most authentic French cooking Mary Frances would ever eat. Nearly every Sunday, Madame Rigulot's parents, Papazi and Mamazi, would arrive for a huge midday meal. Together the group ate the finest cuts of meat and beautiful vegetables. They enjoyed rich, creamy soups, garlicky snails, and airy soufflés. They chased slices of truffled goose breast with champagne and ended their meals with brandy-soaked cakes, chilled fruits in wine and cream, and Papazi's tarts, which were "big as a cartwheel, with all the apple slices laying back to belly to back in whorls and swoops." For Mary Frances, the convivial dining was a welcome diversion. At the loud, messy table she enjoyed herself so much she forgot her budget woes, the distance between Dijon and Whittier, and the widening gap in her marriage.

The lunches that stretched into suppers were so extravagant that Mary Frances, Al, and Larry were compelled to sneak away from the table. But there was no good excuse—they couldn't tell Madame they were full. She just shook her head and insisted they sit and eat just a little more. Eventually they decided it was easier to stay at the table and risk indigestion than to refuse a second or third helping.

Madame Rigulot liked Mary Frances: She gave her grease-stained, handwritten recipe cards and offered to teach her what she knew. But Mary Frances declined, writing that she felt threatened: "I was too shy, and too absorbed in Al Fisher and being away from home. I felt I couldn't have anything interrupt the little pattern I'd made of being very much in love and working hard." It was a flippant choice, and one she lived to regret.

MARY FRANCES AND Al continued celebrating weekly wedding anniversaries, cramping their budget with private parties: a movie, a drink out, or a small bouquet of flowers. Al's romantic gestures fed Mary Frances, convincing her that Al was truly invested in her and her happiness. Yet she failed to fully realize that his wooing verged on mania: After ignoring her for days, he would return with vigor, energetically leap up the stairs, and surprise her with small treasures like "two smooth round tomatoes, still pink with newness" and a little pile of salt he'd set on the table.

But some celebrations were not so convivial. One evening, Al knocked over a glass while getting up from the table and then tripped over his own feet on the way out of the café. A slight embarrassment was made far worse by his worrying that the locals would think him a drunken American. Outside Mary Frances scolded Al—not for having fallen but for his bad French accent as he apologized. He was mortified— so mortified that he wrote Rex and Edith, recounting the moment in exhaustive detail. He ended his tale by reporting that "happily the night was dark and the air cold." The darkness hid his red face and anger over his wife's scorn.

On Rex and Edith's wedding anniversary, Mary Frances and Al fêted them from afar with a meal out and a special wine (funded by Rex and Edith's donations). Later Mary Frances wrote to her parents, thanking them for being such a good example of marital commitment: "We both decided that the best thing we could wish for would be to live together as long and gracefully as you have, and above all to make our children as happy as you've made us." She kept her unhappier sentiments deeply buried.

Just as it had been the year before, the couple's Christmas holiday was a welcome break. Without the structure of school, Al relaxed and was free to devote more time and attention to his wife. The two experienced a romantic revival on a trip to Germany, which Mary Frances called the "most perfect trip we've ever taken . . . Every moment of it was good." Mary Frances loved the holiday squares filled with Christmas finery: trees and wreaths of all shapes and sizes, booths of lebkuchen, tree ornaments, and candles. The shops offered beautiful foie gras in fantastic shapes, and tiny edible pigs fashioned from sausages. Mary Frances thanked Rex and Edith profusely for having bankrolled the trip. Again, she insisted, they were "quite completely silly about each other and everything we see or do together."

For Christmas, Al gave Mary Frances a chapbook titled Pages from the Ghost. Inside the red, leather-bound volume sat a handwritten note: "Best love to my wife, most precious of all ghosts." It was a striking gift, but Mary Frances surely wished that it had followed more daily reminders of her husband's affection.

With the end of the vacation came a return to the realities of Dijon. As Al's academic standing at the university advanced, so did the number of faculty-related social activities the couple was expected to attend. Mary Frances detested the gatherings, especially the wifely role she was forced to fill. She grew accustomed to dressing up in her proper tweed suits and turning on her charms for a roomful of staid academicians, but she could never learn to enjoy it.

One week had several such engagements: a tea, a birthday party, and a formal dinner in honor of a visiting professor from Yale. In a letter to Anne, Mary Frances compared herself to a puppet—"watch me today and pull wires, dearie"—and ridiculed the party games she would be forced to play with the "intelligentsia of Dijon." She remarked, sarcastically, "Isn't it fun to be a kiddy again?"

Mary Frances had no intention of befriending the fussy faculty wives. But she did care about how they perceived her—especially on the day she showed up at a luncheon in a lovely suit and all the other wives were dressed in swishy black georgette dresses. She also hated how the women wanted to gossip and cackle about everyone they knew. Mary Frances, who had plenty of gossip of her own, always declined. She refused many invitations to ladies-only events, but the women kept inviting her. "I'm something of a curiosity," she wrote. "It's very chic now to know Americans . . . They're really overly nice to me."

Dull university events made Mary Frances worry about returning with Al to the United States at the end of the following school year. She now dreaded leaving France. She hoped that Al might be able to find another fellowship so they could stay in Dijon. Despite her loneliness, she enjoyed her carefree life and didn't want to waste any more time being a wife and homemaker.

But she was also starting to internalize the stories she heard from home. Jobs were scarce—would Al be able to find one? She occasionally felt it didn't matter where they landed, because Al wasn't planning to teach any longer than he had to. As soon as they had enough money to buy a home and to care for children, he would stop working and they would "race for the beach—any beach." It wasn't clear what Al would do to keep his future family afloat, but neither he nor Mary Frances seemed particularly concerned. Perhaps they believed he could soon support them all as a poet.

In late January 1931, Mary Frances got a strange letter from her mother. Edith wrote to her daughter suggesting she spend the following summer in Whittier. Mary Frances found the news "exciting—and disturbing too." She didn't want to go—she wanted to stay with Al and help him finish his thesis. But she knew that her mother would likely persuade her to make the trip.

She worried that she would be "miserable without Al" and recalled the loneliness she'd felt the previous summer. Her worries were exacerbated by her uncertainty about Al—she couldn't decide if he thought she should leave. "He may want it," she posited, "but be afraid he'll hurt my feelings if he intimates it." She wondered if it might be "good for him to bat around alone for awhile," to focus on his work uninterrupted. A summer apart might prove to Al how important she was to his happiness and productivity.

Al, to her surprise, encouraged the visit. But Mary Frances had a second worry: that another departure would convince the Dijonaise that she was "absolutely no good as a spouse." With Al's support, she decided that as long as her husband liked her, she shouldn't care what anyone else thought about her marriage or the time she spent away from it.

A few weeks later Mary Frances wrote Edith a cheerful letter: "So you've decided to have me come home! Al and I have already begun to kiss each other goodbye but we're both awfully glad—he for me, and I for myself." Once again, Edith had exerted a subtle force over her daughter's marriage. The young couple, not even married two years, was facing their second extended separation.

There were several possible reasons for Edith's continued dominance over her daughter's life. One was that she sensed the trouble in Mary Frances's marriage and wanted her home so that she could nudge the flailing union in the right direction. Another involved concerns for her other daughters: Anne had been thwarted by her Occidental beau and had taken up with a young man named Ted Kelly, whom she seemed dangerously close to marrying. Neither Rex nor Edith cared for the match and hoped that Mary Frances might divert Anne's attentions.

A third concern was Norah—money was short and Rex and Edith weren't sure that they could afford to send her to a boarding school of the same caliber that her sisters had attended. Ever reliant on her eldest daughter, Edith seemed to need Mary Frances nearby, to help her cope with everything in her life that was unsettling.

But as soon as Mary Frances heard that the expense of her visit might prevent Norah from attending private school, she was quick to respond. "Why on earth don't you postpone my trip home until times are better?" she wrote. Delaying her trip would allow Rex and Edith to use the money to send Norah to boarding school for at least a year.

To convince Rex and Edith that she shouldn't come home for the summer, Mary Frances urged them to prioritize the needs of Anne, Norah, and David. She hated the thought of Norah's enrolling at Whittier's public high school, competing with snobbish wealthy girls or, even worse, being forced to conform to their vapid codes.

Mary Frances claimed she would no longer need her parents' financial support. But her calculations were based on Rex supplying her with money equal to her last two years of college. They were also hoping Al would win another fellowship. Either way, she said, they were going to stop living on other people.

The plans for Mary Frances's trip and the question of what to do with Norah weighed on Mary Frances and Edith. For several weeks, communication between the two was brief and mundane. Mary Frances turned her attention to her studies at the university. She dedicated herself to preparing for her final papers and exams. She had decided long ago that her diploma from the University of Dijon would be worthless without the addition of an American college degree. Still, doing well on her final tests would offer tangible proof that she hadn't completely wasted her time abroad.

And so she was horrified when the school's examination results were posted publicly. Her name appeared in the lower echelons, an *assez bien* (fair) beside it instead of the *très bien* she'd wanted. Having barely passed, Mary Frances realized that, yet again, she had never truly taken her classes seriously or studied hard for anything her entire life. She was embarrassed by her performance but glad she had at least passed. Besides, she rationalized, she had no plans to continue her academic career.

In mid-March 1931, the couple got good news—Al had received the fellowship he had been seeking. Their stay in France would be extended for another year. "Doesn't it sound perfect?" she told her parents. "It will be nice for you, too—because you won't have to support me."

With the couple's whereabouts for the next year settled, the topic of Mary Frances's summer travel plans arose again. She grew increasingly blunt with Edith. She didn't tell her mother that she wouldn't come home, but she did tell her that she didn't want to stay in Whittier as long as her mother hoped. "I see how a month's trip or less than two months' stay seems pretty silly," she wrote. "But I can't ignore the fact that Al and I are married . . . three months away seems like a long time no matter how nice the vacation is." Perhaps worried about how Al would respond to another extended absence, she vowed to make herself so clingy and annoying before her departure that Al would gladly wave goodbye.

Al was more conciliatory with Rex and Edith, thanking them for having suggested the trip, which he said he supported, if a bit mournfully. His letter sped on to the news of Mary Frances's examinations, the translations she was working on, and her housework. The tone was dutiful, disengaged, and decidedly unemotional—he reported her achievements and praised her as if she were a student, not his wife. He also casually mentioned that if Rex and Edith wanted to send Norah or David to school in France the following year he would welcome a second or third Kennedy.

Mary Frances, too, was turning her attention to her younger siblings. In one letter to them she traced the history of wine in Burgundy. "Burgundy is the most famous wine district in the world," she wrote, "as I hope you'll find out for yourselves some sweet day." Next she told them about an excursion she and Al planned to take—a long walk in the French countryside culminating in a large meal. "It's amazing what delicious things you can get at some of the darkest and tiniest little village restaurants," she wrote. But the hill they'd climb after lunch with its views of the blooming countryside was most exceptional: "you are almost miles above the rest of the world," she wrote, her lines reading like a gentle sigh. She thought of them every time she experienced the sweeping beauty and freedom of France, but hoped that "[i]n a few years you will be over here too . . . after you have finished enough school to satisfy first the Authorities . . . and later on, Yourselves."

As she left for her summer in the United States, Mary Frances felt as if she'd already been separated from Al for weeks: "I've been inhumanely busy," she told Edith, "with hardly time to be decent even to my own husband—much drinking of tea and straining of smiles."

Would time away from her marriage confirm the nagging feelings that she wasn't entirely happy and satisfied? Or would a break prove to Al that he didn't really need her? Either option seemed heartbreaking and terrifying. She was equally worried that Rex and Edith had another, self-serving agenda for her trip home, though she wasn't sure what it was.

Mary Frances traveled back to the United States on a ship that was much smaller than the *Berengaria*. The ride was dark and long, and she slept in the bowels of the boat. She was desperately lonely and surprised to find that she felt Al's absence acutely. Her lurching emotions made her seasickness even worse.

She felt "damnably sick" nearly every day that she was on the ship—but held her composure, believing that if she "unloosened enough to be sick, the way my body wanted to be, and scared and lonely the way my heart felt, I'd never be able to stand the rest of the summer!" She could never admit her unhappiness to her parents and family; she vowed to keep it all inside.

Mary Frances wrote little about that summer in Whittier. There are no accounts of family meals, good or bad, nor are there breezy descriptions of the typical Kennedy summer activities: days at Laguna Beach, bonfires, cookouts, hikes. Did Rex, for instance, lecture her about money? Did she and Anne fight like schoolgirls? And what about Edith? Mary Frances's relationship with her mother had always been contentious. Much like her relationship with Al, Mary Frances wanted attention from her mother, which wasn't given freely. Trapped in the webs of both her mother and her husband, Mary Frances felt manipulated and was occasionally forced to pick sides. Edith and her pocketbook almost always won. It's interesting to wonder what advice about marriage Edith administered to her daughter over that long summer—and if any of it was good.

At the end of August, just as Mary Frances was packing the stacks of new clothes she and Edith had purchased into her trunk, her parents made an announcement. They had decided that Norah would not be attending high school in Whittier—or anywhere in Southern California. Instead she would return to France with her older sister and begin school there.

Mary Frances consented to take Norah back to Dijon with her but would claim, in a book she wrote much later, *Long Ago in France*, that the situation had been forced upon her. But the idea for Norah to return to France with Mary Frances had been hers, whether she was willing to acknowledge it or not. On April 4, 1930, Mary Frances had written to Edith, emphatically telling her again that Norah must attend a reputable boarding school, not the Whittier public high school: "unless you decide to let her come back with me for eight months," she wrote. "That would be the perfect thing to do." Her contradictory response (begging for companionship then withdrawing when it was offered) is typical of Mary Frances and what she learned from living with her mother and Al. The ability to withhold affection gave her a power she couldn't otherwise muster.

Mary Frances found herself on another slow boat abroad in late July 1931. Though enraged by the unsteady vessel, Mary Frances enjoyed the time with her fourteen-year-old sister, who spoke gravely about poetry and fashion and kissing. Mary Frances told Rex and Edith that Norah was "more interesting than anyone I've seen so far" on the ship. But she was hesitant to leave her alone, telling her parents that she felt responsible for her welfare even though she was "so damned sensible and intelligent that I'm not at all oppressed by the weight of being a guardian."

Because of her devotion to Norah, the trip was hardly different from the first journey Mary Frances took with Al. Aside from the occasional visit to the bar for a cocktail or coupe of champagne, she did little more than walk, read, sleep, write letters, and focus all her attention on a single person. Instead of large, gluttonous meals, however, she and Norah escaped the heat with iced consommé and fruit.

She described herself as being in a "frightful twitch." She hid her feelings from Norah; it was Norah's first sea voyage and she was transfixed by the details of ship life that Mary Frances now found stale. Instead, Mary Frances was "terribly excited" to see Al and said she was so sick of the summer's food that the first thing she planned to do once she got off the boat was to order a sizzling plate of snails. She couldn't wait for the "lovely exotic meal with many wines and then liquor."

But the thought of returning to their pension on Rue du Petit Potet made her "physically sick." She wrote to her mother, announcing that she had decided they must move out of the Rigulots' boardinghouse. She wanted to live somewhere with more privacy and hoped a new apartment might include a kitchen so that she might try cooking a bit. She was clearly hopeful that a change in location and the start to a new academic year might revitalize her two-year-old marriage.

As she spotted the shoreline, Mary Frances became even more anxious and "gnawed around the edges." Her words flag her nervousness about seeing Al and her concern over how the time away from each other had influenced their marriage. She left the boat, however, with her usual grace. She was happy to feel her feet land on sturdy French soil, and her eyes danced as she searched for Al in the crowd. But inside she was deeply worried about what awaited her, hoping Norah, or anyone else, wouldn't notice.

6

The Pain of Absence

"THE GREAT EVENT has happened!" Al wrote in a letter to Edith and Rex shortly after Mary Frances and Norah had arrived in France. "MF is home to me!"

Though Al never acknowledged it, he seemed finally aware that his relationship was at an impasse. After she left for the summer, he became concerned that Mary Frances might be so content in Whittier she would decide to stay. But was he really saddened by the idea that his wife might leave him, or simply anxious about how it might appear to his family and friends if she did?

Either way, as the date of Mary Frances's return approached, Al worried. He shared his fears with Larry. "Is MF really back?" Larry wondered in a letter. "And is there honey still for tea?" He too was nervous her affection could have wilted in the weeks away.

But in spite of her apprehension on the ship, Mary Frances said she'd never been so glad to see Al. He, Mary Frances, and Norah took the train into Paris and fell into their hotel beds at the Quai Voltaire, sleeping till noon the next day. They took Norah on a tour of the city, visiting the

Louvre, cruising the Seine, and dining at the famous Brasserie Lipp. Mary Frances wrote that they had a "simply wild and gorgeous time punctuated at regular and numerous intervals by large and exotic meals."

The reunited couple seemed happy, but Mary Frances returned to her marriage emotionally wounded, and Norah later said that her older sister may have subconsciously welcomed her presence in France as a "shield against her feelings of betrayal." But at the time, Norah was oblivious to her role, dumbstruck by the sights, sounds, and smells of France. She looked up to her brother-in-law and was excited to see him. "He was always remote, kind and beautiful," she said. "A man I was confident would eventually be acknowledged as a new Keats or Andrew Marvell."

Over the summer, Al and Larry had been together, as Larry described it, "day and night, walking, talking, studying, drinking, smoking." Larry claimed that Al was "crazy with grief" over his wife's absence. Anxious, or perhaps enjoying the summer and the time away from school, Al stopped work on "The Ghost." He had completed only twelve books of the poem and would never finish the remaining fifty-four. Nevertheless, his manuscript still measured more than six hundred pages.

Al described his poem as having been "swallowed up," and he blamed Mary Frances for his inability to write: "the sailing of my wife had as much as anything to do with it." He added, "MF went home to America in 1931 in June. From then until now . . . I have written nothing on The Ghost." Even after the two were reunited, he never returned to the poem, telling Larry that he couldn't maintain his passion for both his wife and the verses. Later he would admit that he wasn't exactly sure why he stopped writing.

When Mary Frances returned to Dijon, she was dismayed to discover that Al had made new friends over the summer, people he didn't want her to meet. He seemed happy in a way he never had before—and, despite his contentions, unconcerned with her long absence.

Mary Frances felt forgotten. Her feelings worsened when she over-heard Al imply that she had killed "The Ghost." "I went home and vomited," she told Larry years later. "I felt as if my heart was being torn out . . . I was still completely in love with Al, [but] I realized that in spite of his eager protestations, [made] to everybody who would listen except me, that he loved me more than life itself, he did not." She believed that "if a thing has life in it[,] it will live . . . The pain of absence, if it is real pain and not an excuse for something else, will nurture beauty and poetry and music."

She finally expressed her suspicions of why Al had encouraged her to leave him for the summer. "Did anyone wonder what my own grief was, when I waited and waited for Al to show in any way, that he wanted me to stay with him when my mother suggested I come back to America for a summer?" she would write to Larry. "I was naive, of course, and unskilled, but I used every wile I was capable of to get Al to show, no matter how, that he would rather me stay than go . . . Finally I went away, watching until the train left Paris for some sign that he would rather spend the summer with me than you."

Mary Frances hoped that moving to a new apartment might jar her and Al back into marital happiness—or, at the very least, the mild satisfac-tion they had enjoyed for two years. But first she had to settle Norah in her new city. For the first few days in Dijon, Norah slept on the couch in Mary Frances and Al's second room. But in their brief time together it became clear that the trio could not live together for long. Even if they got a new and bigger place, Al still needed room to study and the couple needed pri-vacy. Norah was a physically large girl—already over six feet tall—and her addition to the small French apartment made it feel even more cramped. Finding a school and a separate place for her to live was a necessity.

Edith had sent Norah to France as if she were a little girl. Mary Frances helped her younger sister find more adult clothes and appropriate shoes to match. She marveled as people stopped to watch Norah as she strolled down Dijon's streets. She appeared "almost seven feet tall in the bright red fez with the long black tassel she had bought in Paris." Soon Mary Frances had made arrangements for Norah to live and attend school at the nearby Convent Notre Dame des Agnes.

The convent was strict—Norah was allowed out only on Thursday afternoons and Sundays, though Mary Frances could visit her whenever she wanted. When she did visit she watched Norah closely: Mary Frances was deeply concerned about her development as a French student and as a young adult. Yet no matter how hard Norah tried, it was never good enough for her older sister's exacting standards. Mary Frances told Edith that she thought Norah was lazy and reported that she made "no effort to speak to anybody, or read in French, or do anything. She just sits and eats."

It must have been a challenging transition for Norah. All of her classes were in French. She was constantly reprimanded by the mother superior, first for not saying hello to the other students, next for not standing when her elders entered the room. Mary Frances remarked that Norah was "perfectly willing to do anything she's asked . . . it just doesn't occur to her to do anything without being asked." In fact, Norah simply didn't understand the cultural standards. The result of her strict daily life and seemingly unending criticism from Mary Frances must have made Norah feel as alone in France as her sister.

ONE OF THE first things Mary Frances had asked Al while on the train from Paris to Cherbourg was if they could move out of the Rigulots' boardinghouse and find an apartment of their own. She said that at first Al thought she was crazy for suggesting it. But he soon relented, and later agreed that she'd had a brilliant idea. "You can't imagine how marvelous it is," she wrote to Edith after finding them a new place to live. "After two years of eating with nasty people, to be alone . . . to eat what we want, to invite Larry and Noni and anybody else to eat with us, not to eat if we aren't hungry, to eat three meals a day at once if we are . . . but especially to be alone." She hoped their private quarters would help inspire the newlywed intimacy they'd never experienced on Rue du Petit Potet.

Their new apartment, at 46 rue Monge, was in a poor Dijon neighborhood. A tramline ran outside the building, and their windows looked down on a large square that had once housed a guillotine but now had several community pissoirs, or urinals, and the occasional wandering sideshow. Their building was large and airy, perched three floors above a pastry shop called Au Fin Gourmet; the pleasant smells of burnt almond, cinnamon, and vanilla wafted up into their apartment in little clouds. Best of all, they had a kitchen—their first as a married couple. It was small but serviceable, with a two-burner gas plate and a tin oven. The small kitchen window was her favorite part. Later Mary Frances would say, "What I saw and thought and felt as I stood in it with my hands on the food for us, those months, will always be a good part of me."

She described the first week as a cook in France as being almost too difficult—she had to learn how to keep butter cold, how to make fresh vegetables last more than a day, how to buy milk and cheese in the right amounts and from the right vendors. It was the first daily food preparation Mary Frances had ever done, and she said it was only slightly less complicated than performing an appendectomy on a life raft. Later she found that once she got used to hauling water to cook, lighting the oven, prepping and preparing courses, and setting a table, her role as cook and housewife was fun.

The couple slipped into an easy meal routine engineered by Mary Frances. They had milk and fruit for breakfast, meat and salad or a vegetable along with more milk and fruit for lunch, and a vegetable dish or salad with still more fruit and milk for supper. Eager to enjoy food at its finest, Mary Frances went to the market twice a week for produce and picked up fresh dairy products each morning. She found a store that baked the brown bread they loved. She told her family they ate "quarts of cream and milk and pounds of butter and dozens of eggs and whole fields of beans and lettuce . . . We eat just what we like and rather a lot of it. We're both growing moon faced."

Mary Frances described her cooking style as "so reduced to vegetables you could hardly call it cooking." She never made cakes or pies or elaborate dishes of any kind—they could be purchased if necessary. She and Al liked their simple meals and thrived on their diet, based on exceedingly fresh market vegetables. She particularly loved making a casserole from fresh white cauliflower, piles of grated gruyère, and cupfuls of fresh cream. She served the heady dish with salad, crusty bread, wine, and cut fresh fruit for dessert.

For Norah's visits Mary Frances bought fresh milk and fruit, honey, and *pain d'épices*—Dijonaise gingerbread. The sisters would sit by the open window, listening to street sounds and playing records on the Victrola. Now that everyone was settled, Mary Frances enjoyed spending time with Norah and relished their girlish intimacy. Norah adored her afternoons at her older sister's apartment and ate her food offerings, Mary Frances remarked, with "the slow voluptuous concentration of a devotee."

When Larry visited from the Rue du Petit Potet, he brought a bottle of cheap red wine and his charming grin. Just as they had in the couple's previous residence, the three would sit for hours eating, drinking, and talking. "Al and Lawrence planned books about Aristotle and Robinson Jeffers and probably themselves," Mary Frances wrote, "and I planned a few things too."

But after only a few weeks, she began to resent the responsibility of meal planning and preparation. She told Edith that she was "not wildly enthusiastic about marketing and fixing vegetables and doing dishes. I never will be." Despite her dislike for her extra daily work, she considered the effort worth it if it meant that she and Al got to live alone. And yet the household's maintenance was not her sole responsibility. A woman came three times a week to do the cleaning, dishes, and all of their laundry—even Norah's, which she'd leave at the apartment. All that was left for Mary Frances to do was fix three meals each day, wash the occasional dish, make the beds, and shop for food.

Edith Kennedy had never been a typical housewife; she related to her daughter's dislike of chores and worried she was exhausted and overworked. It was a silly concern. Mary Frances had the time to keep up with her daily chores; she just didn't like performing them. Mary Frances put her mother's mind at ease by telling her she wasn't slaving away in a sordid kitchen. "I'm quite shameless about staying out of one all that I can," she said, "and when I'm forced to be in one I reduce my time to a minimum."

The couple's privacy, however, did little to help their floundering marriage. Al still spent his days at the university, and Mary Frances struggled to keep herself busy. With Al's thesis finished and at the printer, and his final examination scheduled for early November 1931, the couple began to think about their move to Strasbourg, in northeastern France near the German border, where Al would continue his studies. Mary Frances looked forward to leaving Dijon. She thought they were stuck in a "comfortable little rut." After enduring two years of his hard work and intense creative drive, she was ready to begin enjoying the fun parts of being married and living in France.

Though she had vowed never to return to the classroom, she toyed with the idea of getting a master's degree in Strasbourg. She continued to believe that the equivalent of a college diploma could only help when she returned to the United States. She told her mother that she "didn't regret having stopped school to be married . . . but I wouldn't mind having a [college] diploma too." She was beginning to view education as a means of both independence and security, even if she didn't actually like it.

She and Al were also beginning to think more carefully about their plans for life after France. They hoped that Al could get a contract from a publisher and begin writing a book. They would live in Laguna for the winter and have a baby. "That would be ideal," she wrote to Edith, with no hint of irony or any acknowledgement that things in her marriage might be anything other than perfect.

MARY FRANCES AND Al left on the midnight train to Strasbourg after a long and wine-drenched farewell dinner with Larry. Only a week before, Al had successfully defended his thesis and the University of Dijon had made him a doctor of letters.

The overnight ride felt endless and the two arrived in Strasbourg tired and cranky. After stumbling through the station, they found the nearest hotel and slept for twelve hours in a bed so soft and wide Mary Frances described it as being like the "meadows of heaven." When they woke they were disorientated and surprised to discover that it was nighttime. They dressed and went out to eat and to see a German movie. It had been months since they'd felt this relaxed and content. "Al had his precious doctorate," Mary Frances wrote, "and we were in love, and Strasbourg lay before us."

Germany had annexed Strasbourg during the Franco-Prussian War but returned the city after World War I. The Germanic influence was everywhere: Grand boulevards were lined with apartments that had ornate façades and beautiful large windows. Humbler neighborhoods were filled with buildings and homes framed in black-and-white timber.

Mary Frances and Al found that the citizens, too, were more German than French. The Strasbourgeois had blue eyes, light hair, and were friendly and boisterous. Mary Frances described them as having a fondness for "children, large dogs, beer, and thumping waltzes." Communicating with them, however, was problematic. The couple discovered that almost everyone spoke German or Alsatian (the regional mix of German and French); only a few spoke the pure French that Mary Frances and Al had learned. The challenge inspired Mary Frances to investigate German classes at the university.

They rented an apartment near the Orangerie, a beautiful park that housed the city's zoo. The flat was in the attic of what she described as a weird building miles from the center of town. There were two large rooms, each with a stove and windows offering views of large trees. There was plenty of natural light, gas electricity, and running water. Mary Frances wrote that the apartment offered "the most luxurious quarters of our marital existence."

She ached for the comfort she hoped a more organized home life would provide. "This last lap of three months has been one of the messiest in my rather messy life," Mary Frances wrote her brother, David, in early December 1931. "I feel all chopped up, and am just beginning to jolt into something that resembles a whole again—like a kaleidoscope, but not so pretty."

She blamed her anxiety and "chopped up feeling" on the understandable stress of moving and culture change. Never in any of her writings from the period does she remark on how the stress of an unsympathetic husband contributed to her discomfort, quite possibly because she didn't realize how deeply the lack of devotion hurt her emotionally. Instead, her discomfort manifested itself as a continued low-level dissatisfaction with herself and her surroundings.

She decided against working toward a master's degree and spent most of her days at home trying to write. She quickly grew to detest her new, once perfect apartment, claiming that upon closer inspection she had discovered it had dingy walls, stained floors, and unreliable heating. One day she woke to discover icicles hanging from the skylight in the kitchen. The small, dank room had poor lighting and was hard to keep clean. No amount of scrubbing seemed to remove the layers of dirt that had accumulated on the cupboards and stove. The cost of living in Strasbourg was higher than they expected, and paying for heat meant there was no money for travel or fun. At least she still liked the setting and the fabulous natural light that streamed through the living room windows.

But after a while, Mary Frances admitted to Edith that her dislike for her new living situation was becoming harder to suppress. She said she "hated to spend time cooking" and tried not to do it any more than was necessary. Meal preparation was also inconvenient: If she wanted to cook, she had to hike three miles to the market for ingredients. Often Al would bring meals home, and occasionally she would walk to the café on the corner, using its phone to have groceries delivered—a luxury that was not in their meager budget. When she did cook, she found it was "discouraging to have to put on my fur coat and gloves to cook a meal in the little kitchen, where steam would stiffen into ice as soon as it hit the sloping uninsulated ceiling." She didn't seem to care that she was undoubtedly the most glamorous hausfrau in all of Strasbourg.

She told Edith that she couldn't help that she was a "child of luxury. I can't get over the joy of having things delivered. I get sick of going to market and lugging milk and stuff around the streets."

On Sundays, when Norah was free from the boarding school she attended in Strasbourg, the three would go for long walks and end their days with a large meal in a café or beer hall. Mary Frances liked sausages, kraut, Alsatian beers, and the crisp and heady white wines from the region. But whereas Norah had bloomed like a "beautiful young pine tree" in wintery Strasbourg, Mary Frances despised the cold. She told Anne that although there was much she wanted to do in the city, it was too hard to face going out. "The truth is that I am too scared to be cold," she admitted. She hoped that she would get used to the weather and was irritated at herself for whining—she had a maid to clean her apartment and a husband who brought home food and never seemed to care if the meals she made were late getting to the table. The couple had hoped to vacation over the Christmas holiday, as they had for the two previous years, but lacked the funds. Mary Frances decided their best option for enjoying themselves was to stay in Strasbourg and pretend they were visitors to their new city. She contemplated getting a hotel room to make their pseudo-vacation feel even more authentic, and planned for a big dinner of roasted goose in a swanky restaurant downtown.

Al brought home holly and mistletoe, and they put up a small but perky tree. Rex and Edith did send money for Christmas—it had become an annual duty—and the trio spent it on dinner out, the movies, and the rent. Al hoped that Rex and Edith wouldn't think they had mistreated their gift by using some of it on food and frivolity. He wrote that their monetary present had already given the two an extraordinary amount of pleasure. "I want to thank you with all of my heart," he wrote, guilty again that he was unable to provide for his wife.

AFTER THE HOLIDAYS, Mary Frances grew increasingly neurotic. She spent her days cooped up in the attic apartment, which was so cold she had to break up the frozen toilet water. "It's cold as hell here," she wrote. "When I'm cold I'm miserable . . . I can't talk myself into believing that I'm not." She had frequent nightmares about the beggar she often saw in front of their building. The man had a peg leg that would pound against the sidewalk as he escorted his prostitute mistress. The two were constantly bickering, and Mary Frances dreaded the sound of them. Even more upsetting were the birds in the aviary across the street. Their slender claws would freeze to the perches, and they would lurch around and squawk, struggling to free themselves from the ice. When they urinated, the liquid would drip down their spindly legs and freeze into a further trap.

In an attempt to brighten his wife's spirits, Al decided one day to make a tamale pie. He spent days gathering the perfect baking dish, the best greek olives, chili powder from Paris, and cornmeal from an obscure health-food store.

The tamale pie was warm and soft, with subtle heat and spice from the exotic chili powder. They ate it for lunch one day alongside an endive salad and a bottle of wine. It should have been a happy afternoon, yet after eating, Mary Frances began to cry. A hot meal was the kind of attention she'd always longed for from her husband. But she knew Al hadn't made tamale pie because he loved her, or because he was concerned about her emotional well-being. It was his attempt to placate her; to quiet her constant, unhappy banter.

In *The Gastronomical Me*, Mary Frances wrote that this was the first time that her husband had ever seen her cry. The claim seems unlikely. But it may have marked the first time that Al saw her cry without understanding why she was upset—and without trying to soothe her. "I simply sat wordless," she wrote, "held in a kind of stupefaction, too limp to put a handkerchief to my drenched cheeks. I was humiliated, but without the energy to hide myself."

Al asked, "What have I done?" But then, without waiting for an answer, he set a glass of brandy in her hand and left for the university. Mary Frances sat in the room that was growing increasingly cold thinking of "my whole past the way a drowning man is supposed to." She pondered the circumstances that had pushed her marriage to this impasse: their brief courtship and engagement, their nonexistent sexual intimacy, Al's narcissism, and her desire for a more loving partnership.

Mary Frances's mood was so sullen that the couple soon decided that they must move yet again, to a new apartment in Strasbourg. She would do anything to avoid sewing and cleaning, so a return to a pension seemed best. She blamed Edith for her lack of interest in her chores and the failure of her domestic life in Strasbourg. "I'm a hell of a housekeeper, Mother," she wrote. "Why didn't you raise me to love this sort of thing?" She also worried that she wasn't the kind of woman who was happy to stay home and make meals for her husband, again blaming it on her upbringing: "after twenty years in your establishment I have a taste for nice things . . . I like to be comfortable," she wrote Edith.

Their new lodgings, at Pension Elisa, were larger and more expensive. But they were much closer to the university, and Mary Frances could more easily attend classes and study German if she wanted.

Al told Rex and Edith that he believed that getting out of the house and attending the university was a better use of his wife's time than housekeeping: "It does seem more reasonable to me that she should be doing this than keeping house. It has disadvantages, of course, but on the whole it is perhaps the better of the two for her . . . But we shall see." He hoped that in a new environment, creative success "will come for both of us." It is more likely, however, that Al hoped that writing success would come for him and that Mary Frances would adjust her moods sufficiently to become the calm and responsible wife he needed.

At the pension, Mary Frances's demeanor changed immediately. On one of the first afternoons in their clean and bright home with decent heat and hot running water, room for books and sweeping views of trees, she settled into a long bath. After soaking in the hot, lavender-scented waters, doing her nails, and brushing her hair, she sank gently into a chaise lounge in their new living room. "I'm so beaming with comfort that I hardly feel capable of writing a coherent letter," she wrote.

The best part of Pension Elisa was the meals: The food wasn't spectacular, but Mary Frances didn't have to prepare it. She claimed that she was saving her homemaking energy for their return to the United States and hoped that having her own well-stocked kitchen might make her more interested in the task. "Nothing makes me as furious as spending money for foul things like pots and pans," she wrote. "Perhaps I may cultivate a little interest in it when I get home . . . but I doubt it."

Her creative motivation briefly returned after the move. She worked on various short stories but put most of her energy into writing a children's book. She wrote her father and asked if he might be able to help her find a publisher in the United States—she was ready to find somebody who might like to read the sorts of things she wrote. Al was still at work on a novel, and for a brief time the two were happy, working side by side and making trips to museums, cathedrals, and cafés. In a letter to Edith, Mary Frances wrote that she and Al were getting along beautifully—they were healthy and rested, sleeping well in their separate beds.

It's interesting to ponder what made this brief time so enjoyable— was it Mary Frances's happy mood and feeling of creative fulfillment? Or was it the fact that neither she nor Al was burdened by the demands of real life? Whatever the reason, they were more eager to engage with each other.

But soon doubts returned, as they always did. Mary Frances began to realize that Strasbourg was strapping her marriage financially and, as a result, emotionally. For the first time, she looked forward to an end to their time in France. She was fed up with her life of dirty apartments and mean proprietors. She craved California orange juice, and sliced avocado on rye crisp crackers. Though she hated the thought of "settling into middle age and the responsibilities of a family," she found comfort in the notion that wherever she lived, France would always be with her. "There's something about this life, which I feel will go on forever," she told Edith.

Perhaps because they disliked being alone together, she and Al were suddenly eager to have children. They considered starting a family in France, but there simply wasn't enough time. Even if Al was granted a fellowship for another year they would still need to return to the United States at some point, and the idea of making a boat trip with a baby was unimaginable. They decided to remain childless while they mapped out their return to the United States—and would "do a rabbit act" once they got home.

She clearly believed that Al, for better or worse, would be her husband forever. And she hoped they could have their family soon, while they were young and spry enough to withstand the shock of becoming parents. She was also considering what she might do after she became a mother. Her time in France had taught her that she wouldn't be content to be simply a housewife. Children or not, she wanted to work when she returned home: "If I don't have children, or if I do, as soon as they are old enough, I want to work too. I would like to work on a newspaper or in a book store or something like that."

Knowing the end of their European life was in sight, Mary Frances told Edith they were going to "have all the fun we can while the money lasts." They could live frugally when they got back to the U.S.—but for now, they were going to revel in having few responsibilities. She hinted that if Rex and Edith wanted to send some money, she and Al would happily invest in furniture—a truly frivolous purchase for a couple who could hardly pay their rent and were returning home jobless in months.

Soon the couple's financial situation became dire. Mary Frances wrote to Edith and told her that she was "really alarmed" about their expenses. "We should never have come here," she said, referring to the Pension Elisa, the main cause of their financial troubles. "It's all my fault." Regardless of if Al's fellowship was renewed, they had hoped to stay in France until August, but they didn't have enough money. "What do you think we should do?" she asked Edith.

Mary Frances wondered if they should return home early. "Would Al have the slightest chance of getting a job for the summer—ranch work or anything? Please tell me what you think . . . We have enough money to last us through the middle (maybe) of May." It's hard to imagine that Edith knew exactly what to say. Her daughter was asking for her help with a set of loaded questions.

Mary Frances decided the most reasonable choice for the three was the South of France, which was warm and less expensive. By early March of 1932, she had picked their spot—Cros de Cagnes, a small fishing village only four miles from Nice. It was rumored to have beautiful waters for swimming, friendly people, and wine like liquid gold. It was the perfect destination while they waited to hear if Al's fellowship had been renewed.

Mary Frances, Al, and Norah left Strasbourg quickly, and arrived in Cros in the middle of March. After learning that Al had not won a teaching post for the following year, they decided to stay in the south until their money ran out, then sail for the States. Mary Frances and Al had secret hopes that with their lowered cost of living they might be able to enlist Rex and Edith's help in subsidizing additional time in the

Mediterranean. It was beautiful and warm there, and they fantasized about staying endlessly, writing and enjoying life.

The couple settled in a pension right on the beach. Their room was on the top floor and had a little balcony. There was heat and running water, and the food was remarkably better than it had been in Strasbourg. But the views of the water were the best. Mary Frances loved to stand on the balcony and watch the entire gulf, from Nice to the small town of Antibes. In the waters immediately below them were groups of small fishing boats with their nets stretched out for the day's catch. The town of Cros was small, only a few stucco buildings, but there were several good cafés, and Al had already adopted one, going each day to write at a table on the outdoor terrace under a canopy of grapevines with sunshine soaking through the cracks.

Mary Frances found a boardinghouse for Norah on the other side of town. She had decided that a bit of distance was for the best—Mary Frances and Al weren't fond of the familial atmosphere Norah's presence encouraged. Mary Frances told Edith that she and Al "haven't such a need for conversations and so on." Norah had once been a welcome addition, her youthful chattiness helping to bring the couple together. But now Mary Frances and Al seemed to want quiet and space; Norah only accented their marital disconnect.

They had all begun hearing more and more about the Depression at home and it haunted them: the breadlines full of well-dressed men, the PhDs working as Macy's clerks, the Southern California oranges being sold roadside for ten cents a crate. They were especially worried about Al's job prospects. They had written to the heads of English departments at universities throughout the West Coast, but his chances seemed grim. Mary Frances said Al was willing to take any kind of job—anything that would pay. She joked that when they returned home they would live near Rex and Edith so at least they could get oranges and artichokes for free.

Larry joined them for a few weeks in Cros to begin writing his the-sis. He described Al as being in a "withdrawn and interpretive state." Larry wrote every morning and took long walks on the beach or went hiking in the hills every afternoon. He regularly invited Al to join him, but Al never did. Perhaps feeling spurned by his best friend, Larry found himself drawn to Mary Frances and the two became even closer in Cros. Larry denied that the two ever touched or even exchanged intimate words. But he did admit that Mary Frances longed to join him on his rambles and didn't, fearful of what might occur.

In spite of everyday stresses, Mary Frances and Al found Rex and Edith's financial stability reassuring. So the couple was shocked when their Whittier allowance dwindled. Instead of the $125 the couple had expected, Rex and Edith had sent only $50. Their shock turned to despair when they pooled their resources and discovered they had only three hundred francs—far less than the seven hundred and fifty they owed for the pension.

Mary Frances, Al, and Norah went into what Mary Frances called a "family huddle" and decided the only option was to wire Rex and Edith and demand more money. "This is the way our finances are," Mary Frances wrote. "Noni's [Norah's] money is all gone, and she is about eight hundred francs in debt . . . Al and I have twelve dollars." Mary Frances hoped that their stern request, which she thought per-fectly explained and justified their situation, wouldn't anger or strain Rex and Edith. She seemed unaware of how petty and aggressive their request might seem.

Within hours, however, Mary Frances thought better of her demands. With no money and little hope, she and Al tore up the cable, and began composing another letter to her parents. This time, they asked nicely for a thousand dollars to use to pay rent, tie up loose ends in France, and purchase tickets home to the United States on a boat that would leave in ten days. "We hate to leave," Mary Frances wrote. "But we might not have as much fun if our last five weeks were one long economy." With no money, and no hopes of finding any more, the best thing to do was head home.

They ate their last meal—bouillabaisse—in Marseille. They dined outside on the cobblestone square of Marseille's Old Port, basking in the late spring sunlight. In *The Gastronomical Me*, she would describe how the rich and saucy fish stew let off tendrils of "potent saffrony steam"—and how the three of them dunked chunks of rustic bread into the soup and "sucked a hundred strange dead creatures" from their shells. They drank well from the owner's private stock of wines and toasted continually to themselves and their time in France.

THEY TOOK A ship named the *Cellina* to the United States. The small Italian freighter carried only a few dozen passengers and moved ever so slowly, stopping in numerous ports. The entire trip would take more than three and a half weeks. The trio did little but lounge and sit in or around the small swimming pool on one of the upper decks. It was horribly hot, and the nights were the worst—the bugs came out, and few could sleep.

Mary Frances described herself as being wiser on her return home than she had been on any other of her journeys: "I knew a lot about myself and what I wanted and what I had to do. It made me soberer, and I was much less shy." Not even twenty-five years old, Mary Frances believed she was in her last glimmer of youth. The insouciance of being a new bride in Paris had long since faded, and she doubted that her early feelings for Al or her marriage could ever be recaptured. Al, too, was quiet, staring at the water, chatting occasionally with some of the other men on the ship, and—in his narrow, tight handwriting—filling his favorite notebook. Mary Frances described him as being "[v]ery good to look at . . . But inside . . . I don't know at all."

She spent most of her time on the ship by herself, knitting and reading and thinking: "I had found out several things about my relationship with my family, and to other men than Al . . . while the ship rolled slowly forward across the waves." She claimed that she had discussed some of her anxieties with her husband but that he didn't really hear her.

But even if Al was listening, what could he say? What could they do? They had been married nearly three years, all of which had been characterized by a "happiness" that most other couples would have considered misery. Norah was left to ricochet between Mary Frances and Al, both ambivalent friends for the young girl. She suffered from terrible earaches on the trip and hated the tropical bugs that seemed to infest every object aboard. She turned fifteen on the boat, and the three celebrated with champagne that was too sweet and too warm. It was a hot and steamy evening and before taking a sip they had to bat away the gnats that were drawn to the alcoholic nectar.

The one bonus to the *Cellina*'s frequent stops was the food in the ports—it was immensely better than the ship food they'd endured on their previous travels. They were lucky enough to have meat nearly every day, and surprisingly good cheeses and breads. The wines, however, were coarse and heavy in comparison to the austere and elegant burgundies they'd loved. Al didn't like them, and in *The Gastronomical Me*, Mary Frances described how she gave him her beers in exchange for "dark yellow wines" and "bluish red ones" that were just what she wanted— "simple and straightforward in all the lush heat of the coastal waters."

No matter her location or level of emotional anguish, she always noticed the meal in front of her. From her first salad on the rumbling train into Paris, to the inky wines that swayed in her glass on the *Cellina*, the colors and flavors of great food and wine brought her incomparable pleasure. Writing about culinary delights became a means of survival: letters, journals, and other creative efforts tuned her prose and masked an existence bruised by sadness. She had learned to nourish herself in France. That skill, along with the ability to articulate why it was important, would soon be more valuable than she ever imagined.

She described the papayas on the ship, for instance, as "cold and smooth as butter." There were large oranges and bananas, coconut milk drunk straight from the fuzzy fruit, and the avocados that she had been craving. One evening, while the ship was docked in a strange city, the three ate dinner on a patio managed by a tiny gray-haired man and two small children. They were served an array of unrecognizable dishes: chewy meats, sweet cooked fruits, flat morsels that, according to Mary Frances, "could have been bats' ears or sliced melon rind." They ate and ate, and by the time they'd finished their coffee and paid the bill, the night was black. As they returned to the ship, a crew of prisoners, their shackles clanking, walked past them. The sound was haunting, and the image resonated deeply with Mary Frances, who felt shackled to her marriage.

For Mary Frances, Al, and Norah, the long trip from France to the United States that summer was characterized by silence. Their consolation: They were convinced that their future in California would be filled with sunshine and easy living. Little did they know that their time there would often prove far more challenging than even their poorest, coldest days abroad.

7

Depression

LMOST AS SOON as they arrived in Whittier, they needed an escape from the Kennedy family, a crew that had grown to include Ted Kelly, Anne's new husband. Days at the ranch were fraught with small misunderstandings, hurt feelings, and the subtle bad moods born of too many people sharing small quarters. So in August 1932, Mary Frances and Al took an impromptu drive along the California coast. The couple sped through a string of small towns, their arms burned scarlet from the sun. It was so hot they pulled to the side of the road and took off almost all their clothes before cracking open a large watermelon and eating chunks of the pale pink fruit in the warm air. The crisp flesh bathed them in a delicious rapture that, for Mary Frances, ended too soon.

The two "ate, slept, bathed, [and] loved each other." The interlude belied the fact that Mary Frances and Al's romantic life—never very fruitful—undoubtedly slowed to a halt upon arriving in the States and moving in with Rex and Edith. Mary Frances's lack of private time with her husband only made her want him more. She was eager to prove to her family, most of whom had never seen her interact with her husband, that she and Al were compatible and that their marriage was a loving one. Al, however, remained typically distant. He engaged with his wife only when he desired her affection, and spent most hours in search of solitude and creative inspiration.

As they drove back to Rex and Edith's, Mary Frances worried how she would ever manage her "unruly wants" for silence and privacy. Her family sapped the energy she needed and wanted to devote to her husband. "It's Al and our life that count for me," she wrote.

The couple found that California had changed immensely during their time away. There were scant employment opportunities, decreased purchasing power, and subpar living standards. It was a dramatic shift from the life they knew in France, where they could live reasonably well on very little.

The two bounced between the ranch and the family's vacation home at Laguna Beach, never fully unpacking or settling in either place. Rex and Edith provided for the couple almost entirely. They also supported their other three children and Ted, and sent money to Rex's ailing aunt and uncle. The family's economic pinch did not go unnoticed—once David asked Mary Frances if the family was getting poorer, and at times Norah appeared saddened that she could not attend fancy boarding schools like her older sisters had.

Their bleak finances weighed on Mary Frances and Al: They knew that Rex and Edith had helped fund their time in France believing that upon their return, Al would become a professor at a university and begin to provide for his bride. The situation was not working out as anyone had planned. So they tried to keep busy. Mary Frances and Al supervised Norah and David frequently. The teenagers hardly needed babysitting, but it was a reasonable exchange for the couple's free room and board. They both made some money cleaning houses and performing light maintenance work on vacation homes in their Laguna Beach neighborhood. It irked Mary Frances that Al made more money doing the same job she did. She wished she could find a real job, a position that might be economically valuable and provide a sense of self-worth. But there were hundreds of people for every position, and it was especially hard for women to find employment.

Meanwhile, Al applied for dozens of jobs. One day he interviewed for a position as a ditch digger, trying to convince himself the work might be a potentially "interesting experience." The idea of her husband digging ditches made Mary Frances sick: "Now is his time for writing. And he must exhaust himself to feed us. I wish I could do something."

Still, she relished the simple moments that their quiet lifestyle afforded them. One late summer day she and Al, Norah, and David took a picnic to the beach. They grilled hamburgers and slid the cooked meat into buttered round buns. Mary Frances marveled at the perfect moment when the sky turned pink and the hills and the water began to look soft and muted. After dinner, she and Al lay on the beach and looked at the stars; occasionally Al kissed the top of her head gently. Their private life was the most valuable thing to her: "That I will fight for," she wrote in her journal. "It is important and should live."

She secretly hoped that Rex might hire them both at the *Whittier News*. It seemed a logical fit: Al was a practiced writer and Mary Frances dreamed of being published. But Rex never offered either of them positions, apparently reticent to have them working in his conservative newsroom.

Though he was giving them free room and board, Mary Frances was still hurt by her father's snub. She worked on few writing projects during this time and instead put her Beaux Arts education to work, carving elaborate tables, stools, and keepsake chests to sell or give as gifts.

Larry Powell had returned to the United States from Dijon, and Mary Frances was dismayed by her subtle attraction to him. She maintained that it wasn't sexual but wrote that Larry had a way of looking into her eyes that made her want to touch him. "I would have been glad to lie with my arms around him or my hand in his," she wrote. She was "glad to have him back, [and] to see him by me" but dismissed the significance of her emotions, believing that despite her desire to be near Larry, she was not at all moved by him sexually. Dismissive of the ambivalent emotions she had for her husband, she easily ignored the confusing attraction she had for her friend.

Al also was happy that Larry was back, even though his friendship with the couple posed complications. One day the three were supposed to travel to Laguna, but Larry called and canceled because he had a job interview. Mary Frances lied to her mother about Larry's change in plans, not wanting to suggest that Larry had job prospects and Al had none. Just as in France, Larry was easily the more charming and compelling of the two men.

To save their money and sanity, Mary Frances and Al decided to spend the winter at the family's Laguna Beach house. Al could write there, and she would be free from the menial daily tasks she braved at the ranch. It seemed the perfect solution for a strained marriage.

Mary Frances worked on building a life for her and Al in Laguna, believing that a well-kept, cozy home might promote marital bliss. She constantly moved furniture and shifted pictures, trying to make their living space more comfortable. Though she had been a poor and reluctant homemaker in Strasbourg, she now committed herself to the task, ignoring her creative urges. She hoped Al would notice, but he didn't seem to.

She captured Laguna's languid days in her journal. She became increasingly observant, acutely and sensually aware of even the simplest actions and images. One night she detailed the experience of eating an exotic passionfruit. She described the palm-size yellow orb as a "new" fruit from Australia. It was small and dark and uncompromising; she needed a sharp knife to cut the shell. Inside was a "vivid yellowish mess, all filled with olive green hollowish seeds growing neatly from three sides of the shell." The insides were to be sucked out or eaten with a spoon; the taste it left in the mouth was pleasant long after the few tart bites were finished. "It is a delightful fruit," she wrote.

Shw was swimming in creative energy so intense and new that she didn't know how to manage it. Her insights likely stemmed from her isolation. In France there had been streets to wander, markets to visit, and shops to marvel over. In Laguna her world was limited to the beach cottage, her husband, and the endless stretch of sand, water, and sky right outside their door. She wrote down, in her estimation, more than half the things she did or said or thought each day. "I can see the words on a sheet of paper," she wrote, "and can see the pen writing them. And in my head, a voice, a kind of silent reading voice, reads them not from but to the paper."

Regardless of how much she wrote, she believed much of it was trivial—which kept her from recording meals in detail. She may have also been limited by her environment. Not only was money very tight, Laguna lacked Dijon's great variety of food. Her diet was stifling, and cooking for Al a bore.

She constantly observed him, hoping that something he said or did might provide some sort of clue to his inner emotions." I know that when he sits looking at his pipe or talking so nicely to any person, his head is working hard on some mad paragraph," she wrote. "And when he needs, suddenly, a little nap, I for some reason am as proud of him as if he had climbed a high mountain, because I suspect what tired him." She described herself as eating, talking, and living full of the consciousness of Al. "He is all through me, like a virus," she said. "I doubt if I ever get over him."

The relentless monitoring of her husband and the never-ending hope that he would choose to engage in their relationship drained her. Even recording her own movement became exhausting. She wished for more exciting things to report, but her reality was far from inspiring. Her mind was usually preoccupied with the mundanity of what to make for dinner or wondering if she should try to curl up alongside Al in the hope of a few intimate moments. She took a job tutoring at a school but quit because she couldn't stand interacting with the children—she liked watching them from afar but hated their "dirty noses and their bitter fingernails . . . I hate their guts in other words."

IN MARCH 1933, a moderate earthquake struck Southern California, and in the minutes that followed, Mary Frances and Al rushed outside. There, amid a community of Laguna neighbors buzzing with fear and curiosity, Mary Frances and Al met Dillwyn and Gigi Parrish. In an act of friendliness that would change the course of both couples' lives, Mary Frances invited the two into her home for a post-earthquake drink. She lit candles and opened a bottle of wine, pouring an ample glass for each. It was the start of a deeply personal yet dramatic friendship.

Dillwyn was a slight thirty-nine-year-old man with blue eyes and graying hair; he was born on July 25, 1894, in Colorado Springs to a family of artists. His father, Thomas Clarkson Parrish, was the part owner of a silver mining company and worked by night creating detailed etchings. His mother, Anne Lodge, had studied in Paris in the 1870s and became known as one of the great portrait painters of the American West. Dillwyn's cousin was the artist Maxfield Parrish.

When Dillwyn, who was called Tim or Timmy by close friends and family, was four years old, his father died and his mother moved the family from Colorado to her hometown of Claymont, Delaware. Later Tim attended Harvard, where he was friendly with the writers John Dos

Passos and e.e. cummings. He enlisted in the army in September 1917, and worked as a volunteer ambulance driver and soldier during World War I. But his tenure was unsuccessful. His last post was at a hospital where he became a patient after collapsing while carrying laundry. The diagnosis: severe undernourishment.

Even after leaving the hospital, Tim was frail. He was thin and suffered from a hacking cough—the result of habitual cigarette smoking. He found himself increasingly drawn to creative pursuits and began working with his sister, Anne, illustrating children's books. He also found work as a tutor for a wealthy New Hampshire family with three children. He fell in love with his youngest pupil, the beautiful Gigi. He was twenty-six and she was only thirteen. Still, Tim was compelled to propose to Gigi. Horrified, her family responded by dispatching her to Europe. Tim followed, and three years later, when Gigi was sixteen, the two were married. Shortly afterward, in 1929, they moved to California.

When Tim and Gigi met Mary Frances and Al, the Parrishes had been married for about five years. A seemingly happy couple, their relationship sometimes suffered due to their age gap and periods of long separation. Gigi was a starlet, working in Hollywood as a Samuel Goldwyn girl. She often toured with a performing company and was on the road for weeks at a time.

Tim floated from job to job. He was the proprietor of a tea salon and also operated a small restaurant, where he made simple meals for his customers. He was passionate about food but found the routine of the restaurant business exhausting. He eventually moved on to the business of buying and restoring homes. Despite California's economic troubles, he was able to live off the combination of family money and the income generated by the quick buying and selling of properties. He and Gigi were renting a home next door to the Kennedys' Laguna Beach home when they met Mary Frances and Al.

The couples became fast friends, socializing and working on creative projects. Al and Tim collaborated on screenplays they hoped they could sell for a large profit. Since Gigi was gone a lot, Mary Frances was again the lone female among two highly intelligent and dynamic men. As Al and Tim worked, Mary Frances watched, wishing she was more productive. Occasionally she remarked on their progress in her journal, subtly taking note of how the two seemingly brilliant minds worked.

IN ADDITION TO Mary Frances and Al's economic stresses, they were experiencing personal woes: Al's father had been diagnosed with Hodgkin's disease. The two men had never been exceptionally close, but the illness was a shock, and Al began to travel as frequently as possible to Palo Alto to spend time with his family. While there, he ventured into San Francisco to look for work, but usually came home from his excursions depressed. He couldn't find a job anywhere, and on one trip his pocket was picked and he got itchy and painful bedbug bites from staying at a seedy hotel. His mental anguish kept him from writing, and he retreated from Mary Frances in the hope that space and quiet might recharge his creativity.

Meanwhile, Mary Frances noted in her journal that she really wanted to write and knew that she could write. But she didn't believe she was driven by a fire intense enough to make her say "to Hell with A's supper." She believed that a willingness to forgo her daily responsibilities in support of her craft would be a sign of her true creative commitment. After all, this was how Al worked: To conquer his muse, he ignored everything else.

Mary Frances, lacking similar obsessions, felt defective. "I make beds and clean and wash and manicure my nails because I want to be clean for him and make him comfortable," she wrote. "If I really were an artist his comfort and his opinion of me would be secondary things. And so would my own. I'd work, and if I did not starve first, perhaps do something very fine. As it is now, all this sincere but ineffective piddling with chisels and journals is to keep me limber. I won't be all stiff and dulled, when my time comes. If it does." She mulled how strange it would be to keep living her life doing things she didn't really want to do, "always feeling that they were just a substitute for what I was really meant to do, and never finding what that was."

As she felt herself dropping into a deep hole of unemployment, financial woes, and relationship and family stresses, she wondered if it was time to abandon her dreams of being a writer. "I've had so many big ideas," she wrote. "But I want to pull out. It is necessary for Al and me. We're sinking now, slowly."

SO MARY FRANCES and Al were ecstatic when, in April 1934, Al received a letter from a professor named Ben Selter. He asked if Al might be interested in working as a part-time English instructor at Occidental College for the fall semester. Al, who had been looking for work for eighteen months, leaped at the chance. Mary Frances, meanwhile, felt invigorated by the possibility of a move and a change. "I am becoming conscious," she wrote. "Gradually I see myself shaping up, forming. For years I've [been] fetal, in the egg shape. I've known it all along. Now I begin to hear, to smell and feel . . . Now it begins to be me."

She was working hard for the first time in many months, on a whimsical investigative article about Laguna. It focused on its future as a haven for artists and writers. To avoid community strife and ostracism upon publication, she disguised the town as the fictional "Olas," so she could write more critically, depicting the uncertain future of any resort town in straitened times. She described the small coastal enclave as "erratically lovely" and wrote of the "blue sky, yellow sand, and foam sprayed cliffs." Mary Frances also worked on drawings to accompany the article and hoped that when the two were finished she might sell them, making money that she could contribute to her life with Al. She sold her compilation to *Westways* magazine for $35. The thrill of seeing her work in print confirmed her belief that she "must either draw or write, to justify taking up space."

With her earnings from *Westways*, Mary Frances bought four books, repaid her mother $10, and took Rex, Edith, and Al for dinner in Hollywood. They had cocktails and a big meal with wine and coffee. Mary Frances reveled in the opportunity to treat her husband and parents to a fancy meal in a nice restaurant; it made her feel capable and proud. She set the rest of her paycheck away to use for groceries.

The experience helped her decide she wanted to work once she and Al got settled near Occidental. She liked the feeling of self-worth it provided and was eager to contribute to their life together. In the meantime, she canned quarts of chili sauce and relish to stock the pantry. She wrote in her journal about her "weakness for old odorous recipes" and happily remarked that she felt like she walked the house in a cloud of vinegar fumes.

WHEN MARY FRANCES and Al arrived back in the United States, Mary Frances returned to her diary writing because she believed that their life as a young couple in the midst of the Depression would make an interesting and valuable story. But almost a year later, she looked back over her entries and realized that it wasn't. Their personal devastation was due to more than just economic hardship. It was due to "almost unrelated inner things that I cannot or shall not write about."

She was vague in describing her marital troubles: "They are bitter and tragic [things] and damning and very beautiful, too, and hopeless with the hopelessness of all human passion, and they must stay locked in our own silent hearts." Her journal entries never elaborate on what she knew was chipping away at her marriage's already unstable foundation.

The couple found a small home in Eagle Rock. On one side of the hill was the Occidental campus, where she'd lived for a semester in college, on the other were views of the mountains. The house was a fixer-upper but was peaceful and quiet with views of green grass and trees. Mary Frances believed that their new home would provide a fresh start. Once again, she looked forward to a space that belonged just to them and was filled with only their things. She hoped that finally being alone in their own home would be comforting to the couple that had been coasting for so long: "The new place will be ours . . . [It] will build over us like the sky an inviolable armor."

With Al happy, Mary Frances believed she would be happier too. But their move to the home in the hills fell through. Mary Frances was disappointed but they quickly found a house in the community of Highland Park that was large and filled with light. They worked to move in before the start of the academic year.

Their new home was big enough for Al and Mary Frances to have separate workspaces. She set up her carving table, and he escaped into his writer's room. His strict work routine continued, and Mary Frances recorded her observations of him with astounding specificity: "Al taps on the typewriter or writes minute tracks on little scraps of paper. He smokes a pipe with a kind of absent minded sensuality, or holds a cigarette gingerly in his fingers. His hands [have] . . . the irreality of great carving. He frowns slightly." Mary Frances tiptoed around Al; she moved softly down the hall into the bathroom and hoped the flushing sound of the toilet would not disturb his work.

At night the two ate simple but large meals by candlelight in their new dining room; it had white walls and yellow curtains that often moved in the light breeze that came in from the hills. After dinner, Al would retreat to his study to continue to work and Mary Frances would read, write, or take long hot soaks in the tub. They'd often meet again in the bedroom—but only to read before sleep. Their sexual life does not appear to have improved in their new living space, but by this point regular intimacy had been absent from their relationship for so long that the lack of comfort or caress seemed normal.

Mary Frances soon found a job at a small shop in Los Angeles. Al would drop her at the bus station, and she would travel into the city, often arriving several hours before the start of her morning shift. So she began to visit the Los Angeles Public Library, to prove to her husband that she wasn't wasting time on a park bench every morning as she waited to go to work.

At the library, she was drawn toward the medieval cookery section, thanks partly to an elderly hobo who often sat next to her with copies of Elizabethan cookbooks. "They smelled so good," she said. "The leather, old paper and good ink . . . so I began to read the quaint old things." Inspired, she also began to write about the cookbooks and their odd and ancient recipes. She wrote a piece or two a week, and showed them to Al, who found them amusing.

But there was someone else she hoped to entertain: Tim Parrish. Mary Frances, Al, and the Parrishes remained good friends, and Mary Frances was in awe of the glamorous couple. She was especially taken with Tim, whom she described as a man "destined to draw out anything creative in other people." Soon Mary Frances's composition of brief essays eclipsed her journal writing, and she began to focus on short culinary pieces that she shared with Tim every time she saw him. She stopped making regular entries in her journal after moving in the fall of 1934, and would not return to its pages until January 1936.

ASIDE FROM HER new interest in essay writing, there was another reason for Mary Frances's turn away from her intimate journal. Increasingly bored with her husband and his listless approach to their marriage, Mary Frances looked to Tim for attention and creative motivation. At first, Mary Frances's interest in Tim didn't seem to bother Al—he was consumed with his own work. But Al eventually found it agitating. Surprisingly, he seemed less concerned with Mary Frances and Tim's interest in each other. Instead he was jealous of the interest Tim expressed in Mary Frances's writing. After all, Al was consumed by his desire to be a successful writer. The positive attention Tim, whom he considered a friend and creative equal, paid to Mary Frances's work incensed him. But perhaps Al should have been more concerned with Mary Frances and Tim's mutual admiration, because the two were falling in love.

IT'S NOT SURPRISING that a twenty-five-year-old Mary Frances would have been attracted to Tim Parrish, who was thirty-eight. He was oddly distinguished and demonstrated more interest in her and her creative work than Al ever had.

But it never occurred to her to do anything about her developing feelings. "I loved my husband," she said, "and was by nature and training unprepared for adultery." Such a statement, however, is difficult to believe: In her personal writings, Mary Frances indicated her unhappiness with her marriage and her subtle interest in Tim and Larry Powell. But although she had been married for more than five years, Mary Frances was hardly mature enough to understand her shifting emotions. Her understanding of what a "good marriage" entailed may have been clouded by her lack of experience.

Mary Frances may have been emotionally unprepared for adultery, but her physical attraction to Tim was undeniable. And one evening in the fall of 1935, she confessed her love: "Suddenly I told him that I was deeply in love with him. This was awful, for me. To say such a thing was for me a complete break with what I had been fighting for many years. DP [Tim] remained cool and well bred, as I'd known he would."

Mary Frances considered her overture excusable because Tim and Gigi were in the midst of a divorce. Gigi, married so young and often away, had fallen in love with another man, a screenwriter named John Weld. Tim was deeply depressed over the loss of his beautiful wife. Mary Frances had been longing to comfort Tim and confess her romantic feelings, but worried her affection might mar their friendship. Moreover, she was confused—she had been raised to respect fidelity and honor her marriage vows.

Perhaps she believed that she and Al might eventually salvage their relationship. They remained under extreme economic pressure, and Al remained endlessly devoted to his creativity. Maybe Mary Frances thought that once the difficult early years were over, and Al had become a successful writer, they'd construct the life they dreamed of: writing and poetry, good food and wine, intellectual discussion, and progressive thought. After all, she believed they'd been in love once, and she couldn't really understand what had happened and why their marriage didn't appear to be working.

A different tale of the seduction is told in Joan Reardon's book *Poet of the Appetites: The Lives and Loves of M.F.K. Fisher*. Reardon reports that Tim met Gigi at the train station and told her that "[a] funny thing happened when you were away." According to Gigi in this account, Mary Frances asked Tim to dinner one night, never making it clear that they would be dining alone. After eating, the two separated, but not for long. Tim went home to bed, and was surprised when soon after, Mary Frances entered the house through an unlocked door, crept into the bedroom, undressed, and eased herself into bed with him. Tim never asked Mary Frances to leave his bedroom, a choice that signals his desire (or at least complicity) in the intimacy.

Regardless of whether Mary Frances intended to embark on an affair, and what consequences (if any) she saw for her marriage, she slipped quietly and easily into a romantic liaison with Tim. And despite his medical issues, their relationship was emotionally and physically intense. With Tim, Mary Frances discovered the type of pleasure she had never experienced with Al. This only heightened her affection for Tim. Her lover adored her sharp mind, nourished her creative spirit, and feasted on their sexual connection.

BY THE TIME she picked up her journal again, early in 1936, she could more freely acknowledge Tim's influence in her life. "For seven months now I've written to Timmy, instead, really, of writing in a journal," she admitted. "I value my friendship with him." She doesn't elaborate on the nature of their relationship, nor does she say how this friendship affected her marriage.

From Tim, Mary Frances had gained confidence as a writer. Her mind was streaming with words, and she was eager to begin work on a novel about the founding of Whittier. In her journal she casually mentioned that she had "no experience" in book writing "except for the book I wrote last winter."

She failed to mention that last winter's manuscript was more than just another stab at writing: It was a collection, nearly finished, of culinary essays inspired by her mornings at the Los Angeles Public Library. Tim had shared the manuscript with his sister, Anne Parrish, who saw promise in Mary Frances's work and gave it to her editor at Harper & Brothers, Gene Saxton. Saxton was impressed with the unknown author and curious subject. He wanted to see more from her.

It was a huge accomplishment. Yet Mary Frances makes no mention of it in her journal, insisting she had no interest in selling books or even seeing her work in print: "I believe there are too many books, too many people writing, above all too many women writing." She claimed her writing was not a career but a compulsion, something she did simply because she had to. "I write, without really wanting to," she declared in her journal. "I write probably ten hours a day, mostly in my mind."

In reality, she had dreamed of being a published writer for years. The promise of a finished book should have brought her a feeling of deep accomplishment. But it was underwhelming, perhaps because of the intense personal issues that continued to divert her.

Despite her love affair with Tim, she and Al, ever clueless to his wife's infidelity, continued in much the same fashion as they had before. The two had even begun to discuss having children again. Mary Frances was now less certain about parenting with Al. Her unsatisfying marriage coupled with her interest in Tim made becoming a mother seem daunting. She wondered, "[A]re we fools to get a child? Will we breed a fiend or adopt an idiot? Would it be better to grow old alone, unbothered, dry, inverted?"

And yet she also believed that children could bring great joy—joy that might outweigh the nuisance of child-rearing or the negative influences of an unhappy marriage. In a moment of rare honesty, Mary Frances admitted that her six years alone with Al had "given me a fortitude that I know will withstand any torture." It was a searing indication of her true feelings about the relationship.

She carried on with her marriage—it seemed that that was what the world expected of her. And besides, Tim was no longer in California. After spending the summer traveling in Switzerland with his sister Anne, he had returned to Delaware indefinitely. His extensive travels had temporarily halted their correspondence.

Without Tim or his letters to occupy her, Mary Frances wrote in her journal about gardening, errands to run, a new purple dress, and social obligations. "This is a good life," she mused. "I have a fairly good body, an active if insignificant mind, a charming house to live in, and most important, all important, my dear love by my side and all about me."

But who, exactly, was "my dear love"?

8

Unspeakable Thoughts

*I*N EARLY JANUARY 1936, Tim sent Mary Frances a letter with a bold proposition. He was planning an extended trip to Europe with his mother and wanted her to be Mrs. Parrish's traveling companion. Mary Frances was wise to the plan's undercurrents. She had "been in love with [Tim] for three years or so . . . I was keeping quiet about it; I liked him and I liked his first wife who had recently married again, and I was profoundly attached to Al." But Al raised no objections when Tim broached the idea of taking Mary Frances to Europe for most of the spring. In fact, to her "astonishment and chagrin my husband eagerly, or so it seemed, urged me to go."

It was the third time that Al had agreed, apparently easily and happily, to a long separation. Yet Mary Frances still professed strong feelings of love and responsibility for her husband, saying that even as she packed her bags for the trip she was "making plans for the next years with him, the rest of my life with him."

She continued to imagine that she and Al would have or adopt children, garden and raise animals, and have interests and friends that extended far beyond the walls of academia. Yes, she was bothered by her stifling role as a faculty bride. But she believed that she was elegant and intelligent enough never to be trapped in the drudgery of wifedom and motherhood that she feared.

Perhaps this was why she agreed to the trip: It seemed plausible, at least for a moment, that she could travel to Europe with her lover and then return home and quietly resume life with her husband. But the odds of her weak marriage to Al surviving infidelity, and then beginning to flourish, were very slim—something that Mary Frances was slow to accept. Although it seems far-fetched, her sheltered upbringing and the standards of the time made Mary Frances believe that her marriage was healthy and could survive its battered state.

But while traveling east en route to her departure for Europe, her thoughts veered again, and she came to a chilling realization: Her future had been decided. If she stayed married to Al, she would indeed become a staid faculty wife, trapped in a loveless marriage, slowly losing her creativity and her soul. After a few more years of the regimented routine, she'd be "wearing brown satin afternoon dresses and wearily eating marshmallow salads at committee lunches with the best of them." The thought turned her stomach—and made her ever eager to continue her romance with Tim.

AFTER ARRIVING ON the East Coast, Mary Frances spent a few days with Tim and his family amid the glitter and sophistication of Manhattan. The Parrishes' wealth secured opulent hotels and champagne-drenched dinners. She was so taken with her surroundings that she failed to update her family about her travel plans. Al sent her a letter that hinted, lightly, at the bemused anger he and others felt at her silence. He told her that Edith was "greatly worried that she did not know where you are or what, precisely you mean next to do. In order that she should not feel isolated in her opinion I agreed it would be fine to know where you are going and where you are going to stay." Finally, Al admitted concern. It must have been gratifying to his disillusioned wife.

After their few months apart, Mary Frances found Tim even more dashing. He had started dressing entirely in navy blue: flannel shirt, tie, trousers, socks, and muffler beneath a navy double-breasted coat. She found it "really handsome, very becoming to D, and very sensible, and comfortable. I like it." With Tim's slight build, shock of nearly white hair, and blue attire, he attracted second looks wherever he went. Mary Frances liked the mystery that surrounded her lover.

Thoughts of Al, however, were never far from her mind. She voiced her conflicted feelings subtly, writing her husband that there was something "unreal and of no true importance, stuck into the truth of you and me." But the truth was that her feelings for Tim were a wedge in her marriage. By agreeing to leave her husband to travel with her lover, she chose to take her fate into her own hands. She tied her future to Tim Parrish when she stepped aboard *The Hansa* on a cold and ice-heavy February night.

Mary Frances vowed to be "good, noble, and high-minded" while on the ship—a feeble attempt to honor her attachment to Al. Her resolutions quickly shattered. She plunged back into her love affair after only two days: "I found myself standing alone in the cold moonlight, with spray everywhere and my black cape whipping, and my face probably looking a little sick but covering, I am sure, wild and unspeakable thoughts. Suddenly I seemed so ridiculous, so melodramatically mid-Victorian about my Hopeless Passion, that I blushed with embarrassment, straightened my hair and went down to the bar . . . We celebrated, with the first of ten thousand completely enjoyable drinks." It was the official start of their love affair.

She was at peace with her transgressions. She enjoyed visiting the Ladies' Salon, where she marveled at the concert grand piano that was painted creamy pink and "looked like a monstrous raspberry in the pistachio mousse decor." She took long baths and read book after book, enjoying the dramas of fictional lives.

Each night, when she arrived back at her cabin after dinner, there was a small sliver tray piled with "thin sandwiches of rare beef, a pepper mill, and a tiny bottle of cold champagne." After her midnight snack, she slept fitfully and late, usually skipping breakfast. Instead, she started each day at noon by meeting Tim in the bar for a beer. Next came a late lunch with Mrs. Parrish in the ship's restaurant, a large room with big windows that looked out to the sea. The menu regularly saluted a different country: the foods of Mexico, Sweden, Italy, Russia.

Mrs. Parrish was witty and entertaining. She was also smart—and skeptical of her son's relationship with her traveling companion. In a letter to Al, Mary Frances said Mrs. Parrish "can't figure Dillwyn and me out." She was sure that Mrs. Parrish believed her frequent declarations of love for Al and that she was happily married. But it is more likely that Mrs. Parrish quickly realized Mary Frances and Tim were romantically involved and decided to ignore their infidelity.

The three liked to lounge and watch the other guests eat and drink—a sport that Mary Frances had also enjoyed while traveling with Al. Many of the other passengers were German, and before beginning their meals, they cheered wildly and toasted the restaurant's portrait of Hitler. Aware that war was likely coming again to Europe, Mary Frances noticed that her shipmates seemed to devour the "whipped cream and pressed ducks and pâté de foie gras" as if they "would be stored somewhere in their spiritual stomachs," tiding them over during forthcoming hungers.

On the last night of the trip, the passengers gathered for a forest-themed feast. The dining room was dressed in pine boughs, and the kitchen served blue trout and wild boar, delicacies that hardly tasted as if they'd been carried frozen across the ocean. Mary Frances felt fetching and seductive in a dress she described as far too daring for chaperoning dances with Al at Occidental. At the end of the banquet, drunken passengers dissolved into a series of silly games: Toy wooden pistols were fired and poufs of cotton balls were tossed through the air. Mary Frances, Tim, and Mrs. Parrish ended the night drinking buckets of champagne in the Ladies' Salon next to the ice-cream colored pink piano.

MARY FRANCES WROTE Al regularly, telling him how much she missed and loved him. Tim's constant presence, of course, made her realize her love for her husband couldn't endure. But each letter she sealed and sent made her feel less guilty about her infidelity. Her marriage was unhappy, but she was serious about the vows she'd taken. The prospect of Rex and Edith's response if they discovered her betrayal made her sick.

After landing in Cherbourg in early February, the three traveled through France and Switzerland before arriving in England. They all won attention wherever they went: Mrs. Parrish was old and aristocratic, Tim was dramatic in his navy blue clothes, and Mary Frances was taller than most French women and stylish in her American fashions. It was clear they were foreigners, and though Mary Frances usually preferred to blend into her European landscape, this time she enjoyed the stares.

In Switzerland, Mary Frances visited the small plot of land that Tim and his sister Anne had recently purchased. The property had been christened Le Paquis, French for "the pasture," and was located in the Lavaux wine region of Switzerland, near the villages of Vevey and Chexbres. Mary Frances loved the area so much that in *Gastronomical Me*, she would refer to Tim Parrish as Chexbres. She called it a "private joke"—Chexbres was also the old Swiss word for mountain goat.

The Swiss landscape stunned Mary Frances. The clear, blue waters of Lake Geneva inched up to terraced vineyards that were centuries old.

Le Paquis was the one plot of land in the area that had not been planted as a vineyard. Instead, the relatively level ground was planted with fruit trees. A narrow brook, lined by willows, traversed the property. From a small field there were views of vineyards, mountains, lake, and sky. The air was crisp and fresh.

Tim sent Al a letter recounting an early springtime afternoon excursion with Mary Frances. "We wandered to the far end of Vevey," he wrote, "then up through the stepped vineyards to the Cafe du Terrance. It was clear and crisply cool, but not too cool to sit on the high terrace on the lake side of the café. Relaxed, at peace, we gazed down at the lake, the town, up at the snow covered mountains. Primroses and crocuses grew in the path side grass. A fat old woman wandered through her tiny kitchen garden picking greens for a salad while she munched a big white onion . . . We drank white wine (1934) and ate cheese with coarse peasant bread."

It was bold of Tim to write such friendly letters to Al. His musings were so complimentary they can't help but appear tinged with a falseness that borders on pity. "You know I think of you," he told Al. "You, Mary, Anne—the people I love. I want no more. I am blessed and I am happy in having you. Don't work too hard; try not to be lonely. Bless you."

In comparison to Al's tightly rendered prose, Tim's writing was effortless and unrestrained. But often, Tim's openness was careless and cruel. "We touched glasses and looked into each other's eyes," he wrote after an afternoon spent hiking in the Alps with Mary Frances, her "long, cool fingers" touching his arm lightly. Tim taunted Al from afar, seemingly boasting about the prize he'd won. Yet he was careful never to betray the true nature of his relationship with her.

Al didn't suspect the affair. But he wrote back to Mary Frances, happy and relaxed, in letters more overtly adoring than any she had ever received from him. He addressed them to his "Sweetness," his

"Dearest Love," and his "Precious Little One." It was a textbook attempt to manipulate his wife by showering her with a kindness that, conveniently, never required supporting action. His letters recounted the mundane tasks of his days: visits to the ranch for dinner with Edith and Rex, trips to the market and the resulting home meals, money woes, and his constant attempts to work and to write. He mentioned often that he was "terribly lonely" for his wife and "missed her help and presence" more than he could say.

In one long, undated letter, Al revealed himself to his wife in a way he never had before: "You don't know how I miss you," he wrote. "It isn't any one thing—talking to you when I come from college or reading in the same room with you or eating together or waking up in the morning to see you there so sweetly or making love—it's none of the particular things, nor all of them together. It's you as a person and a presence that I so miss and need. I'm distracted inside."

Suddenly, Al seemed to long for the marital intimacy that he had resisted for years. Perhaps he recalled the long letters and romantic sonnets he had sent to Mary Frances from Wyoming—and hoped that his current musings would work the same magic.

The fact that he had agreed so easily to her departure now haunted him. In one letter he told her: "you know, of course, and without my saying anything about it, that I would not have had you miss going to Europe for the world . . . I wanted you to go and I'm glad you went . . . But I cannot help feeling . . . so alone. This aloneness is not the 'great loneliness' of a romantic, nor the solitariness of the wan young poet in college. It is something profound and real."

Al always ended his letters by proclaiming his love for his wife and for Tim: "All my best love always . . . and give my love to Tim too. I suppose I'm fonder of him than I've ever been of anybody but you. I worship you." Just as much as Mary Frances and Tim wanted a relationship without him, Al was convinced that his future happiness was firmly connected to both his wife and his good friend.

As Mary Frances's trip with the Parrishes progressed, she wrote Al less and less. He became increasingly distracted, awaiting news from his wife. When three letters and a small packet arrived from Mary Frances before a weekend trip to the Kennedy house at Laguna Beach, Al reportedly shook with joy. He decided that he wanted to delay the pleasure of reading them until he returned home.

That's when Al lit the fireplace, found a cigarette, and settled himself on the couch, intent on "prolonging (what kind of sexual perversion is it? . . .) my pleasure." After years of dismissing his wife's creativity, intimate life, and often her mere presence, Al was now eager to savor every word she wrote. He used Mary Frances's lines as a way to connect with her in a way he'd never wanted to before. "Little do you realize," he wrote, "[h]ow you have really eaten each meal twice . . . been twice as seasick . . . little do you realize how much pleasure I have in knowing you are on such a luxurious trip."

Mary Frances was dismayed by Al's mournful letters. But her concern over his loneliness was short-lived. "I didn't sit brooding over your sadness," she wrote. "I know you're glad I'm here, and so am I . . . And soon I'll be home again—chez moi, in your arms."

Al's anxiety sprang from the news that Mary Frances was inching toward a book deal. In early April 1936, she wrote to Al detailing her visit to the offices of Hamish Hamilton in London, where she had discussed gathering the essays inspired by the Los Angeles library into her first book, a volume called *Serve It Forth*. Hamilton, the American editor Gene Saxton, and Mary Frances had decided that she should "write a 45,000 word book . . . No contracts signed, no mention of money, only a very firm demand for more, more, more, soon, soon." She said that despite the fact there'd been no talk of money or contracts, Tim had told her that the conversation meant the book had been sold. "I think we're set!" she told Al. "I know you'll be glad."

The book would be published under the pen name Mary Frances had developed when pitching her first article to *Westways* magazine. Just as Edith signed her checks E.O.H. KENNEDY, Mary Frances would write as M.F.K. Fisher. From Mary Frances's first visit to Hamish Hamilton's office, the lore surrounding the moniker of M.F.K. Fisher was born. In none of her letters does Mary Frances ever mention any discussions with her publisher of how she would be billed on the cover of her first book. But later she spun a vivid tale about Saxton and Hamilton's surprise when she arrived as M.F.K. Fisher the woman, not M.F.K. Fisher the corpulent male gastronome. She claimed that she had "upset them both by appearing as a young woman in a Paris hat instead of the willowy Oxford don they imagined the writer to be."

It's difficult to believe that Mary Frances's gender was never mentioned in any of the letters of introduction that were written by Tim and Anne Parrish. But the confusion over her name made for a spicy tale. And in spite of the surprise over who the true M.F.K. Fisher was, the men still believed in her writing and wanted to publish her work.

Gene Saxton would edit the American edition, which would be published by Harper's. He, Hamilton, and Mary Frances agreed that M.F.K. Fisher was a fine name for an author who did not write about the pleasures of the table in "correctly female and 'home economics' fashion."

In early May, Mary Frances had another meeting with Hamish Hamilton, and they formalized her contract. The publisher wanted a larger version of her original manuscript with the "same easy and interpersonal history of food." She told Al that the goal was to publish it "not as another pleasant gastronomical chat, but as an important work!" She said that Hamish Hamilton believed "there's no such thing in print at present . . . no definite and chronological survey of man's rise to civilized dyspepsia." She felt excited, amazed and "somewhat panicky" at the prospect of writing something that her editors and publishers believed could prove seminal.

Al claimed to be pleased by the news of Mary Frances's writing success. "It's a good book," he told her. Yet the announcement made him frantic that his wife's successes were about to eclipse his own. Al wrote and told Mary Frances that he had met the dean of Smith College, in Northampton, Massachusetts, and that he had offered him a job teaching advanced composition. "Would you be willing to go to the best women's college . . . in America if we had the chance?" he asked. He also mentioned moving to Europe. He was increasingly bored with academia and dreamed of more exciting projects like working in a Swiss chocolate factory and then writing a book about chocolate.

Next he subtly requested that she not "sign anything or make plans for the summer" before first speaking to him. After years of holding the power in his marriage, Al was now grasping for attention and authority. He wasn't pleased that Mary Frances, who was living a life he knew only through the occasional letter, was becoming so independent. Nor was he pleased that she seemed so happy without him.

Mary Frances had her own response to Al's fledgling plans. "Fisher, I'll soon be home," she told him. "Hold everything and don't tie yourself too tightly for this summer . . . Who knows?"

She tried to appear enthusiastic but dreaded her return to California. She told Al that "the thought that I'll be with you almost as soon as this letter is almost more than me and my tummy can stand. It makes me quite sick." She was facing a bitter truth: She wanted a divorce but wasn't sure how to ask Al for one.

MARY FRANCES'S TRIP back to the United States, in May 1936, was slow and thoughtful, not unlike other contemplative voyages she'd taken at sea. But instead of merely pondering major life changes on the ocean, this time she was determined truly to begin a new course.

She was intensely preoccupied with sorting through her feelings and beginning to make plans for a future without Al. She described herself as being "almost in absentia, like a woman concentrating on bearing a child." Her metaphor was apt; after years of focusing on Al's needs, Mary Frances was ready to begin birthing her true self. She believed that her life with Al, the life that she had planned to go back to upon her return from Europe, no longer existed. She realized now that perhaps it had been over for a very long time. But she was stuck wondering how she could help Al realize the truth of their relationship and see that their marriage was dead. She also wondered what sort of life she would want for herself if she was no longer married to him.

Mary Frances got off the train in Chicago, determined to stop there permanently. She planned to look for a job and then write and ask Al for a divorce. But then what would she do? She was deeply in love with Tim. But she was frightened—Tim did not seem to want to do much about solidifying their relationship. It was unclear if leaving Al meant beginning an honest relationship with Tim, or just living alone as a shamed divorcee. The uncertainty terrified her. Ultimately, she decided to return to California. She hoped that seeing Al would help her decide what to do next.

UPON HER RETURN, Mary Frances found her husband "much changed." From the tenor of Al's letters, it is easy to imagine that during the four months Mary Frances was gone, he morphed from an aloof and self-absorbed man to a needy husband, terrified of losing his wife to another man. His behavior mirrored Mary Frances's in Dijon. Married too young, far from home, and lacking in affection and emotional depth to make their marriage work, what the two really desired from the other was not love and devotion. It was attention.

While Mary Frances was away, Al's father died. The loss of his stern, religion-loving father affected Al, sparking emotional highs and lows unfamiliar to Mary Frances, who was accustomed to the constancy of a distant and uninterested spouse.

Though he may have been eager to repair his marriage—or at least prevent losing his wife to another man—Mary Frances rebuffed Al's advances. Al struggled with impotency during this time, and was horrified by his inability to be sexual with his wife. But for Mary Frances, it was a relief. After so much intense time with her lover, any attention from Al, especially overt affection, made her feel uncomfortable and guilty.

The death of Al's father focused Mary Frances's attention on the unvoiced expectations that Al had for their marriage. She began to realize that when the two met, Al had seen in Mary Frances "proof to his omnipotent father and family that a woman could read 'daring' books and still be a lady." But as their marriage evolved, Al grew tired of his wife's more creative and bohemian side and began to want conventional things like "roast beef and mashed potatoes and chocolate cake for Sunday noon dinner," food she felt he'd been raised to think were "concommitment with Marital Happiness." It was all so clear to her now: He wanted a limp companion to care for him and engage emotionally and physically on his terms. Mary Frances wanted passion, an equitable partnership with a man who valued her creative urges.

Al was in love with what he wanted her to be: "the ideal he'd built in the East Adams Presbyterian Church, of a girl who was well bred, but that did everything he had been taught was not so: smoked, drank, wore lipstick, read T. S. Eliot. Liked Picasso." He was so taken with this idealization that Mary Frances claimed that as their marriage dissolved, Al was sleeping with a photo taken of her at sixteen. Mary Frances considered this proof that Al had fetishized her into a vaporous dream woman.

Their lives differed so dramatically from her newlywed hopes: "gone were Proust and the grilled lamb chop and green salad. Gone were the nights when a few of us sat with some wine . . . and talked and read and sang. Instead Al and I went almost every night to a double feature movie, and ate chocolate bars, and came home drugged with bad air and drivel, and were too tired to 'talk.'" Their life was no longer literary, bohemian, or even remotely exciting.

Upon returning to California, Mary Frances found that she lacked the strength to exit her marriage. Al had become attached to her, suddenly eager to know her innermost thoughts and pressing her to continue planning their future together. Tim was in Delaware, and his absence was unnerving. She couldn't be sure that she'd have his support if she divorced.

The stress and uncertainty was overwhelming, and Mary Frances waited gingerly for something to happen, a small push of fate to help her decide what to do next.

Mary Frances and sister Anne, Christmas Day, 1911

Aunt Gwen and swimming companion with Mary Frances (center), Anne, and baby Norah

↑ Edith Oliver Holbrook Kennedy with daughters Mary Frances and Anne

→ Grandmother Holbrook with Mary Frances and siblings Anne, Norah, and David, 1919

⬆ Graduating class of Miss Harker's School, Palo Alto, 1927. Mary Frances is fourth from left (The Schlesinger Library, Radcliffe Institute, Harvard University)

➡ Mary Frances on her wedding day, September 5, 1929

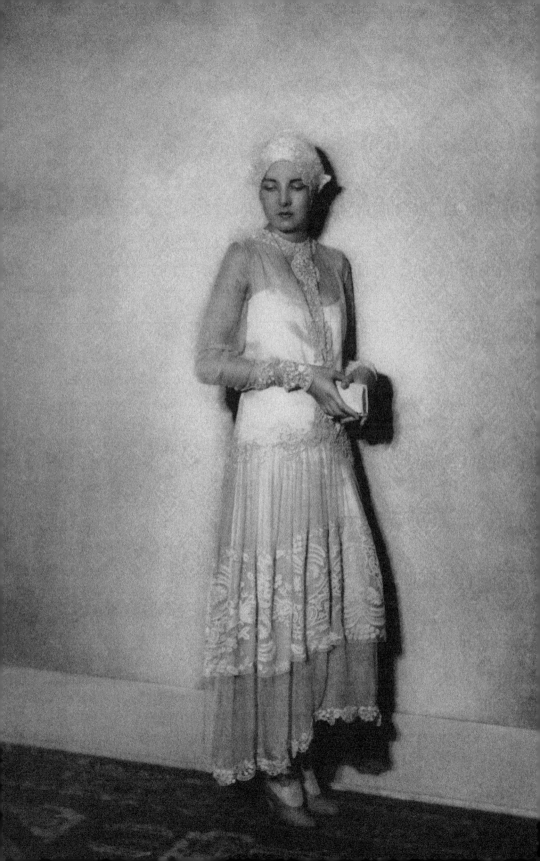

 Alfred Young Fisher

 Mary Frances on ship to
France, 1929

Mary Frances and Lawrence Clark Powell, Dijon 1930

Mary Frances; photo taken around 1931

↑ Mary Frances and Al,
Laguna Beach, 1932

← Mary Frances and Norah, in Paris
at the Colonial Exposition, 1931

↓ Mary Frances, Al, and Larry
Powell in Cros de Cagnes,
France, 1932

Tim Parrish gardening at
Le Paquis, 1936

Mary Frances relaxing in
vineyard at Le Paquis, 1937

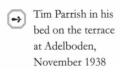 Rex Kennedy,
Al Fisher, Tim
Parrish in Vevey,
Switzerland, 1937

Norah Kennedy, Tim, and Anne Parrish picnic
at Le Paquis, summer 1938

Tim Parrish in his
bed on the terrace
at Adelboden,
November 1938

A sketch by Tim Parrish done in the
hospital on October 1, 1938, titled
"First Night—Dreams of Suicide"

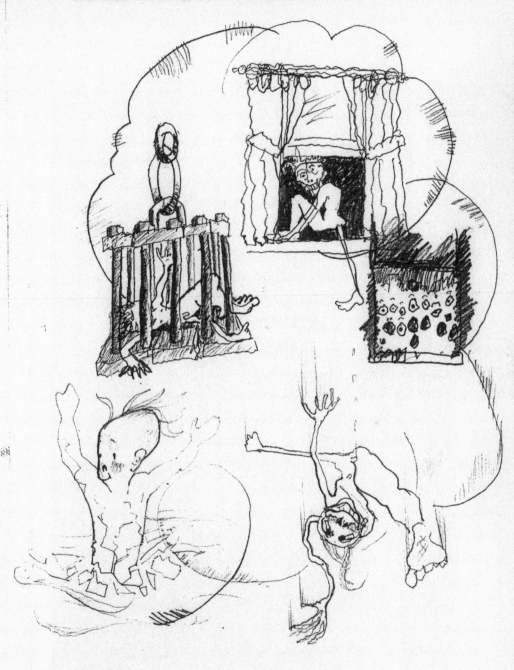

First night - Dreams of Suicide

IV
1.X.38

Mary Frances and Tim, Bareacres, 1941

Tim on the porch
at Bareacres

Mary Frances with
siblings Norah and
David, and David's
wife Sarah, in
Mexico, 1941

Mary Frances and Donald Friede in Atlantic City on the day they were married in May 1945

Mary Frances at work

Mary Frances and baby Anne, 1944

Mary Frances, Donald, Anne, and Kennedy, Bareacres, June 1946

Mary Frances in her Bareacres kitchen. The photo, taken in 1944, was part of a shoot for Harper's Baazar

9

The Edge of Ripeness

OMETIME IN LATE spring 1936, Mary Frances got another letter from Tim. She unfolded the thin pages and read that he was moving to Switzerland, to Le Paquis. He asked her and Al to join him, live communally off the land, and work freely on their creative projects. He had plenty of money; and Tim hoped eventually to have enough space to invite a cadre of like-minded academic, literary, and artistic companions to help him build a bohemian artists' community alongside Lake Geneva. Mary Frances and Al could be the first to sign on.

Al, wanting to recharge his own creative life and escape his career in academics, decided they should go. Mary Frances was shocked and frustrated. She never imagined that Al would be attracted to the idea of the two of them moving abroad to live with Tim. She hoped that Al would simply encourage her to go to Europe without him, just as he had earlier in the year. But Al was in denial—not only about his marriage but also about the nature of Mary Frances's relationship with Tim.

She couldn't persuade her husband to remain in California. Al was intrigued by the opportunity to help launch something bohemian and new, and was happy to be invited back into what he perceived to be Mary Frances and Tim's insular friendship. Al also desperately wanted to try living in Europe again; he had decided that he loathed Occidental and teaching. Mary Frances recalled that he "remembered how happy he'd been in Dijon, young, in love, free." He couldn't wait to pack and leave.

As soon as Mary Frances realized Al was serious about moving to Switzerland, she began to feign benevolence, suggesting that she was deeply sympathetic to Al and his unhappiness. It was a revisionist history that would endure—even late in life she would claim that she and Tim had Al's best interests at heart when they suggested a move to Switzerland. She wrote that they "felt it was terrible for a man as fine as Al to be so miserable as he felt at Occidental." That the two never considered how terrible it would be for Al when he realized they were lovers went unmentioned. Mary Frances said she "honestly thought it would work."

The two traveled to Switzerland in the fall of 1936 on a small Dutch passenger freighter. There were fewer than two dozen travelers on what Mary Frances called the "realest ship she ever knew."

They took the long route to Europe, traveling through the Panama Canal and Central American ports to Rotterdam, in the Netherlands. Al said that when he was not reading he was "lazing, and perhaps, musing rather too steadily in an erotic mode." But he wasn't thinking erotically about his wife. The two traveled in distant tandem. They chatted with the captain and crew of the ship regularly, and made friends with an elderly widow—anything to avoid being alone together.

The food on this trip was "different from the almost lavish cuisine" of the other ships. It was plain but good and fortifying, complemented by vegetables and salads that the staff somehow managed to preserve and keep serving all the way across the ocean. Mary Frances especially liked a thick green soup brimming with cabbage, potatoes, leeks, and sausage that was perfect for brisk and windy days at sea. Another odd favorite was a dish called Hodge-Podge, a sludge of vegetables and chunks of ham that she described as good in a "simple crude way that might offend or bore sophisticated palates." She liked it for its comfortable honesty. The solid, unpretentious food and drink helped pass the time between ports and fortify Mary Frances and Al for the challenging weeks on land.

The couple traveled by train to Switzerland, arriving in Vevey via tracks that hugged Lake Geneva and steep, terraced vineyards bursting with October gold, red, and orange. Tim's friend Otto Trettma met them at the station and took them to a pension where Tim had left fresh flowers, liquor, and cigarettes.

They bathed, unpacked, and tried to rest. Relaxing was hard—Mary Frances described herself in her journal as "jittery, for more reasons than can be written." She fretted about Tim and their reunion—"Would he still like us?" she wondered. "Would he want us to live with him when he saw us?" She worried not only about seeing Tim after a few months apart, but about Al and Tim's reunion. Would Al be able to instantly see the affection between the two?

Tim arrived on the evening train, looking healthy, strong, and handsome. Mary Frances noticed that Al seemed surprised by the change in Tim's appearance and demeanor. The last time Al had seen him, he was bereft, broken from his divorce from Gigi. After driving Tim to the Hollywood train station to begin his trip east, Mary Frances and Al had worried about his physical and emotional health. Now Tim was calm and happy, and Al noticed the change immediately. Mary Frances was pleased that her husband noted the new confidence Tim exuded, even if it put her slightly on edge.

Mary Frances and Tim politely "kissed and touched each other," trying, she wrote, to see "months in a few seconds." Their reunion's intensity was amplified by Al's presence—the couple wasn't free to do or say what they really wanted. From their brief interactions, however, it was clear that their desire hadn't died. The three went to dinner, where they nibbled at their meals, talked too loud and fast, and nervously laughed at nothing. Later they went out drinking, consuming several bottles of the local Vin de Vevey with anxiety and anticipation. As they began their life in Switzerland, she and Tim tried to subvert their romantic interest, hoping to keep their relationship hidden from Al. For Mary Frances, the choice was intentional and selfish. She sought to protect herself at all costs, never daring to reveal the truth until she was ready to face it, even if it meant hurting those closest to her.

The morning after Al and Mary Frances arrived, the three visited Le Paquis. It was a cool, clear day, and the thin autumn sunlight dappled the yellowing leaves of the vineyard. Mary Frances was surprised to find that the property, which she had visited only once before, felt comfortably familiar. She wandered through the house's two small rooms and the surrounding plot of land. She looked at the trees and vines flourishing around her, and felt grounded in a way she hadn't in a long time. "It exists," she wrote in her journal. "And so do we." She was very happy, seemingly unaware of her supremely odd living arrangements. Later, though, she would admit that "before we'd been there for five hours Al knew that even my exaggerated talks of how difficult it would be were not wild enough."

The next few days were busy. The three went wine-tasting in the cellars of Fribourg, a neighboring vineyard, and drank a bottle from the 1934 vintage. By the end of the visit, Tim and Al had decided that Al should begin to study winemaking. "Why not?" Mary Frances mused in her journal. It seemed as good a creative pursuit as any other. That night they had what Tim described as a "wine dinner without the dinner," consuming white country wine from Switzerland, red wine from Burgundy, champagne, and various liquors till they were weaving and shaking.

As the days passed, Mary Frances, Tim, and Al worked together on plans for improving Le Paquis's rustic structure. Tim wanted to remodel and expand the small cottage with more rooms and French doors opening onto terraces with views of the lake, land, and sky. The three also discussed moving out of their pension and into a temporary apartment in Vevey. Mary Frances believed that it would be good for the three of them to live quietly together in an apartment—it seemed more permanent and settled.

In pensions, her main impulse had been to keep busy at cafés and museums and shops; it felt less like home and more like a vacation. Now she wanted a place where she could simply be still, enjoying the quiet and the landscape. They decided to sign a six-month lease on an apartment on the market square in downtown Vevey and worked together furnishing and settling into their new space. As their daily tasks unfolded, Mary Frances recorded them in her journal.

She was hesitant to write anything too personal. Yet she was also afraid of writing an account of her life in Switzerland that was stiff and boring. "How to write of three people with complete impersonality?" she wondered. The result was a colorful, detailed account of life at Le Paquis that was comprised almost entirely of vegetables bought, chamberwomen hired, and meals consumed. Her raging personal strife went nearly unrecorded, though an undercurrent of tension is apparent in her alternating terse and lyrical lines.

She made vague mention of trying to veil the confused heaviness she felt in Tim's presence. She believed that when she could "answer my own questions I shall be able more clearly to ask them of others, and more firmly too." Undoubtedly this is a reference to the perplexity she felt living with two men, her building desire to ask Al to leave Switzerland, and her uncertainty about how to do it.

The stresses of the trio's living arrangement quickly mounted as Al began to realize that Mary Frances and Tim were romantically involved. Usually confident, Tim seemed to suffer from the stress, perhaps fearing a confrontation. While at the theater one evening, Tim grew anxious and shaky. He managed to leave the auditorium before collapsing on the stairs outside. His face turned gray and his eyes rolled back; he was unconscious for close to a minute. As the incident occurred, Mary Frances was calm. But after going to bed, she tossed and turned in a "half-waking nightmare" that troubled her until morning. She had a feeling that the spell, which she described as a "nerve-bile-crisis" from which he quickly recovered, was related to Tim's numerous stresses, including living in a house with her and Al.

Money was another complication. Tim had it; Al and Mary Frances did not. Though Tim had invited the couple to live in Switzerland on his bankroll, he still expected that they would chip in for food and other household items. Mary Frances felt a "prick of resentment" at Tim's desire to purchase expensive things when he knew Mary Frances and Al couldn't. What's more, while traveling in Europe with the Parrishes, Mary Frances had grown used to traveling stylishly, at their expense. She was irritated by Tim's expectation that she now chip in.

"My only excesses are mental," she claimed. Yet her physical maladies belied stress. She suffered from frequent stomachaches and slept excessively, to "escape reality." Her slumber was often interrupted by nightmares or flashes of panic that left her wide awake and shaking, alone in her bedroom.

She used cooking to escape the daily life that both thrilled and confounded her. The local cuisine was a heavy, wintery diet influenced by

Switzerland's German and French neighbors; it inspired Mary Frances. She loved wandering the local market and searching for the next meal's ingredients and floral arrangements. "The cabbages and salads and all the leeks and leaves and colored things were like flowers," she wrote. She marveled at the bread in big piles, onions woven into necklaces, and mounds of potatoes.

But whenever she returned home with her goods, she confronted the household's tacit unhappiness. Al was restless; he thought he needed isolation to write but actually loved company to spur his creativity. He left the house daily for a walk or in search of breakfast brioche—anything to occupy him. Tim was equally itinerant but was clearly the head of their small household.

Mary Frances, however, did her best to remain composed. In previous years she had proved that she could live contentedly without Al's affection. Having subordinated her sexual needs while living with her physically distant husband, she was sure she had her desires "well in control" when she set off for Switzerland. She also believed her trip abroad with Tim proved she could be with him regularly without setting off any "bonfires."

The remodeling at Le Paquis began early in 1937, and Mary Frances filled the pages of her journal with mundane updates about the construction and more colorful lists of the vegetables she was planting in the garden: asparagus, tomatoes, eggplant, and, later in spring, carrots, lettuce, and onions.

Occasionally, she mused about how much she loved the slow pace of life in Switzerland: "On my window sill, to catch the rare sun, is my little garden, two pansies, a deep blue cineraria, two pots of spindly morning glory sprouts I hope to raise." She wrote in her journal while sitting in her sunny bedroom and sipping on a bottle of beer. In the next room, Tim wrote and sketched at the dining room table. Al was chopping wood at Le Paquis, after which he'd walk into the village of Chexbres for a bowlful of hot soup for lunch. The activities were typical of their life together in Switzerland: deliberately quiet living with an undercurrent of emotional confusion.

Despite her alliance with Tim, there were times when Mary Frances was the odd woman out, watching Al and Tim drink beer, play games, or discuss literature and art. Those moments were reminiscent of long evenings in Dijon with Al and Larry Powell, and she hated them.

THOUGH MARY FRANCES searched for ordinary things to record in her journal, there's never any mention of her forthcoming book or edits to the manuscript she might have been expected to work on during the winter and spring she lived at Le Paquis. Only once did she mention her correspondence with Gene Saxton, hopeful that he would be pleased with a new batch of writing she sent to him. She also mentioned the idea of applying for a Guggenheim grant, believing that the prestigious award could fund additional time working in Europe.

She was tempted, she said, to begin writing a personal book. She felt her life was "strange, complicated, and interesting," and perhaps worthy of deeper consideration. But she worried that her deep distrust of personal revelation would prevent her from being able to dig more deeply into the aspects of her life she found herself continually pondering. Perhaps Mary Frances thought that if she put the most intimate and painful parts of herself on the page she would begin to understand who she was and why she occasionally made such curious choices. Perhaps she was worried about what she might discover.

IN APRIL OF 1937, after a long and emotionally arduous winter and early spring spent tiptoeing around each other, Al made a big announcement. He was tired of living with Mary Frances and Tim, and was ready to leave Switzerland, return to the United States, and resume looking for a teaching position. He had realized, after months of observation, that his wife and Tim were lovers and that her affection for Tim was great enough that a return to their marriage was unlikely.

As the months at Le Paquis passed, Al had increasingly found himself alone with his sheaves of rain-colored writing paper, a headful of ideas, and persistent confusion and anger about the state of his relationship with his wife. Her drifting from him, and their shell of a relationship made him realize, finally, that their marriage was over. Later, Al would tell Larry Powell that as he watched the new Le Paquis rise, he became certain that he would never really live there.

When Al announced his intention to leave, Mary Frances told him she would not return with him to the United States. She asked him to stay with her until Rex and Edith's upcoming visit to Switzerland, and then depart. He agreed. It was a necessary deception; she had never told her parents about the strife in her marriage or about her deep feelings for Tim. The letters she wrote to her family had remained typically cheery and vivid.

Mary Frances, who decided to greet Rex and Edith alone in France, lied to Al and Tim about their arrival date and escaped to Paris a few days early, eager to leave the men behind. Apprehensive about her parents' arrival, she prepared their hotel room with flowers, mineral water, and good English novels. She repeated the same words in her head, over and over, to calm herself as she wandered Paris. "Flagons and apples," she said, trying to vanquish the thoughts in her jumbled head. The words were a reference to lines from the Bible's Song of Solomon: "Stay me with flagons, comfort me with apples: for I am sick of love."

In an autobiographical essay she wrote after her visit to Paris, "Stay Me, Oh Comfort Me," Mary Frances described herself as tired and confused. "I wanted love," she wrote, "but I was tired of it, wearied by its involutions, convolutions, its complex intraplexities. I had fled from it, leaving there in Vevey the husk and the bud." She tried to write to Al and explain that she was happy and well. Presumably, she wanted him to know that she was content with the shape her life and future were taking, even if he was not.

But she could not finish the letter. She knew that running away from their marital troubles had not helped them at all, and perhaps had even worsened their living situation and her feelings of anxiety. She wrote that she "loved him too much to lie" about the person she saw herself becoming. But she also knew she did not love Al enough to continue living with him. As she waited for her parents to arrive from the United States, she knew that she had to find some way to tell them that her marriage was over.

But she wasn't brave enough. It was Rex's first trip to Europe and a rare extended vacation for her devoted parents. After a week of touring and tasting in Paris, Mary Frances, Rex, and Edith traveled to Vevey. Her elaborate guise continued, and Rex and Edith, floored by the beauty of their daughter's life in Switzerland, were happy to serve as guest actors in Mary Frances's intricate play.

One of the group's most memorable moments in Switzerland was an evening picnic. It was early summer and the nights were growing soft and warm. At the end of the day, after the workmen had left Le Paquis, Mary Frances, Tim, Rex, and Edith spread a tablecloth on a table under an apple tree. Tim and Rex picked fresh green peas, and Mary Frances and Edith shelled them as quickly as possible before cooking them in a heavy casserole over a small fire, swirling them with butter as they gently cooked in their own steam.

They ate the tender peas alongside cold cooked chicken, good bread, and local white wine. As the sun set and the breeze began to blow from the lake, the group packed up their things and returned to the car. They drove the vineyards' winding roads until they reached Vevey and their protected apartment terrace where they sat drinking bitter black coffee in the dark. It was a glorious evening. Rex and Edith left Switzerland shortly after the meal; they returned to the United States knowing only that Mary Frances and Tim seemed to be very close friends. They had no idea that Al planned to leave Le Paquis shortly after they did.

In spite of his injured pride, Al was undoubtedly glad to be free of his binding ties to his wife and her lover. Later Bob Spackman would declare that Al's indifference to Mary Frances and their marriage was clear from what he had allowed to occur. "First," Spackman said, "MF spent a summer abroad with Parrish and his mother as a 'companion' to old Mrs. Parrish, and then at Parrish's suggestion (and on Parrish's money) the Fisher's and Parrish's [sic] set up housekeeping in Switzerland."

Spackman claimed that he was too embarrassed to ask Al much about the trio's life abroad and the "terribly unhandy form of adultery" that he had observed. Ultimately he knew few details other than that "nobody's nerves stood it for very long, and in due course Fisher walked out."

In an unpublished manuscript, *For the Record*, composed years later, Al gave a brief synopsis of the triangle at Le Paquis. He wrote that Mary Frances "fell in love with my then good friend Dillwyn Parrish." But he couldn't decide if he'd felt a "sense of guilt about readily yielding my first wife to a friend." Even years later, Al's true feelings about his life in Switzerland were vague.

After leaving Le Paquis, Al wandered Nazi Germany for a few months before returning to the United States and a teaching job at Smith College. Tim funded his travels. Spackman was astonished that his friend was willing to "sell his wife" to Tim in exchange for travel and living expenses. But if Tim did give Al money, it wasn't so that he could "own" Mary Frances. Tim wanted to help Al get on with his life while Mary Frances and Tim continued their love affair. Mary Frances did feel some remorse over Al's departure. In a letter to Larry Powell, she asked that he write Al: "He'll be lonesome for awhile."

After Rex, Edith, and Al left Le Paquis, Mary Frances stayed, now "plainly the mistress." Their life was blissful. They worked daily on their land; Tim, who loved gardening, read books about farming and experimented with crops and planting. Mary Frances said that he seemed to keep the feeling of "growth and fertility and the seasons in his bones and flesh." It helped that the old soil at Le Paquis was dark and thick, "bursting with life." The couple grew greens for salads, herbs, onions, and garlic, which Mary Frances braided into "long silky ropes" and hung from the attic rafters.

They often had more food than they knew what to do with. She canned tomatoes and beans and vegetable juices; made pickles and catsups; preserved plums, peaches, and other fruits; and made endless jams and fruit liquors. Bins were filled with root vegetables and shelves lined with cabbages and apples and tomatoes. Mary Frances loved looking at her growing collection; it was a "reassurance of safety against hunger" she found "primitive and satisfying."

From neighbors she learned to cook vegetables in their own juices with "sweet butter or thick olive oil to encourage them a little." Tim fried tomatoes so that the thick slices were "dark brown and crisp all though," yet still delicate and tender. Occasionally they would make corn "oysters," round fritters crafted from dried corn they'd brought from the United States. The two would "sit right by the stove and lift the shaggy little cakes from the hot butter" to their plates, and then "float them down with beer chilled in the fountain." Their love of food fed their romantic passion; so did their endless conversations. Mary Frances would later say that because of the intense time they spent together, Tim was the "only man I've ever really known."

In the summer of 1937, shortly after Rex, Edith, and Al left, *Serve It Forth* was published. It won great acclaim, but she hardly noticed. "I was so involved emotionally [with Tim] that I paid no attention to it." She was concerned mostly with the money and financial stability she hoped the book would provide, telling Larry in a letter, "To hell with esteem."

A brief review in *The New York Times* began, "This is a book about food; but though food is universal, this book is unique." It was a "delightful book . . . erudite and witty and experienced and young. The truth is that it is stamped on every page with a highly individualized personality."

It was also reviewed in the *New York Herald Tribune* by Lucius Beebe, a well-known writer and gastronome, who gave his blessing despite his apparent shock upon discovering M.F.K. Fisher was not a man. "Women," Beebe pronounced, were "supposed to confine themselves to home economies." And *Serve It Forth* was hardly a book about home economies, written for the American housewife.

In its introduction, Mary Frances wrote that her book was about "eating and what to eat and about people who eat." It was a collection of short essays on food history, recollections of past meals and pleasures, and musings on the relationship among people, food, and desire. The essay titles were provocative and unconventional: "Let the Sky Rain Potatoes," "Fifty Million Snails," "Pity the Blind Vegetable," and "The Social Status of the Vegetable." Recipes—there were only a few—were strategically sprinkled. Mary Frances wanted them to be "like birds in a tree," present only "if there is a comfortable branch."

The few negative reviews came from American critics who thought M.F.K. Fisher lacked the culinary training to conjure food in such a literary manner. They also worried the book was biased against American and regional cuisine. There was some truth to this: Most of the essays did focus on European, specifically French, gastronomy. The attention that was paid to the European aesthetic seemed, to her detractors, to assert that America lacked such "high art" cooking. Moreover, Mary Frances unsettled critics who found her far more evocative and seductive than was appropriate for female food writers. In a piece called "Borderland," she wrote about the pleasures of eating just what she wanted. For her, it was tangerine sections broiled on the radiator during the long, cold February days she and Al lived in Strasbourg.

She described the ritual, telling how to prepare the tangerine for broiling: "[I]n the morning, in the soft sultry chamber, sit in the window peeling tangerines, three or four. Peel them gently; do not bruise them . . . separate each plump little crescent. If you find The Kiss, the secret section, save it for Al." Next she described her pleasure at eating the hot, crisp, sweet-and-sour fruit: "I cannot tell you why they are so magical. Perhaps it is that little shell, thin as one layer of enamel on a Chinese bowl, that crackles so tinily, so ultimately under your teeth. Or the rush of the pulp just after it. Or the perfume. I cannot tell." Her lines introduced readers of both sexes to the private pleasure she derived from eating. Never had a woman written so sensually about her intimate enjoyment of food.

AT THE END of 1937, Mary Frances traveled back to the United States to tell her parents about her impending divorce. Tim believed that a letter was an adequate way to communicate the news, but Mary Frances wanted to do it herself. It was a "kind of castigation for hurting good people," she believed.

The trip was rough. She felt "flattened" and "boneless" and believed her feelings stemmed from the despair of having left Tim behind. After all, her every trip away from Al had brought disaster. But she also feared her parents' reception: She knew that the end of her eight-year marriage would shock Rex and Edith.

She traveled home surrounded by Jewish refugees who were fleeing Europe in the face of anti-Semitism and war. Most were doctors, lawyers, and other professionals confronting a vastly uncertain future. Though they played cards and smiled, they were resentful, anxiously wondering how they would begin anew. Many had already endured moves from Austria to Holland before embarking to America; some had also spent time in Nazi labor camps. They had packed tools, books, and other small belongings they hoped to sell for seed money to restart their lives.Watching them heightened Mary Frances's misery, and she occasionally felt as emotionally exiled as her shipmates. To rally her spirits, she decided to do and act just as she wished on the trip—even if she became an object of curiosity. She made the unconventional request of her own private dinner table to avoid annoying companions. She ate and drank whatever she wanted, whenever she wanted. She discovered she preferred to eat alone, "slowly, voluptuously, and with an independence that heartened me against the coldness of my cabin and my thoughts," rather than dining with companions who might offer up uninteresting stories or need advice.

"I know what I want," she wrote, "and I usually get it." She ordered meals that were "more typically masculine than feminine, if feminine means whipped-cream-and-cherries." She ate lettuce hearts and buttermilk dressing for dinner, and slowly savored rich slices of paté. She drank good wine, and heaped appreciative praise on her attentive waiters. The ability to eat alone, quietly and calmly, would save her again and again.

The trip to the United States forced Mary Frances to face the problems in her life directly, something she had never done before. If she could simply have ignored the end of her marriage and carry on with Tim, she likely would have. But she wanted a divorce, and in California, it took a year to get one. She needed to get the papers filed. But this, too, was complicated: Al had already moved to Massachusetts and begun teaching at Smith College. Meanwhile, her friends and family lamented their separation and began to question the nature of her friendship with Tim Parrish. She detested the gossip.

While Mary Frances was home, the Kennedys took pleasure in being together in their usual comfortable way. After a few days of family meals and outings, she told her parents that she would be divorcing Al—and was surprised that they supported her choice. Her parents had grown fond of Al Fisher and were worried about their daughter's future, but they had watched the trajectory of their relationship: the shotgun wedding, the constant need for financial assistance, the frequent trips home. They had also witnessed her happiness with Tim and hoped it would continue. Yes, her marital troubles slightly embarrassed Rex and Edith, community leaders in a small town; Mary Frances noted that they were ultimately "dignified and unquestioning, very good indeed" at dealing with the news.

But for Mary Frances, that wasn't enough. She had also expected Rex and Edith to take pride in her publication of *Serve It Forth,* which she had gladly dedicated to them. Her accomplishment failed to resonate, however, and again Mary Frances felt incapable of getting attention and validation from the people she loved most. She left the United States for Switzerland convinced that no matter what she did, good or bad, her parents would react with blind acceptance—and the overwhelming belief that no matter what, everything was going to be just fine.

Back in Le Paquis, Mary Frances felt compelled to return to her journal. She had temporarily stopped writing, unable to reveal her private thoughts amid the triangle that had trapped her. She remarked that "for a long time it was better to write nothing" than to continue with the "stiff comments she had permitted herself" in past journal entries. Life at Le Paquis had moved fast and "inevitably toward an undreamed conclusion . . . The house was built, and much we had built or hoped to see grow in it was forever broken." She was still trying to understand "what grew in its place, in our several hearts." Her journal helped her sort out these feelings.

She was working on new projects, too. She sent fresh pieces to her new agent, Mary Leonard Pritchett, and awaited feedback. She toyed with the introduction to a gastronomical bibliography that had been commissioned to write by Jake Zietlin, a friend of Larry's who owned a bookshop in Los Angeles.

The focus of her life, though, was Tim, with whom she was completely in love. "My whole existence has become more completely physical than ever before in my life," she wrote. "I eat, sleep, listen, even cook and read with an intensity and fullness that I have never felt until now." She was completely absorbed in herself—"but myself as seen through Timmy." She reveled in the feeling but knew, somehow, that the happiness could not continue.

10

A Pendulum of Desire

O N THE TERRACE of Le Paquis, French doors opened to expansive views of Lake Geneva, gently sloping vineyards, and the pointed outline of the Alps. When the weather was warm enough, Mary Frances and Tim loved to eat outside, the reflection of the bright sun off the lake nearly blinding them.

Meals eaten on or near the terrace often left Mary Frances awestruck by the beauty that engulfed her. Occasionally she watched the landscape in the reflection of a mirror hanging on her living room wall. "If the lake seemed too wide, the Alps too high, we could look into the great mirror opposite and make them less remote, less questioning of us," she wrote. Observing her surroundings through the smaller lens of a framed mirror made the beauty in her life seem easier to appreciate.

Mary Frances and Tim were happily oblivious of those who might frown upon their romance. They entertained often, abundant dinner parties with French-Swiss neighbors and expatriate guests. The menu for a winter fête was a "masterful stew," served alongside a big salad and a basket of crisp rolls. For dessert, Mary Frances presented small dishes of chilled pears topped with honey, kirsch, and cream.

The couple wanted their home to be a gathering place, and the two were content being their kitchen's cook and servants—an oddity to their European neighbors. One night, a visitor insisted they must be hiding a cook in the cellar. He couldn't believe that she had made the meal he'd just eaten. Mary Frances was bemused; she wasn't convinced that the stew she'd made was that impressive. But it was honest, simple, and served in a beautiful setting. That alone made it transcendental.

After a grueling day in the garden, Tim made a dinner reservation at a fancy restaurant in one of the large casinos in nearby Evian. As she dressed, Mary Frances worried that she had grown too used to her rustic surroundings. Her nails were rough, and she was thin and sinewy from her outdoor work. She was much too slender for the dress she wanted to wear and embarrassingly brown from her days in the sun. Her high-heeled shoes felt strange and stiff.

After a boat ride across the lake, Mary Frances relaxed. She felt "more beautiful than possible" and knew that Tim, who was dressed in his white dinner coat and topknot, felt just as attractive. The two ate an astonishing meal, drank heady wines, and enjoyed their roles as spectators at the opulent casino.

But as the evening drew to a close, the couple was still glad to leave, cross back over the lake, and wind up the steep road to home. They arrived at Le Paquis so late it was almost morning, the shy sunlight just beginning to rise. Instead of going to bed, the two shed their evening attire and changed back into dungarees. They both felt they had been away from the garden for too long and ached to return to the dirt.

As her relationship with Tim deepened, so did the bond between food and love. Mary Frances had reveled in the meals and flavors of Dijon, but Al had not been her culinary match. Now, as she dove into her second major love affair—and the first in which she had experienced true passion—food became her language of intimacy and seduction. Tim was glad to play along.

After an Easter dinner with a visiting American friend, Mary Frances and Tim snuck away from the table and retired early to separate rooms. She was pink with anticipation. Earlier that afternoon she'd found a big sheet of drawing paper on her desk. It was heavily decorated with scrolls and banners and the outlines of fanciful creatures. Elaborate writing on the page invited her to Tim's art studio at midnight for an intimate snack.

As she waited, she made herself beautiful, putting on a clean dress and dotting her cheeks with blush. At twelve o'clock she traveled to Tim's room carrying a small nest she'd fashioned from the grasses in the pasture at Le Paquis. She found Tim's studio filled with candles and flowers and her gift—a large tin of beluga caviar—in the center of a pale yellow plate. In a wreath around it were fragrant apple blossoms.

She swooned: "I think apple blossoms are perhaps the loveliest flowers in the world," she wrote, "the mysterious way they spring so delicately from the sturdy darkness of the carved stems . . . they were the loveliest that night, in the candlelight, in the odd shaped room so full of things important to me." The two whispered and laughed and piled pungent black beads on triangular points of toasted bread that they washed down with sips of brisk gin.

When they were nearly done, Mary Frances stood up, wiped the crumbs from her clothes, and thanked her lover for the meal. Tim was surprised at her sudden departure—the two had hardly touched. But Mary Frances was feeling coy. She adored mystery and the disguise of playing shy. When she returned to her room she heard "long gusts of laughter" as Tim marveled at her affected flight from the exquisite pleasure of his table.

The summer of 1938 promised to be monumental: Norah and David Kennedy planned an extended visit to Le Paquis, as did Tim's sister Anne, and her friend Mary Powers. Mary Frances found Mary Powers neurotic and difficult to be around, but the group reveled in the Swiss summertime. They had picnics and parties, toured the countryside, and deeply enjoyed each other's company.

It was to be their last summer at Le Paquis. The cost of maintaining the land and the house had become prohibitive for Tim, and he had reluctantly announced that the property was for sale. Soon, Tim and Mary Frances accepted a bid and agreed to vacate in October. Where they would go next was unclear.

The political events unfolding in Europe threatened to disrupt their lives. Mary Frances had monitored international politics since her days in Dijon, and knew the possibility of war loomed ever closer. What she didn't know was that soon her world would be rocked by a devastating incident that was far more personal and frightening than the global conflict that brewed.

In late summer, while on a weekend trip to Berne, Switzerland, Tim became very ill, experiencing severe cramping in his left leg that could not be assuaged. He was admitted to the hospital, where doctors diagnosed a blood clot involving the veins from his ankle to his pelvic cavity. In a three-hour procedure, surgeons made an incision in his lower left abdomen and removed a three-inch embolism from the main artery. The next morning they operated again, removing several more small clots.

Four days later, Tim's left leg began to discolor. His foot, now porcelain white, withered and his toes turned brown. Nearly two weeks after becoming ill, his left leg was amputated just above the knee.

A month after the amputation, Tim still lay in his narrow hospital bed. Mary Frances tried recording the experience in her journal from a small hotel near Viktoria Hospital. She looked out the window to see the outline of the wet Kornhaus Bridge and the dull shape of buildings that stretched into the sky. Sipping a glass of brandy, she managed only a few sparse sentences. Occasionally, she paused to look into the mirror above her light stand to see if there was light reflected from Tim's hospital room. She hoped he was resting. He was in constant pain, already dependent on a myriad of drugs. That evening he had been given two ineffective pain pills, then a powerful shot of a drug called Analgeticum. He was in a narcotic sleep that would last only a few hours.

The source of Tim's illness was, at that point, unknown. While serving in World War I he had faced repeated enemy gas attacks, which could have contributed to the circulatory problems and clotting. Now, as his health diminished at the hospital, he battled to maneuver without his left leg. For a man who loved hiking and gardening, an immobile life would be devastating.

There were other troubles, too. With the threat of European conflict, American citizens had been urged to leave the area. Tim's physical challenges made travel impossible, but Norah and David were scuttled out of Switzerland on the day the Munich Pact was signed. Her siblings' departure was traumatic. Mary Frances didn't want them to leave, but Rex and Edith insisted: They couldn't bear having three of their four children trapped in Europe as war approached.

Anne Parrish was also forced to leave Switzerland: Mrs. Parrish was ill and needed her back in Delaware. Before their departure, the group of siblings were able to help pack the couple's belongings and move them from Le Paquis. Mary Frances gathered the few things she would need to keep comfortable while nursing Tim. Everything else was taken to a temporary apartment outside Vevey, which she hoped they might inhabit soon.

Mary Frances spent most of her time in the hospital room with Tim. Often she helped his nurse, a nun named Irma, with his care. Other times she retreated, trying, often unsuccessfully, to rest and write. One late fall afternoon, Mary Frances lounged on Tim's hospital-room balcony, wrapped in Tim's thick gray coat. The smell of the coat brought back memories of their happy times together, moments she tried to vanquish. Through the crooked glass of the door she could see Tim, "distorted as one of his own drawings of pain, being bathed by Sister Irma." He was thin and ashen. Watching his struggle saddened and terrified her. The small man with the cheerful shock of white hair she'd met in 1933 now trembled constantly. And there was nothing she could do to make it stop.

Despite his pain, Tim tried to be jovial and took up smoking a pipe. It would help him look distinguished, he reasoned, and would be an excellent complement to the cane he would need. Mary Frances bought him a pipe and cleaned it carefully. The Swiss doctors, however, somehow failed to realize that smoking would significantly worsen Tim's prognosis, encouraging further inflammation and injury. Indeed, the doctors still hadn't determined what had caused the clot in Tim's leg. Meanwhile, Mary Frances, who considered the pipe one of Tim's few pleasures, endorsed his new habit wholeheartedly.

WHILE CARING FOR Tim, she often found herself numbing her anxiety with alcohol. It helped her relax; after a drink she often penned the longest, most searingly honest entries in her journal. "I am drinking what is left of a bottle of bad champagne," she wrote one night. Dull music played in the background and she thought first of her family, and next of Tim, who "rocked in the dark opiate arms of [the drug called] Analgeticum, lulled by the weariness of a shot of Pantopon." Finally she thought "vaguely and not too close, for safety's sake, of myself here, there, drugged or alive or dreaming or hysterical." She viewed her world through the lens of Tim's excruciating pain. His optimism was shattered: He shook and cried, and they both dreaded his nightly bouts of anguish. Mary Frances described him as being in "ceaseless agony" and herself as being "weary and so often frightened."

It had been five weeks since the amputation. On that terrible day she had wished, mercifully, that he would die. Now she did all she could to care for him, holding him by his "beautiful blue-white hair while he bobbed helplessly" in the hospital bathtub.

Though hospital-bound, the couple made every effort to pursue their pleasures. If he was feeling well enough, Tim would dress for lunch, and they would eat together. One midday feast featured sweetbreads with eggplant, a roasted pigeon with rice, cooked vegetables, and a salad accompanied by a glass of wine. For dessert they nibbled on a tart stuffed with the purple half-moons of sliced plums.

Eventually, Tim was allowed out of bed; to increase his mobility, the two made small jaunts away from the hospital. Tim maneuvered the streets with his new crutches, moving always with meticulous grace. Mary Frances was more anxious, watchful, and worried that he would place his crutch into a deep pocket of cobblestone or sidewalk grating and fall.

But the excursions were often too strenuous. After returning to the hospital one afternoon, Tim climbed into bed, wild with pain. Mary Frances wrote that he whispered "craftily to me, for the hundredth, the thousandth time, that now was the time to help him die. Then he yelped and chatted like a hyena." Tim's pleas sickened Mary Frances. Neither of them was sure that his extreme pain was worth living through, but neither, despite Tim's exhortations, was entirely ready to act.

After two and a half months at Viktoria Hospital, doctors advised Mary Frances, Tim, and Irma to move to Adelboden, a small town in the

Alps renowned for its health resorts. Unsure of exactly how to diagnose Tim or the proper way to improve his condition, the medics hoped that Adelboden's higher elevation, clean air, and restful environment would be curative. But the recommendation was another dose of bad advice. The increased altitude would mean decreased oxygen; less oxygen in the blood could impair healing and further damage Tim's already compromised leg tissue.

Mary Frances wondered if there would be an adequate pharmacy and how she'd move Tim from place to place. But she hoped a new environment might be good for both of them. She was growing weary of Tim's increasingly anxious state. One evening in the hospital, he had cried for hours, screaming that he couldn't remember "one goddamn distinguishing feature!" of his leg. She knew she couldn't fully appreciate the pain or the loss, but wished she could help him more. Yet she also wished she had time and energy to focus on herself and her needs. She had a deep desire to write, but was overwhelmed by the stresses of her everyday routine. "What can I, what should I say?" she wondered. "Why in hell, why . . . should I write anything?"

In late November, just before leaving the hospital, Mary Frances and Tim went out for lunch at a restaurant called Cafè du Theatre. It was the same place Tim had first felt searing leg pain a few months before. They planned to order caviar, or perhaps oysters and champagne to celebrate the beginning of what they hoped was a quick recovery. Instead they decided on thick grilled steaks with potatoes and a bottle of red wine from burgundy. They were ready, with high hopes, to move on.

A FRIEND HAD hired a hired a chauffeur for the trip to Adelboden, but Mary Frances was too skittish to let him drive. So she personally motored him, Tim and his new prosthesis, and Irma up into the Alps. After arriving, Mary Frances and Irma hurried around the room unpacking and settling, pausing frequently to stare at the dominating mountains just outside their windows. The Alps reminded her of the mesas of the American West, "hard and sculptured against an infinite blue sky."

The new environment invigorated her. After giving Tim his shots and putting him to bed, she slid into her own narrow bed with her journal. "My cheeks burn," she wrote. "My eyes too. I am excited yet half asleep, eager to wake early to watch from my window the sun upon the mountains." She was smart enough to know that their troubles were far from over, but already felt that the crisp and clean mountain environment was a fresh start.

On the third day in Adelboden, Tim developed a fever and complained of pain in his right leg. Mary Frances called a doctor who diagnosed congestion in the main artery of his remaining leg. The possibilities were devastating and Tim lay in bed, tears dripping down his cheeks. "Now and then," Mary Frances reported, "he shakes violently and clutches me and sobs." She was beginning to wonder if Tim might die. She knew that if he did, she would regret any moments they spent apart. Her guilt and grief kept her from writing—she could think of nothing else.

It was their lowest point. At Viktoria Hospital, the bad days had been followed by occasional reprieves. Now Tim seemed to be withdrawing from the world. Mary Frances felt he was "saving all his various strengths to fight the weariness, to hold at bay the bouts of pain, to keep himself on the right side of hysteria."

She found that it helped if she ignored her sadness and fear, a skill she had honed during her last years of marriage to Al. But her emotional retreat also halted any attempts she made to work on new projects. She subsisted by writing in her journal, but even that was vapid. "There is so much I can never write about," she acknowledged. "All this is superficial."

Though Tim had helped Mary Frances explore her creativity, she still did not believe she had a talent for writing. She worried that if she were a "real writer (predestined), I'd work in the face of everything." But she couldn't. "I truly don't feel keen enough," she wrote, "to be able to put aside all thought of the present while it is moving and moaning ten feet to the left of me."

Soon, however, she began a new project inspired by her despair, a piece so intimate that she couldn't show it to anyone but Tim. The fictional tale was based on Tim's illness and the highs and lows of their past summer in Switzerland. Mary Frances's reborn creativity calmed her, and she began to enjoy caring for herself and her lover. At lunchtime she would prepare a small snack for Tim—often a cupful of soup with crusty bread broken into bites—that she would deliver to his bed on a tray. Then she would return to a private dining table to sit and enjoy her own meal while she studied the mountains just outside the windows. Her palate was teased by a rich consommé followed by ravioli with tomato sauce and cheese; roasted chicken with potatoes and brussels sprouts; wine; and chocolate cream pierced by thin wafers.

She ate slowly, stopping briefly to make Tim another plate with some of her sliced chicken and a cup of applesauce. Finally she returned to the table, finished her lunch and dessert, and ended her meal with coffee and cognac. She wrote in her journal that she was interested in the "slowness and this solemnity" of being wholly present. "I suppose it is a desire to escape," she wrote. "To forget time and the demands of suffering." An appreciation for the pleasure rendered from being aware of life's smallest and most essential moments would continue to weave its way slowly but deliberately into Mary Frances's emerging creative work.

BEFORE LEAVING THE hospital, Mary Frances received a letter from Larry Powell, who had recently seen Al for the first time since his departure from Switzerland. "He has likened himself to a wounded dragon," Larry wrote. "To an empty hole that is now filling in and of itself—and [he] continually expressed a kind of bewilderment at your having left him." He and Al had spent a long afternoon together; during that time Al had told Larry the "whole story, from his point of view." His confession led Larry gently to query Mary Frances: "I really wonder, did you think you could continue to live in the same house with two men, both in love with you?"

The subtle assault on her character wounded her. She had heard from mutual friends that Al was exposing astonishing details about their intimate life: her infidelity and supposed nyphomaniacal tendencies. But she, too, had gossiped: Maliciously, she had told Larry that Al had suffered from impotency after the death of his father. Al had defended himself by remarking that Mary Frances "SHOULD HAVE BEEN PATIENT" with him—not coped with their insufficient intimacy by starting a relationship with Tim. Larry told Mary Frances that he had gently reminded Al that sexual distance was "not the way to keep a wife."

One of the couple's closest friends, Larry realized that Al's impotency had less to do with grief than with the couple's passionless relationship. Larry told Mary Frances that as their relationship died, Al had used a "large measure of ripe flesh," both in Switzerland and the United States, to cope with the injury to his male vanity.

The letter upset her. Despite her happiness with Tim, she thought often about her first marriage and the reasons it had ended. "I will always have a feeling of unfulfillment about our life together," she told Larry, "a feeling that his past came too soon, too strongly between me and what I knew was there in him." She hoped that something she gave him "(because I gave him everything I had) . . ." would help make him "easier to know and help and love . . . and to make him easier with himself."

In the meantime, she was excited that Larry was helping to publish Al's finished portion of "The Ghost." It made her feel strange to know that something that was once "so intimately a part of my life" was now happening without her having any part in it. She enclosed a check for her copy of the book, and looked forward to getting it from Larry when she returned to the United States.

After a few bad days in Adelboden, Tim seemed to care only about his next painkiller. He lost weight quickly and needed constant care: massages, drops, injections, and other medications. It became impossible for the couple to have a normal conversation except when Tim was in his rare lucid moments, just after an injection. Mary Frances was tired of listening to him moan and cry, and occasionally she longed to snap at him and tell him to "buck up" even though she knew he had little strength left.

One evening, she stepped out on the balcony to look at a gleaming moon rising far above the Alps. When she turned to go back inside, she was struck by the sight of Irma sitting beside Tim's bed. She was massaging his "white smooth rump, rubbing rhythmically." The curtains framed the two, and Mary Frances caught a bit of her own reflection among the shadows created by the afterglow of the full moon on the door.

By mid-November the pain had abated; Tim no longer had a fever and his pulse was normal. He still suffered from phlebitis, and his aching sciatica was being treated with an unguent of bee venom that helped the pain a little and spread a delightful herbaceous incense through their hotel room.

The biggest challenge was his "theoretical foot"—the phrase Mary Frances and Tim coined for the intense pain he felt in his missing limb. The medical term was "phantom limb pain"—constant cramping, burning, and stabbing torments. The pain, which had begun shortly after his amputation, radiated from his left leg and made it seem as if the limb were still there. It reduced Tim to a "twitching hysterical wreck" unless he was mildly doped.

Despite small improvements, the change in altitude that was supposed to help Tim had nearly killed him, and Mary Frances decided they must return to their apartment outside Vevey. As soon as the holidays were over and Tim had stabilized, they would sail for America.

IN EARLY 1939, the couple boarded a small ship called *The De Grasse*. By this point Mary Frances was sure Tim was dying. They traveled across the ocean in "revolt at the whole cruel web of clinics and specialists and injections and rays" that they had endured in Europe.

The De Grasse carried only twenty passengers, and Mary Frances was the only woman. The couple was traveling without a nurse, which made her the sole provider for Tim's care. It was a rough crossing, and she would later recount the horrors of preparing hypodermic needles amid the rolling seas. The couple stayed in their room most of the time, getting up for meals only when the motion of the ship permitted it. Then Tim would "invent dances down the empty corridors on his one leg and the crutches, so that when we went into the dining room we were always laughing wildly." Everyone on the ship was aware of Tim's delicate health and of the stress that traveling caused the couple. The ship's chef wooed them with dishes that weren't on the menu, and at the end of the voyage the captain gave Mary Frances a large tin of caviar with a note that read, "pain cannot touch the loving hearted." It was a kind sentiment, but she had little faith in it.

After docking on the East Coast in the spring of 1939, Mary Frances and Tim traveled to Delaware to meet with Harold Springer, a physician who had treated Tim in the past. They hoped he might be able to help them with the pain Tim felt in his missing limb. Dr. Springer's report of

Tim's health is revealing. Written in 1940, and added to Tim's bulging medical files, Dr. Springer claims that he treated Tim's tuberculosis by removing his testicles.

A man who has been castrated is still capable of intercourse, but over time, due to a decrease in testosterone, may experience a loss of sexual desire. According to a detailed description of Tim's health penned by Mary Frances, Tim's castration occurred in 1935, roughly two years after he and Mary Frances had met, fallen in love, and become sexually involved.

Mary Frances's frank record claims the operation actually improved her lover's health. He gained weight, drank and smoked less, and his sexual pleasure increased. Nonetheless, the couple's romance, though intense, was sexually unconventional—just like her relationship with Al.

Mary Frances had escaped her poor marriage and occasionally impotent husband for an ambiguously sexual relationship with Tim, a man with whom she felt a deep emotional and intellectual connection. Her continued insistence that she did not leave Al for a lusty affair with Tim was correct. Their relationship was a rarity: The two had a deep intimacy that often transcended physical desire.

That Mary Frances would have a relationship with Al Fisher, who was uninterested in sex, followed by a relationship with Tim Parrish, who was incapable of typical intercourse, is fascinating. It wasn't because she was frigid—M.F.K. Fisher was a deeply passionate woman who, over the course of her lifetime, had many love affairs. Her writing, especially her prose during the time she was involved with Tim, is deeply evocative, filled with sensuous description and ripe with metaphor. It's clear that her interest in the physical and emotional pleasures of food often masked voracious sexual desire. Writing about food was her way of expressing the fullness of her sexuality, something she could not do with either Al Fisher or Tim Parrish.

The couple's visit to Dr. Springer, however, had nothing to do with Tim's prior treatments. The doctor operated again on Tim's left leg, cutting two inches above his initial amputation. Dr. Springer believed that the sciatic nerve ending was caught in the scars from prior operations. He hoped that re-amputating and re-mending the leg might heal the damaged nerve endings. Ultimately, the procedure offered little relief.

Although Mary Frances was not fond of the East Coast, she did come to love some of the regional food on which Tim had been raised, particularly oyster stew. A bowl at the Doylestown Inn helped her decide the creamy oyster-stocked soup was magical. The stew and the accompanying apple pie topped with a pale, tart local cheese had "flavor, a kind of reality, of excitement about it" she hadn't often experienced while dining in the United States.

The meal changed the way she thought about regional cooking and made her think carefully about the criticism that had been tossed upon *Serve It Forth*: "I know that I was criticized for being supercilious (and superficial) about American cooking—mainly because I wrote that nothing is worse than a bad piece of pie. I still say so . . . And I still feel very sorry and resentful that the average standard of food in my own country is so low."

Even in the poorest villages in Europe the food was good; someone could always scrounge up some nice bread, cheese, and sausage. But in America, she remarked, there was often "listless attention, wretched tough tasteless food." Her musings were the first sign that Mary Frances had internalized the criticism of her first book and was pondering the creation of an American companion to *Serve It Forth*.

WHEN TIM HAD recovered enough to travel, the couple ventured west, hopeful that the dry California air and radiating heat might help him heal. And though Mary Frances thought it might be impossible, she imagined that she could find a spot for them to live where they could replicate what they loved best about Le Paquis: fresh air, gardening, startling vistas, and privacy.

The two arrived on the West Coast in the late spring of 1939, and settled temporarily in Palm Springs, California, where the heat and low altitude did seem to diminish Tim's pain. But the couple's ultimate destination was Switzerland. It was now clear that war was approaching; it was time to shutter their Vevey apartment. Even more important was Tim's need for the painkiller Analgeticum. It had soothed him in Switzerland, but there was nothing comparable in America. To keep him comfortable, they would have to scoop up as much of the drug as they could overseas.

In their rush of planning, the two hardly noticed the publication of a slim book the two had written together under the pseudonym Victoria Berne. The novel, *Touch and Go*, was a frothy story about a woman who finds love in Switzerland with a German émigré. The book was a commercial failure; in a letter to Larry Powell, Mary Frances described the book as "awful trash, but entertaining for [the] hammock."

BEFORE LEAVING THE United States, the couple made their union official, marrying on May 12, 1939. It was a small civil ceremony in Riverside County, California, with no family present, and no party afterward. Instead, the couple quickly returned home to prepare for their voyage, leaving only days later for Europe. It was a grim honeymoon. Yet somehow, despite the terrible purpose of their trip, they found beauty in the chaos of their life as invalid and caretaker. Mary Frances wrote that they were "immune to everything, that summer, that could hurt us."

They traveled on *The Normandie* and spent most of their time in bed, in the smoking room, or the lounge—an airy room with glass walls, views of the water, and attentive waitstaff. They drank glass after glass of champagne and talked while they watched the spread of blue waves. They enjoyed long and luxurious lunches where they ate lightly but well. Tim could not stomach much food; he subsisted nearly entirely on a diet of painkillers, alcohol, and cigarettes. So Mary Frances ate with a resolute enjoyment for the both of them; she knew it was important to continue living decently—or, at least, to pretend.

After an afternoon nap and an evening spent drinking Pernod and still more champagne, reclining on soft chaise lounges while watching films, the two would return to bed. Occasionally they would wake in the night and start talking again. If they were still hungry, they would nibble on the sandwiches, hot consommé, and tumblers of brandy that worried waiters delivered to their door. For the first time in her life, Mary Frances wrote that she felt "beautiful, witty, truly loved." She was "the most fortunate of all women, past sea change and with her hungers fed."

The two knew that they needed to rescue their belongings from their apartment before the war started. But their task was laced with irony. Because of Tim's illness and their regular travel between Europe and the United States, they had discovered they had no real need for possessions. Still, for a brief moment they were happy to use the project as an escape. They returned to the life that had been so vital and happy before Tim's illness, choosing not to worry much about their belongings, the political stirrings that necessitated their move, or their task of securing Analgeticum. Together they "drank and ate and saw and felt and made love better than ever before, with an intensity that seemed to detach us utterly from life."

One day they took the train from Vevey to Milan, something they'd done several times while living in Switzerland. They had fond memories of venturing to the wood-paneled restaurant car and ordering a bottle of Asti spumante, drinking the sweet bubbles as the train rocked and chugged its way through the mountains and into Italy.

On their return visit they were pleasantly surprised when, upon boarding the train, they were greeted by a waiter who seemed to remember them. "Asti! At once!" he shouted, and hurried away after taking a sly, sad glance at Tim's missing leg. It wasn't yet lunchtime, but that didn't seem to matter. The waiter brought a bottle, wrapped in a cheerful red handkerchief, and two glasses to their car. The gesture moved them profoundly, though they wished they could have drunk it in the train's restaurant car, as they'd done before. The cloying sparkling wine was just as they'd remembered it—"warm, almost sickish"—but utterly delightful.

Their happiness, however, was shattered by plainclothes policemen, who arrived handcuffed to a political prisoner who was being returned to Italy. When the prisoner tried to jump through the train's window to his death, the trip seemed ruined. But after a lengthy stop at the border, the train chugged on. When the commotion had finally quieted, Mary Frances and Tim began their slow trek to the dining car for lunch.

The wood-paneled dining car was nearly empty, and the two were greeted with small plates topped with pickled onions, salami, and butter set on a table laid with crisp linens. After sitting down, the waiter brought them a bottle of chianti; it was rich, deep purple-red in the glass, and delicious. The food they were served was just as they remembered it—simple but abundant. There were chunks of bread to eat with the antipasti, big Italian white beans served cold, pasta with herbs, crisp green salad, fresh fruit and cheese. Mary Frances wrote that it was "good to be eating and drinking there on that train, free forever from the trouble of life, surrounded with a kind of insulation of love."

Tim stopped eating for a moment and flagged an older waiter to inquire about the prisoner. "Did he get away?" he asked. The waiter nearly spat on them before turning quickly and retorting that it was none of Tim's business. Mary Frances watched Tim's face pinch with pain. These were no longer the happy days of 1937; they weren't on a frivolous, love-soaked trip to Italy. Underneath the table, Tim's left leg sat like a limp fish. Mary Frances could no longer swallow her food.

Within moments, the waiter who had recognized them when they boarded the train was by their side. He spoke softly and quickly, explaining that when the train had stopped, the prisoner had not tried to jump out the window—he had broken the window and then slit his own throat on the sharp edge of the broken glass.

Mary Frances wrote that with news of what had occurred on the train, the "world seeped in." They were no longer two invisible travelers, immune to personal pain or destructive current events. Tim was a "man with one leg gone . . . a small wracked man with snowy hair and eyes large with suffering. And I was a woman condemned, plucked at by demons, watching her true love die too slowly."

11

Landscape of Love and Sorrow

B Y MARCH 1940, the couple had returned from their har-rowing voyage. They sat hidden in the shade of a large California sagebrush. Beside them was a small radio and the remnants of a picnic; surrounding them were wildflowers and the rolling brown hills of San Jacinto. The sky was milky with clouds and the temperature was unpredictable. One minute Mary Frances found herself chilled, the next she was rushing to take off the coat she'd carried with her for the day.

Earlier she had given Tim a shot of Analgeticum. The medicine made him look and feel better, and it made it easier for him to maneuver the walk from the car up the hill. They'd sat and had lunch: beer, some cut-up celery and radishes, and an artichoke. There was a peanut butter sandwich for Tim, but Mary Frances ate only vegetables—she was dieting.

Far from heavy, she was nonetheless continually exhausted from being a caregiver. This, coupled with her concern for Tim's health, had led her to watch both their diets more carefully. But such a regimen was hard for her to follow. Often she found herself ignoring food for hours before pouncing on the pantry like a hungry wolf. Her bad habits, along with constant stress, had contributed just a few extra pounds that only she noticed.

It was a beautiful afternoon, and they loved being, as Mary Frances described it, "up there in the sweet air . . . looking around at the wild rock slopes and down toward the little house. Bareacres was ours." In early 1940, they had purchased the property, ninety acres nestled in the hills near Hemet, California, east of Los Angeles. As they waited for the current residents, Mr. and Mrs. Dix, to pack and move out of the small house on the property, Mary Frances dreamed about how they would furnish their new home.

They knew that their odds of a long and happy life together were slim. For the past year they had been making regular visits to the office of Dr. Hal Bieler, a Pasadena physician Mary Frances had met through Larry Powell. Dr. Bieler espoused an unconventional (and sometimes untested) approach to medicine, believing that many illnesses could be cured through healthy eating.

Dr. Bieler advised Tim to quit smoking and drinking, and prescribed bland foods. But boring meals of bran muffins and warm milk reminded Mary Frances too much of Grandmother Holbrook. As much as she trusted Dr. Bieler's advice, Mary Frances believed that the monotonous diet would do Tim more harm than good—after all, long meals with decadent foods were one of their great joys. She happily helped him break all the rules the doctor had dictated.

One afternoon, tired of all the restrictions, the two were overcome by a craving for greasy burgers. On their way to visit Dr. Bieler, their appetite was so deep they "saw dark spots in the shape of hamburgers floating before our eyes." The two pulled over at a roadside spot and devoured beer and burgers with "complete delight." Before climbing back into the car, they took swigs of whiskey, and Mary Frances gave Tim another shot so he'd look as good as possible when they arrived.

Mary Frances engaged Dr. Bieler in frank talk about Tim's pain. He had started to require more Analgeticum in recent weeks. Mary Frances had been reluctant to increase his doses, believing that the additional amounts caused a "retrogression on his part." But there were more practical issues, too. They had run out of the Analgeticum they had purchased a few months ago in Switzerland and were now ordering it from abroad. Mary Frances had yet to hear if their most recent order had been shipped—and was worried they might run out of the drug while waiting for the replenishment to arrive.

At the current dosage, they had just enough for fourteen months—if they didn't lose or spill any. After that, life would be especially bleak. "Tim says, if he still needs it, the jig will pretty well be up anyway," Mary Frances wrote in her journal. "(And that is where I am counting on Bareacres to give him strength and more courage and will to live.)"

Administering the shots was an art. "[T]he main idea is to . . . give it to him quickly—to rub his skin hard with the wad of alcohol and cotton and to stick the needle in sharply," Mary Frances wrote. She was exceedingly careful: "I think deliberately, always, of how to pick up the delicate ampules most expertly so that they will not tip or spill." But sometimes, when tired, or after drinking too much, she was clumsy. Then, she wondered if Tim noticed the difference "or if all he minds is how quick relief comes."

As war in Europe developed, the couple watched the news lines with horror. They worried not only about their many friends abroad but about their dwindling drug supply, fretful that the war might keep them from returning to Switzerland or ordering more from abroad. Mary Frances was woeful: "What can I do?" she wrote. "At times I am near despair . . . I see the supply of Analgeticum grow smaller, in spite of our fight not to use more than the absolute necessity, and I know that if the war goes on, it is most likely to be all that we get of it." She hated to think of what might happen if Analgeticum were no longer available.

She was trying to make herself comfortable with the likely outcome of his illness. "I know I could never blame T. for whatever he might feel that he must do to settle this problem that no one else seems to be able to settle for him," she wrote in her journal. Yet she was understandably deadened by the possibility that Tim might someday want to end his own life. She decided that she must try to think of suicide with the "same routine thoughtfulness that it takes to recognize hunger." If she could accept the possibility of his death, perhaps that would soften its arrival.

One night Tim quietly asked Mary Frances to hide the .22 bullets for his gun. She did it quickly, recalling the Swiss hospital—where she realized that if she left Tim's bed too close to the balcony window, he would jump to his death.

Tim had talked of suicide often there and "begged me to help him, to carry him" closer to the edge. She had argued, asking him to give her one more day, or week, even a few more hours. But that night at the Viktoria, she knew that if she left him alone, he would do it. There was a part of her that wanted him to. She almost left the hospital bed to "leave him to what he so desired . . . and then I turned back, and pulled his bed away from the edge, and could not look at him for knowing that I had condemned him to more torture."

In Adelboden, she had even found a razor in their bedside table drawer. She'd crept away with it. Yet they'd also talked openly of how he might kill himself. "No drugs . . . No slashing wrists—so messy and scandalous," she wrote. "What, then . . . what?" They'd made bargains. Mary Frances implored Tim to wait—just a few weeks longer, she pleaded—and then "when it is worse, I swear by Christ crucified that I will help you."

By May of 1940, Mary Frances and Tim had officially moved into their home at Bareacres. Even without heat or electricity, they loved it. But still, Mary Frances anticipated the worst: "When I hear a strange noise or when I hear too long a silence, I think, This is the time: it has happened, and I make myself call out in a quiet way, or walk slowly, unhurried, heavily, to what I may find." Tim's discomfort was so deep, that often when she got up to check on him she had a "wild hope that perhaps this is the time."

Mary Frances also wrote in her journal, "I know how to kill T. and to do it easily and probably so that I would never have to be accused of it." But when she thought more carefully about assisting him so blatantly in his own death, she became firm: "I know that I never will." Ultimately, she believed that if Tim took his life it would be courageous, even if others might find it controversial or cowardly. "Maybe I am wrong to write about this," she noted. The knowledge that "life must be sweeter than it is for Timmy to endure it much longer, even though we are so happy here together" haunted her.

TIM HAD BEGUN painting, working on about ten canvases a week in addition to his pencil and charcoal drawings. Mary Frances described him as "working at a mad pace, but it helps him to get along without too many shots." His work was good, "developing too fast to realize, almost . . . I seem to have married myself to another genius."

Mary Frances had finished the novel she'd begun in Adelboden, now called "The Theoretical Foot." The narrative of a rowdy expatriate summer romp is interspersed with vivid descriptions of the illness that strikes the fictional Tim Garton at the end of the summer, leaving him helpless, in great pain, and missing one leg.

Mary Frances was proud of the manuscript, and she sent it to her brother, David, and Anne Parrish for review. David was generally positive, telling his sister that he did not mind being a character in the book even though the entire plot seemed "a little too obvious, if anything." Nonetheless, he hoped that the book would be published and sell quickly and well, ordaining his sister's reputation as a "brilliant woman in all the best circles."

Tim's sister was far less supportive, telling Mary Frances that she felt horribly betrayed. "I wish I had not read it," she wrote. "I feel as though I had overheard confidences not meant for me . . . And it has turned what was, to me, a beautiful time, into one of almost unbearably revealed suffering." She felt that Mary Frances had portrayed her as cold and domineering, a possessive older sister who sought to control her attractive and artistic younger brother. "I am startled and sometimes shocked to find strange words and emotions given me," she wrote. "The curious theme of possession runs through the book . . . [and it] bewilders me." Mary Frances had hoped to publish the novel, but retreated.

When the news came that the Germans were within seventy miles of Paris, Tim crumpled and then wept, scuttling off to mourn in silence. Mary Frances suffered from a more general depression. She had dreams about the war and was concerned about an old friend, Professor Connes, whom she worried was in a concentration camp.

That spring, Mary Frances received a letter from Madame Rigulot announcing that Papazi had died. As she read the news to Tim, Mary Frances felt her throat close and her voice vanish. She was partly relieved: She hated the thought of Papazi witnessing the invasions and bombings of World War II. But she was also devastated to realize that the Europe she had experienced was gone forever. She was filled with grief; everything that she cared deeply about seemed to be dissolving before her eyes.

One night in mid-June 1940, Tim again begged Mary Frances to tell him where she'd hidden the bullets for his gun. She refused. The next day the two awoke to a hot and bright morning. They lay together quietly, Mary Frances stretching and Tim reading a magazine. Finally, Tim turned to her and said that he'd like to buy a car and drive to visit his sister and mother on the East Coast. He thought they should "use all the Analgeticum I need to be really comfortable, and then come back and finish it up after a good time." He seemed serious about the plan. Mary Frances was upset—Tim didn't usually speak of killing himself in the morning. It was something he longed for at night, when the world was dark and unforgiving. The shift frightened her. She begged him to instead consider visiting the Mayo Clinic, as his sister Anne had suggested. Perhaps physicians there could help.

As July passed, Tim worked on a series of paintings of fruits and vegetables that Mary Frances described as "very sure and rich." She, meanwhile, continued to tinker with an old manuscript of Tim's called *Daniel Among the Women*. She thought the manuscript read well but lacked literary importance. Still, she hoped they might find a publisher so that they could generate some cash.

She had also returned to her idea of chronicling American gastronomy. After a period in which her meals had been routine, food had been on her mind. She snuck pleasurable bites of potato chips when she was not even hungry. She craved champagne for breakfast, and one morning even indulged in a meal of leftover bacon and beer. She described her demeanor as a "strange piggishness, which might be called with more nicety but no more precision, gourmandize." Soon she began to give a voice to her cravings using the language of food. She began writing brief pieces about oysters, a sensual and indulgent treat.

As the hottest days of midsummer drew to a close, Mary Frances and Tim often ate outside. Watching the sun set, she would stare at the "soft coppery brown" hills. It might have been after one of those sunset meals that the two decided to heed Anne Parrish's advice, borrow money from their families, and travel to the Mayo Clinic, in Rochester, Minnesota. It was a final cry for help in understanding and managing Tim's pain. By the end of July they were on the train, arriving at St. Mary's Hospital in early August.

The doctors at the Mayo Clinic told Tim that nobody knew why men with "good" amputations continued to suffer. Their preliminary solution was a procedure that attempted to locate and block the nerve that caused Tim's leg pain; if that worked, they would sever the faulty nerve but Tim's stump would be paralyzed. There would be no chance of his ever having an artificial leg.

But the doctors warned them that there was no guarantee; it was equally likely that Tim's troubles were coming from the spine, not the nerve endings in his leg. They could also be the result of shock or disease. Perhaps, as Mary Frances wrote, "[the doctors] may say there is nothing to do but live partially doped until you die." Still, Tim was willing to gamble on getting help.

The ninety-minute operation was excruciating. Tim was under anesthesia but still conscious. The doctors poked him all over his body trying to discover which nerves were responsible for his pain. When Tim was wheeled into the recovery room on a stretcher, Mary Frances wrote that he seemed to have "shrunken and lay in a kind of boneless way, crying out for me." A short time later, a doctor came in and announced abruptly that the operation had been a failure and that it "proved further surgery was useless." Mary Frances and Tim were stunned.

The next morning, doctors sat the couple down together to tell them that Tim had Buerger's disease, a chronic phlebitis, or inflammation of the veins, that usually occurred in the leg. Mary Frances wrote that the physicians said there was "no way to prevent another Berne episode, a quicker death or, for that matter, a longer life." Mary Frances told her parents, "we regret bitterly that we came here." If they had stayed at Bareacres, she reasoned, they could have continued to live easily and coped with Tim's disability. But now they had been told that Tim should lead a life with "no cigarettes, no action, no excitement, no painting." It was a horribly diminished existence.

The letter to her family included the news that Tim was in great danger of losing his other leg or—if he was lucky—"dying relatively quickly." There was a slim chance that if he lived exceedingly carefully he might avoid another thrombosis, perhaps even improving and living into old age. More likely, however, were further problems in Tim's remaining limbs. If he continued to live, he almost certainly faced great pain and the threat of more amputations—he could first lose his other leg, then his arms, one by one.

Mary Frances, Tim, and Tim's doctors discussed possible Analgeticum substitutes, and the couple learned how to care for Tim's remaining leg and his painful stump. Their instructions, Mary Frances wrote, were that they "must keep certain niggling care of his foot (remaining), and keep absolutely quiet and not smoke (nicotine is very dangerous)." She told her family that she believed that Tim was "working out his own little plan for life. God knows any man of his age . . . should have that privilege."

Against doctors' wishes, Mary Frances and Tim decided to leave Minnesota immediately. Mary Frances hoped that a quick return to Bareacres would rid them of the traumatic memories of Tim's medical assault and terminal diagnosis. She couldn't wait to return to their normal life together, and if Tim decided to cope with his pain in a way that brought an end to his life, so be it.

On their way back to California, the couple stopped briefly in Colorado Springs to visit her brother David at art school. Before leaving for Colorado, David had visited Bareacres regularly. He was a welcome companion to Tim and helped Mary Frances around the property. David and Tim often discussed their artwork, sharing supplies and techniques. Since Rex and Edith didn't support his artistic inclinations, David relied heavily on his older sister and her husband to fuel his creative motivations.

Once home, Tim briefly kept a journal. He expressed both his misery and the comfort that his surroundings brought to him. "This desert-like country gives me immense pleasure," he wrote. "So long as I keep this journal there will probably be much about this world of valley and mountains which will comfort me. Each evening I sit in my chair, the day's painting done, the day's pain made quiet for a little while with an injection of Analgeticum." Mary Frances was happy he had started a journal and hoped he would continue, but ultimately, his entries were few.

In late August 1940, Tim decided that he was going to stop taking Analgeticum. But Mary Frances thought it was a poor idea. Tim's pain had been worse since they returned home. He had a constant backache and was weak and often irrational. He painted violent and twisting shapes and colors and drank increasing amounts of whiskey to numb his leg. She had nearly doubled the strength of the shots she was giving him. She was not looking forward to his detox from the narcotic and wondered if he could endure it.

He could. Without the drug there was still pain, but Tim seemed better able to cope with it. But a letter from Dr. Bieler finalizing that there was no cure for Tim made the couple glum. They had believed that by resisting the traditional practices offered in Minnesota and investing in the alternative theories of Dr. Bieler, they might be able to beat

Buerger's disease. Mary Frances announced the news, becoming sick and hot. Tim cried, but not a lot, before telling Mary Frances that he wanted to begin taking what was left of the Analgeticum. Though he didn't say it, Tim's intention was clear: when the drug supply was gone, his life would be over.

Aware that Tim's time was running short, they began to make plans for a final vacation. They would travel to Delaware to visit Tim's mother and sister; they would also collect some of his canvases, which they hoped Larry Powell would use as he organized a show of Tim's work. Having packed their new Oldsmobile, Mary Frances and Tim set off for the East Coast.

Mary Frances was happy to be away from her family. Anne, now divorced and living with her son Sean, often fought to tears with her parents over money and child-rearing. Meanwhile, though he abhorred David's decision to become an artist, Rex was uncharacteristically supportive of Norah's interest in becoming a writer. His encouragement of Norah frustrated Mary Frances, who could remember when Rex would try to convince her that "journalism is really no place for a woman . . . it toughens and hardens her."

After only a few days on the colorful winding roads of Arizona, Mary Frances wrote that she was "happy now in a completer way than I have ever known to be, alone and unrecognized with my love." They ate regional foods at funky roadside restaurants, stopping at Johnson's Pic-a-Rib in Globe, Arizona, for good martinis, delicious spareribs cooked with sherry, salad with a piquant dressing, and hot french bread. They traveled through Texas, Louisiana, Florida, South Carolina, and Virginia, driving slowly, with short layovers to accommodate Tim. The breaks let them experience more than just restaurants: Mary Frances loved the southern Louisiana towns with enormous oaks, dripping Spanish moss, and big white wooden houses. She described

New Orleans as beautiful and primitive, full of the smells of people and magnolias, wine, and fish.

Mary Frances made notes in her journal about regional eating; she ate at some famous and many average places while traveling, hoping to unlock what made American gastronomy unique. She and Tim found themselves particularly drawn to oysters when they could find them: soft, beautiful, and briny, they ordered them again and again. Decadently fried or slurped on the half shell, the small mollusk intrigued her.

By Christmas, Mary Frances and Tim were in Delaware, and by December 28 they were in the Warwick Hotel in midtown Manhattan, reading magazines in their luxurious suite and wandering through the Museum of Modern Art. Thanks to the Parrish pocketbook, they were vacationing in the highest style. Mary Frances loved eating at the Plaza with its rococo woodwork and deep leather seats. One evening she and Tim began drinking martinis alongside lamb chops and pickled walnuts. They woke in the early morning hours to swallow aspirin—the drinks in crystal cocktail glasses were so good they'd indulged in more than a few.

Mary Frances's letters from this period are reminiscent of her early writing from Dijon. The pages are filled with beautifully rendered recollections of every part of their journey. She is invigorated and in love. There are few mentions of pain or of Tim's illness; he, too, seems to have been uniquely content as they traveled. The couple had always been happy together, but Tim's illness had obliterated the life they'd hoped for. Now, briefly, they were glad for the opportunity to escape and simply enjoy each other. The trip was tinged with even greater intensity, since they both knew it might be their last.

AFTER THE NEW year, the two traveled back to California. They dipped briefly into Juarez, Mexico, for Tim to make some sketches, and arrived in Bareacres at the end of January 1941. It was good to be home—sort of. Everything was just as they'd left it: their little house, the soft rolling hills and intense quiet. But the reality of Tim's illness haunted Mary Frances, as did her mother's increasingly poor health. When her beloved dog, Butch, became sick, Mary Frances became despondent. She knew the dog was ill enough to be put down, but she couldn't bear the thought of it, especially with Tim so weak and Edith in the hospital suffering from compromising chest pain. It seemed unfair and cruel to be able to relieve Butch of his pain when Tim and Edith had to carry on relentlessly.

The handwriting in Mary Frances's journal, always big and loopy, became small and tight. She wrote not because she wanted to but because she was too exhausted to do anything else. Yet the couple was determined to carry on with their Bareacres life. They made plans to build new shelves, oil the floors, and refinish furniture. They looked forward to Tim's art show, a two-week exhibition at UCLA of nearly two hundred sketches, watercolors, litho-pencil drawings, and paintings. On a whim, they bought a piano. It was an extravagance, but as soon as Tim sat down to play and Hayden's sonatas filled the house, Mary Frances knew it was justified.

In late spring, the two became godparents to Barrie Evans, the daughter of Bill and Jane Evans, friends from Mary Frances's Occidental days. She was ambivalent about her role as godmother, worried that seeing and holding Barrie would bring up painful feelings about childbearing. In her journal she wrote that she knew when she held the baby she would "quite possibly cry, wishing it were my own. The sentimentality, the pomp of procreation, and the ceaseless mystery, cannot but affect me."

Mary Frances believed that her failure to conceive was a good thing, and she claimed she was thankful for it. But when she held baby Barrie, Mary Frances was "swept away by stirrings that are as raw and gnawing as any sexual orgasm." The words offer a rare peek into Mary Frances's innermost emotional life. There were things she wanted but never dared hope for, and subtle ways in which her second marriage had failed her just as much as her first.

By the time spring of 1941 bloomed, Mary Frances had completed a draft of her second, American-food-based book, tentatively titled *Consider the Oyster*, and sent it to New York, where it was easily sold to Duell, Sloan, and Pearce. With the help of her agent, Mary Pritchett, she'd also submitted three chapters to *Gourmet* magazine. *Gourmet* didn't care for the pieces but asked if she would consider working on a series of articles about the great gastronomes of history. Mary Frances was glad for the diversion and quickly planned a research trip to Los Angeles.

Meanwhile, Tim was experiencing increased pain in his right leg, which Mary Frances described as a scalded thigh, "like skin held under steam . . . at nights sometimes he howls like a dog." He had been giving himself cobra-venom injections to placate his pain, but they produced only numbness in his leg and a sudden drop in body temperature. Still, Mary Frances hoped they might see an improvement soon. They had ordered more Analgeticum from Switzerland, but it hadn't arrived; she feared it had been held up by tight wartime security. On a whim, Mary Frances even wrote to President Roosevelt detailing their case and pleading with him to do everything he could to get the drug approved in America.

Tim accompanied Mary Frances as she researched her *Gourmet* pieces (which the magazine never published). It had been less than six months since their cross-country adventure, but traveling just a few hours to Los Angeles proved grueling for Tim. He felt worse when they arrived in the city and underwent physical challenges Bareacres didn't present. "Stairs and even straight walking are almost impossible for him anymore," she wrote. "He must stop and rest every few steps, and it humiliates him who, even with one leg, has hopped about like a cricket. He suffers mildly and constantly in his good leg."

THE KENNEDY FAMILY watched from afar, not sure what, if anything, they could do to help. The situation was particularly hard on Norah and David, who had been with the couple in Switzerland when Tim became ill. In June 1941, the two decided to move to Mexico. David hoped to intensively paint, Norah to write. Both planned to use their art as a way of avoiding an adult life constricted by Tim's illness and a world at war.

Watching her younger siblings set off on a creative adventure in another country made Mary Frances feel old beyond her years. Her siblings were not as naive as Mary Frances had been in her early twenties in Dijon. Whereas she had wanted to escape from the stifling binds of family and societal expectations, they were fleeing from a world that seemed to be filled only with hurt.

Mary Frances remarked in her journal that her siblings seemed thin and pallid; "too finely drawn." They had tense lines in the corners of their mouths and deep pockets underneath their eyes. She pitied them both, she wrote, "for they seem finished too soon. They need new blood in them." Longingly, Mary Frances watched them drive away. Often now, she felt used up, too—desperate for invigoration.

By July, she was discouraging visitors from coming to Bareacres. She also wrote Larry Powell that Tim had grown much worse in the past few weeks and that travel was out of the question. "He is increasingly weak," she wrote. "So that he can't walk at all unless I hold him." At least, she said, his morale was good and he managed to work in his studio just a little bit every single day.

Mary Frances did allow Rex and Edith to join her for her thirty-third birthday in July 1941, hopeful that a little party could help her relax. She managed to enjoy cocktails, grilled steaks, and presents, but she was thinking mostly of Tim. The day before, they had seen the doctor and Tim's standing leg had been tested for strength. The physician told them that his right leg seemed to be in good shape, but after arriving home he collapsed, his leg buckling beneath him. The episode had been dreadful, and Tim was miserable all night. She knew he was "abysmally discouraged. His eyes look strangely at me, and even when he is asleep I feel them rolling under their lids, looking for help or me or anything but despair."

After Rex and Edith left, Mary Frances's mind wandered to Norah and David—and Mexico. Imagining the sights, sounds, tastes, and colors, she could see herself next to them "drinking beer and watching the stately sexual parade each night while the band plays. Or working in the hot thin air." The air in Bareacres was hot and thin, too, but neither Mary Frances nor Tim was doing anything beyond watching the bright sun and how it "flung itself against the middle distances of San Jacinto in an intense blow."

She stopped writing in her journal. The days slipped by as she cared constantly for Tim, rarely aware of what was going on in the outside world. Then, on August 6, 1941, she awoke to a single gunshot.

12

The Color of Mourning

*W*ITHOUT WAKING HIS wife that morning, Tim had risen early and crept to the rim of the small canyon that lay just beyond the doors of Bareacres. Then, perhaps after watching the sun rise and bathe the San Jacinto hills in pools of light, he shot himself in the head.

Tim's body was cremated and his ashes placed in a small box that was buried underneath a giant hanging rock near where he had died. Mary Frances did not walk with her neighbor Arnold, who had been charged with the task of interring the tin container, to the burial site. When he returned they shared a large nip of whiskey. It was the only commemoration of the solemn moment.

Mary Frances wrote that after Tim died she was "in flight . . . I would be working in my little office and suddenly go as fast as I could out the door and up the road, until I had no breath left." She couldn't write in her journal or do much of anything besides wander aimlessly from room to room in her house, staring out the windows at the large expanse of brown hills, listening to the silence.

The nights were particularly hard. She used to enjoy turning out the lights and lying alone in bed, watching patterns of moonlight on the eucalyptus leaves outside her window. Now she was afraid of the quiet and the dark. Her mind was "riddled like an old oak chest with loathsome wormholes." She drank hot toddies in bed, and, if she was lucky, the alcohol helped her fall sleep. But usually the rest was only temporary and she woke again, cold and sober, her unwilling mind leaping "like a starved dog at the poisonous meaty thoughts." About one day out of three or four, she managed to sleep heavily until eight in the morning without dreaming of hearing the shot that ended Tim's life. She wrote in her journal that she tried to "live (even asleep!) with what dignity I can muster."

Her family considered Tim brave. "What can I say about Tim's death?" David wrote from Mexico. "Of course it was completely right, as right as everything he ever did. It is better that he was not a victim." Norah told Mary Frances that she was glad that Tim no longer had to suffer: "He was a great man in both his paintings and in his relations to people. So even if I did not love him I would thank you both for suffering so much to keep him alive." Their words echoed the sentiments of the family and friends that gathered around her, but the sympathy did little to relieve Mary Frances's grief.

Edith stayed with her daughter at Bareacres for several weeks, but Mary Frances did not always find her presence comforting. With Edith around, Mary Frances felt she should be writing and trying to drum up some creative work. Though no one around her was pushing her to do anything except grieve, in early fall Mary Frances wrote in her journal that she believed that it was time to stop her "ghastly life of compromise" and "get back to work."

"There are too many things I can't write yet," she noted in her journal as she toyed with returning to it. "They are words in my head, but

I am afraid of writing them." She worried that if she opened herself up to write, her words might "make a little crack in me, and let out some of the howling hideous frightful grief." Later she would reveal that during this time she occasionally wanted to kill herself. "I had unpredictable returns of this frantic necessity to destroy, for about one year," she wrote nearly a decade later in a mental health history she composed for her psychiatrist.

Her emotions were numb, she wrote, but her senses were "bright and alive." She saw colors more clearly, and even the simplest sound seemed to make an exquisite noise. She described herself as eating with a "rapt voluptuous concentration which had little to do with bodily hunger, but seemed to nourish some other part of me." She cooked beautiful meals for visitors, enjoying the process of feeding and caring for others. When she was alone she took just as much care, again preferring solitary dining. Occasionally she would go to a restaurant alone and "order dishes and good wines, as if I were a guest of myself, to be treated with infinite courtesy."

It was difficult to know how to live at all, but of this she was certain: She wanted to be alone. Part of her desire for isolation was her need to confront her new reality: "I am alone, completely, unalterably, and living with other people or having them live with me can never make me any less so, as long as I live." Though Tim had been dead only a little more than a month, it was time to "practice being dignified, all by myself, instead of always having an audience to make it easier."

In the hope of taking Mary Frances's mind off Tim's death, Norah invited her sister to join her and David in Mexico. "Please consider coming down," she wrote, "you could lie in the sun and look at murals, different from life at home." David seconded Norah's plea. "I finally have a studio fixed up," he told her, "half my bedroom, with a beautiful handmade easel and everything within arm's reach. Very cozy."

Her siblings did their best to seduce her with vibrant descriptions of a city bursting with color and life. Norah portrayed Mexico City as a "strange mixture of a pleasant and grubby European town . . . and something much older and more savage than Europe has been for several thousand years. The streets are narrow, jammed with busses, streetcars, lavish American automobiles, women in doorways selling bananas, peons with five chairs and three heavy tables tied to their backs, lottery sellers, babies begging for a centavo, all gathering for long conversations on street corners, horns honking, bedlam." She felt sure that the blistering country with its authentic blend of color and grit would help her sister heal.

Mary Frances, however, couldn't bear the thought of leaving. Bareacres was now hers alone, and in her grief she longed to wrap herself in what she and Tim had built together. In a will composed only a month before his suicide, Tim left his share in their property and all his belongings to Mary Frances and dictated that she should use her discretion to distribute mementos to his mother, sister, and extended family. The brief instructions reminded Mary Frances that in his final years Tim had clung fiercely to her, loosening his relationship with both his mother and his sister. Within months of Tim's death, her relationship with the Parrish family would disintegrate.

MEANWHILE, HER WRITING flourished, fueled by the success of *Consider the Oyster,* published only weeks after Tim passed away. She had written it to entertain her dying husband, and she believed that if Tim had known that it was going to be published so soon, he might have put off his suicide for at least a few more weeks.

The book is a series of short meditations on the brief yet passionate life and death of the oyster. It combines witty stories of oyster lore, personal musings, and recollections of past meals and travels. The pages of the slender book are dotted with recipes for Mary Frances's oyster favorites: Rockefeller, bisque, and stew. There are also recipes for regional finds: San Francisco Hang Town Fry, Oyster Gumbo, and an oyster-stuffed New Orleans po'boy.

The book was extraordinarily difficult to classify, but reviews were uniformly positive. One critic described it as "stories of the pleasures and disillusionments of dreams fulfilled." The praise made one thing clear to Mary Frances: She must always write toward somebody she loved. For years her words had been shaped by Tim Parrish. In the wake of his death she realized that if she was to continue writing, her work would require emotional intensity to make it authentic.

AFTER MARY FRANCES accidentally sideswiped a car one early fall afternoon, Anne told her sister she needed to take a vacation. She bought Mary Frances a ticket to Mexico, arranged for the necessary visas, and bought her sister a new hat. She flew first class from California to Mazatlan, where she was supposed to switch planes and continue to Guadalajara. But in Mazatlan, rain covered the plane's wings with a thin sheen of ice. Passengers were told they would continue their voyage in the morning.

The group was shuttled to a hotel, and Mary Frances checked into an airy room with views of an esplanade that hugged the beach. She changed into lighter clothes and walked to dinner, her high heels making hollow clacking noises on the large tiled stairway. She stopped briefly to have a cocktail with fellow travelers from the plane. Secretly, she didn't feel like being friendly to them, but she felt she must. She ordered a shot of tequila and a small beer and drank quickly, eager to leave the safe and boring conversation behind.

Mary Frances moved next to the dining room at the hotel. It was dark and dull, just as she expected. A waiter seated her at a small table near a door that opened out on to the patio. Occasionally a cool breeze wafted into the room, mingling with the soft conversation of other diners. She ordered another beer and sipped slowly at it until her dinner arrived.

The food was terrible: "a tasteless sopa de pasta, a salad of lukewarm fish and bottled dressing, some pale meat . . . I felt very sorry but I simply couldn't eat it." As she stared at her inedible meal, she caught whiffs of the savory smells that wafted from the kitchen. The waiters seemed to emanate the scent as they walked by delivering food. But what she smelled was not the food the waiters carried; the fragrance came from the men themselves and what they ate behind the closed kitchen door. The quiet of the dining room became even more unbearable as she listened to the waiters and cook staff laughing and talking.

At the end of her meal, the waiter delivered a moist block of pale bread pudding. Mary Frances couldn't hide her disdain. The waiter, sensing her dissatisfaction, leaned down. He whispered to her, telling her that there was a country kitchen next door to the restaurant kitchen. Would she like to try something? She nodded, and the waiter disappeared.

She sat, waiting, the scents reminding her of distant memories: a farm kitchen in the South of France, pungent but with more spicy pepper and less biting garlic.

The waiter delivered a rustic pottery bowl filled with light brown beans that had been cooked with tomato, onion, and many herbs. Later Mary Frances wrote that "the feeling of that hot strong food going down into my stomach was one of the finest I have ever had." It was the first thing, she said, that she had really tasted since Tim died—the first thing that fed her, in spite of the many meals she'd made and eaten since Tim's death. The beans were hot and healing; the piquant tastes reminded her who she was and from where she had come.

She recalled suddenly and intensely her love for travel, for sitting alone in restaurants, for eating magnificent meals. She was momentarily happy, absorbed in the pleasure of the food and the way the simple dish seemed able to completely nourish her. She ate enough food to easily feed three or more people, but she didn't care. After pushing back her bowl, she slowly and contentedly finished her beer. Next she paid for the meal, thanked the waiter profusely, and returned to her hotel room. For the first time in months, she slept well, "dreaming good dreams in my well-being, but hearing the waves when I wanted to through the dreams."

In the early morning, she was back on the tarmac again, waiting for a plane she hoped would take off soon. She watched tired passengers slump on benches and then stumble toward the dim light of a coffee shop where waitresses swept crumbs from countertops and laid out worn breakfast menus.

As the sun rose she boarded the plane, and as the thin aluminum wings lifted into the sky, Mary Frances closed her eyes. She woke to the bustling sound of morning chatter and the noise of stewardesses maneuvering the narrow aisles of the plane with trays of breakfast. There were little cups of steaming coffee, glasses of concentrated juice, and a large orange emblazoned with a fruit company advertisement. Alongside the cardboard cutlery and a paper napkin were two small cellophane envelopes. In one packet was a chunk of grilled ham, in the other, a pale yellow scrambled egg. The floppy yellow mess was nothing like the nourishing egg sandwiches Aunt Gwen had fed her as a girl. Mary Frances pushed the small tray of food as far away from her as she could, disgusted by what others considered a meal. If she pressed her tongue against the roof of her mouth, she realized, she could almost taste the haunting spices from the dinner she'd eaten the night before. She watched the clouds and avoided the eyes of the steward who was convinced that her lack of appetite meant that she was going to be sick.

Almost as soon as they were through distributing and clearing breakfast, the stewards started again with lunch, handing out little paper boxes that unfolded into makeshift trays. Small cups were filled with water, juice, and hot consommé, and a large apple was tucked into a nest of decorative violet-colored paper. Two covered paper cups held a half of a canned pear on a bed of cottage cheese and a bright yellow gelatin salad with gently suspended slices of banana and pineapple. There were three small sandwiches, skimpy piles of meat and cheese packed between slices of tasteless bread, each individually wrapped and sealed.

Mary Frances called for the steward and asked him to remove most of the water from her drinking glass, filling it next with a "mature-sized sip" of bourbon from the flask that she kept in her bag. She looked out the window of the plane and "toasted a cloud and . . . almost at once felt even better than I had before." After drinking most of her cocktail, Mary Frances attacked the sandwiches, layering chicken and ham into a thick, meaty middle bookended by pieces of white and rye bread. She described it as a "pleasant lunch, small yet nourishing," concocted with a "neatness and intense dispatch impossible everywhere but high above the earth."

As the plane dropped, Mary Frances watched "coconut trees poisonously [and] impossibly green in the last sunlight" and the silver waters of the bay, dotted with black boats. It was an entirely different experience to travel by air than by sea. Yet the weightless feeling was the same. Flying took her mind off of her troubles. For a few hours she was a "wingless human . . . much higher than a kite." Then the earth moved up to touch her feet and, she felt suddenly very, very hungry.

SHE WAS MET in Guadalajara by Norah and David. Her brother and sister looked healthy, tanned from the intense sun. They drove through the city and into the open Mexican plains, chattering about ordinary things.

The ride was charged with anticipation: When Mary Frances arrived at the house she would be introduced to Sarah, David's new wife. David's wedding had been a shock to Rex and Edith, but Mary Frances had known when David and Norah left for Mexico that Sarah was planning to join them. Mary Frances wasn't sure that David should have married but believed that there was "something to the theory of gathering rosebuds while you may, especially these days."

When the three arrived in Chapala, Sarah came out to greet them. She was nervous but gentle-looking, with unlacquered nails and a fresh, unpainted face. Mary Frances felt out of place. She was still wearing her stiff shoes and traveling clothes, and underneath her makeup, her eyes were tired. She longed to change into something that matched the feel of her relaxed and friendly surroundings.

After unpacking, she joined David, who was sitting in one of the twilight-lit living rooms with a guitar and two drinks. Mary Frances noticed immediately that David looked different from how he had months before—older. She sat on the floor next to him. As they drank, David asked about Rex and Edith and the escalating war, never directly mentioning Tim's death. Mary Frances asked lightly about David's art and the small village, avoiding her brother's unexpected marriage to Sarah. Despite the gaps in conversation, Mary Frances felt welcome, as if the blanket of grief had been temporarily lifted from her shoulders.

Their rented villa was adjacent to a small square with thick green trees, a wide promenade, and a small collection of women who laid out blankets and sold exotic flowers and small votive candles on nice evenings. They were close to the public market with its sprawling collection of colorful stands. There farmers hawked produce and tried to sell cuts of meat that sat rotting in the sun while flies circled overhead in frenetic patterns. Merchants cooked and made tortillas over a circle of stoves that were planted in center of the market. There were counters for eating just-purchased meals and underneath the stools, circles of hungry dogs and cats roamed, hoping for a lucky bite.

The busy market, however, was unreliable at best. There were days and sometimes weeks where there would be almost nothing fresh available to purchase. Other times there would be just one item in abundance. It was challenging to find enough food for a meal. Some days Mary Frances longed to take an empty bowl to the doors of kitchens that blew delicious smells into the village air and beg to be fed a simple meal of beans and tortillas. She knew those closed doors hid the most delicious Mexican food she might ever eat, and thought regularly of the beans she had eaten in Mazatlan.

She wanted very much to cook, to "fold myself in the comfortable cloud of mix-baste-and-boil." But despite visits to Guadalajara, where they stocked up on butter, bread, lettuces, and other vegetables, she couldn't find enough inspiring ingredients. Her rare evenings in the kitchen reminded her of living in Dijon, and how difficult it was to cook before she mastered the routine of the market and the idiosyncrasies of her simple kitchen.

Mary Frances, Norah, and Sarah were helping David paint murals in Chapala's municipal baths. They spent "several hours every day neck deep in the clear running water of the pools, walking cautiously on the sandy bottoms with pie plates full of tempura . . . and paint brushes stuck in our hair." At noontime they returned home for lunch. They ate bread and butter, "tomatoes and hard eggs and whatever other things like radishes we had been able to find." They drank cold beer, tequila, or Coca-Cola. Their dining room was big and hollow and their voices echoed as they talked, sounding "full and rich, and clearer than ever before." Occasionally David played guitar and they sang, their voices and the music bouncing off the walls until they decided it was time to return to work.

At night they ate at one of the plain restaurants on the village square. They devoured white fish, thick porridges made from rice and herbs, and tortillas. There were no salads and almost no vegetables. Sometimes they would visit a woman who made tortillas, swirling them on big oval pans set over the hot embers of the fire, cooking them just enough that they were carefully wilted, not burned. The limp tortillas were filled with chopped herbs and lettuces and could be eaten in just a few perfect bites.

Every night, as the group sat eating, drinking, and listening to music, they watched young men walking through the streets with pots and platters of food balanced on their heads as they moved slowly home to their wives and children. There were pots of beans, meaty stews, platters of tacos, and the occasional boiled chicken. This was the food Mary Frances craved.

One morning, while the group was sitting around the big table with remnants of breakfast coffee, toast ends, and crumbs strewn about, they heard a loud crash and a piercing cry. Irritated, David got up to see what had caused the sickening sound that Mary Frances said reminded her of a melon being tossed from a window and hitting the sidewalk with a loud and splitting thunk.

When David returned, he reported that a woman from the hills, carrying a big pot of beans on her head to sell at the market, had tripped and fallen in front of their house. The woman had probably walked most of the night with her entire crop of beans in one giant pot.

The news of the woman's accident made them all restless and worried. Mary Frances stared out of Norah's bedroom window to see the beans, pale and nasty, and spread on the stony sidewalk, "mixed with broken pottery and already half-eaten by the starved dogs of the village and a few beggar children." People made wide circles around the woman to avoid stepping in the mess. They didn't seem to notice or care that she sat, "folded into her shawl, with her face on her knees, never making a sound after her first wail."

The woman sat in front of the villa all day, even after the beans had been cleaned up and the broken pieces of pottery laid at her feet as a small offering. David went outside to give her some money, shaking her a bit, as if to wake her from her sorrow. But the woman did not respond, and the coins rolled from her limp fingers. She got up, gathered the shards, and began to walk back home shortly before sunset.

That night, the four went out eating and drinking. They drank and spent more money than usual, an attempt to banish the woman's suffering and the blunt sound of a pottery crock full of beans hitting the stony sidewalk.

On Mary Frances's first night in Chapala, David had introduced her to mariachi music. She was intoxicated by the wild noise—the steady strumming, the soft melodies, and the men singing in rollicking wails. One voice stood out. It was piercing and sweet—a passionately beautiful falsetto. Mary Frances discovered that it belonged to Juanito, a young girl from a hill town outside Chapala who had disguised herself as a boy so she could start a band.

Juanito was slender with pale skin, short, dirty black hair, and a tired and worn look, as if she slept in the dusty streets every night. She was stooped like an old Mexican man, but her voice was young and vibrant.

David was obsessed with Juanito and her music. He knew that Juanito was a woman masquerading as a man, but unlike the priest in the village who frowned on the deception, David encouraged it. He developed an unlikely friendship with Juanito, positioning himself in front of the audience when Juanito sang, the two making concentrated eye contact.

Juanito directed all of her passion to David, and seemed to be singing just for him. And David responded by looking as if "the music had filled him, just under the skin, with some kind of magic wax."

Mary Frances learned that after David and Norah had arrived in Chapala, David had regularly invited Juanito to visit the house. The two would retreat to the living room, where they would play music and sing together. Mary Frances felt sure that Juanito saw that every time she played, David's "exhausted face grew younger." She wondered if they longed for each other. She wasn't sure which version of Juanito attracted David. He'd married a woman, but was taken by Juanito's androgynous look and captivating voice. Perhaps the young singer reminded him of sexual feelings for men he'd tried to escape by marrying and moving to Mexico.

Juanito had responded to David's interest by dressing, for a time, as a woman. But according to Norah, when Juanito learned that David had married Sarah, she violently cut her hair and drank until she could no longer walk, her crumpled, masculine form greeting the newlyweds as they returned to the village.

To David, Juanito was an entertaining curio. And Mary Frances was stunned by how Norah and Sarah encouraged his interest by attending concerts with him and echoing his praise. But their faces revealed their embarrassment and concern. Mary Frances watched the two women as they observed David, their faces "tight under the smooth, beautiful well-bred skin." She noticed that when David whistled loudly in appreciation, or requested another song, Sarah's arm would reach protestingly, hoping to quiet him. It rarely worked.

Though it had only been a few months since Mary Frances had last seen him, it was clear David had been changed by his time in another country. He was the patriarch in Mexico, presiding over a house of young, beautiful women, and sporting a haughty attitude. Mary Frances wondered if Juanito was partly to blame. David had "turned on himself with a concentration I had seldom seen . . . a hard, furious devotion that was at once tragic and admirable . . . His marriage, his imperious gentleness with Sarah and his sisters, even the intensity of his eating and drinking had a remoteness about them impossible to assault." Eventually Juanito began returning to the villa to give David guitar lessons. On the days she came, Mary Frances would stay in her room, "lying in a kind of helplessness . . . listening to David and the singer." The echoey rooms in the stone house sent the couple's voices up to her with clear intensity. Mary Frances could hear how close the two were becoming. She believed that David selfishly viewed Juanito as an "instrument who played music that pleased him," rather than a vulnerable young person. She was also concerned that Juanito's future, and her safety, might not be endangered by a friendship with an older American man.

The unknown nature of David's relationship with Juanito eventually made Mary Frances eager to leave Mexico. She knew she was observing something too private for her to understand, and she longed for her own space. She needed solitude to contextualize her own experiences, and she didn't want to worry about the decisions her brother might make.

After David finished the murals he'd been constructing, Mary Frances was happy to pack her bags and head home. The warm breezes, bright colors, and intense flavors of Mexico had awakened her senses and deeply nourished her, just as she had hoped. Now it was time to return to California and her dusty Bareacres home. It was time to bring herself back to life.

13

A Place in the World

MARY FRANCES ARRIVED home to a jarringly unfamiliar landscape. After several weeks in Mexico, constantly surrounded by noise and people, Bareacres felt barren, brown, and lonely. She began driving her Oldsmobile west, splitting her time between her desolate country house and Anne's apartment in Beverly Hills. She was at Anne's on December 7, 1941, when news came that the Japanese had attacked Pearl Harbor. The United States was plunged into a wartime hysteria that, after several years of living in Europe, was all too familiar.

Shortly after Pearl Harbor, Homer D. King, the publisher of the *Hemet News*, wrote to Mary Frances, asking her about the blackout and air raid precautions she had observed while living in Europe. Her response, a three-page typed letter, was published in the Hemet and Whittier papers.

"Blackout Lessons Drawn from Europe: Woman Who Lived in Switzerland Tells of Air Raid Precautions" underscored the importance of preparation. "We will be stronger and better for whatever preparations we can make," she wrote, "even if they never be used." She advised stock-ing a pantry with easily prepared and nourishing foods: canned soups, coffee, and evaporated milk, and fashioning dark fabric into lightproof window covers. The brief article turned into a popular and reprinted piece, and before long, Mary Frances was sequestered at Bareacres again, working on the manuscript for what would become her third book.

Writing was the salve she needed. "I was still in strong grief," she said later. "It seemed quite natural to do a book exactly as I would do a good report for Father's paper, to earn my living the only way I could." It was the first time Mary Frances was conscious of writing as a means of supporting herself, and after outlining the book in her head while sunbathing at Bareacres, she worked productively and hard, finishing a draft of the manuscript in only a few weeks.

How to Cook a Wolf was penned in the belief that the thoughtful presentation of food and eating were the "true ways to ward off hunger, hurt, or any other wolf at the door." She used her preferred medium of food and gastronomy to address the needs and fears of a nation at war. The weighty book—comprising her characteristic musings, short instructional lessons in cooking, and brief recipes—suggested how to eat well even when there was little to choose.

The chapters had such titles as "How to Boil Water," "How to Keep Alive," and "How to Pray for Peace." Pages offered housewives advice on how to achieve a balanced diet, stretch ingredients, eat dur-ing blackouts, deal with sleeplessness and sorrow, and care for pets during wartime. Simple recipes were written with the idea that readers might have pantries that were limited by war rations. "Sludge" was a thick mix of ground beef, grain cereal, and ground vegetables; it may have been unappetizing but would fill every empty corner in a stomach. Cakes required no butter or sugar. There were instructions for how to make mouthwash and soap. Its tone was occasionally mocking; despite the newspaper article and its success, Mary Frances was aware that she was no authority on how to endure bleak times.

If *Consider the Oyster* had been composed as a love letter to Tim, *How to Cook a Wolf* attempted to obscure the pain she felt over his death. Still, the project focused her swirling energies on something that seemed helpful: survival amidst personal and collective chaos. The book was slated for publication in the spring of 1942.

As she waited for the bound volume to arrive, Mary Frances lived at Bareacres, read constantly, and entertained many guests. Around that time, she began keeping what she called a "recipe book," filled with the food likes and dislikes of the people she fed.

More character profiles than lists, the short entries reveal how carefully Mary Frances observed the people around her. Though her personality was reserved, if she liked someone, she showed it by feeding them, and caring deeply about the foods they liked. She described Norah as a lover of fresh food and "one of very few really enjoyable guests, gastronomically. Tastes are simple but investigatory . . . Much interested in simple but intricately seasoned dishes." But her pen could turn venomous. She noted that Rex, for instance, ate the same breakfast every single day and that in spite of his love for foreign foods, "at home [he] eats according to wife's tastes, which she sincerely believes are his." There are fewer than a dozen entries in the thick book—she simply didn't have enough close friends to fill the pages. Her abandonment of the project was a testimony to both her self-protective nature and her occasionally fleeting interest in creative projects.

When not at Bareacres, Mary Frances spent time in Hollywood looking for a job. She was surprised to find that many of the creative types who had flocked to Europe in the '20s and '30s were now looking for work in Los Angeles. Competition was stiff, and her search was unsuccessful.

The publication of *How to Cook a Wolf* reconfirmed that Mary Frances differed from the women who composed recipes for ladies' magazines, or wrote cookbooks or entertainment guides. It was a revolutionary book that presented food not only as a pleasure but as a necessity. Though some recipes were included, the strength of her narrative lay in her ability to philosophize on the importance of eating and eating well. M.F.K. Fisher had created a genre all her own.

Reviewing the book in *The New York Times,* Orville Prescott wrote that M.F.K. Fisher spun "amusing stories between dishes and colors nearly every page with her own forthright, astringent personality." But he found her philosophy—that mindful eating could help curb hunger— lacking in practicality. "Mrs. Fisher is not accustomed to cooking for lumberjacks, cowboys or even men who have played three sets of tennis or eighteen holes of golf," he opined. It was a valid criticism. Though Mary Frances's book was filled with thoughtful advice on emotional survival during wartime, the recipes she had included weren't suitable for adults working in factories or fields, managing the home front while war raged.

Prescott questioned Mary Frances's love for simple ingredients, thoughtfully prepared, and eaten attentively. He called it the "weird notion that if a soup is rich enough and good enough, it is almost presumptuous to want anything else. Imagine!" For another reviewer, M.F.K. Fisher's belief that food was an integral part of our physical and emotional experience as people was delightful to ponder but far less practical to employ.

How to Cook a Wolf's literary success made it easier for Mary Frances to find a job. A feature about her published in *Look* magazine in July 1942 claimed that studio executives were so enamored with her sophisticated book-publicity shot that they sent a talent scout to tempt her into acting. She scoffed at the suggestion and finally found a job much more conventionally—through friends with connections in Hollywood. In late May 1942, she signed a contract with Paramount Studios and began working as a junior writer.

Her husband had been dead for more than six months, and she was lonely. Though her life was becoming more and more exciting, it was far different from the one she had planned. But she was young and attractive. She got a lot of attention from men, many of whom occupied places of power in Hollywood circles. Later she would say that she worked hard in Hollywood and had some "very good affairs" while she lived there.

Still, she was hesitant to share herself with just anyone and preferred to dine alone most of the time. She described the solitary months: "I have often eaten an egg and drunk a glass of jug-wine, surrounded deliberately with the trappings of busyness, in a hollow Hollywood flat near the studio where I was called a writer, and not been able to stifle my longing to be anywhere but there."

Occasionally Mary Frances was irked by her solitude; she had numerous suitors but none of them wanted to take her to dinner. She was a woman of firm opinions and an expert gastronome. The idea of sharing the table with a woman with such defined tastes made men blanch and turn toward someone "much less written." Mary Frances joked that she was hungry and the vapid girls were inevitably better fed.

She came to believe that "since nobody else dared feed me as I wished to be fed, I must do it myself, and with as much aplomb as I could muster." She ate light dinners while she worked at home in the evenings. She became a regular at two good restaurants and occasionally bought expensive meals complete with an aperitif, dinner, and a small bottle of wine. The meals were never as satisfying as she hoped, so she shifted her routine and started visiting the market on her way to work in the morning, hiding her perishable goods in the water cooler just outside her office.

Her early-morning sprees guaranteed the freshest dairy and produce. She bought the biggest, brownest eggs and the palest sweet-cream butter. She filled her pantry with tins of canned fish and other simple items that could be dressed and warmed in a small chafing dish. She purchased a case of inexpensive but delightful wines.

At Paramount, Mary Frances worked dispassionately from ten in the morning until six at night. There she wrote gags for the likes of Bob Hope, Bing Crosby, and Dorothy Lamour. She found the work remarkably unfulfilling. On one of her first days on the job, her producer asked her to write a three-minute gag line. Mary Frances walked quickly across the lot, into her office, and dictated the gag to her secretary, who typed it and had it delivered back to the producer. The producer rejected the gag and accused Mary Frances of plagiarism, believing no one could write a joke that good in thirty minutes. When Mary Frances asked her agent what she had done wrong, he told her bluntly that she had written too fast. "It should have taken two weeks," he said. Then they would have accepted it immediately.

When done for the day, Mary Frances would travel home and began the elaborate task of feeding herself. She soothed her tired spirits with a glass of sherry or vermouth. She ate salads made from fresh lettuces, herbs, and vegetables. She usually had a glass or two of wine with her main course, often "a big bowl of soup, with a fine pear and some Teleme cheese; or two very round eggs." Other nights she made "sourdough toast with browned butter poured over and a celery heart alongside for something crisp; or a can of bean sprouts, tossed with sweet butter and some soy and lemon juice, and a big glass of milk." She ate it all, slowly, from a big tray set properly with china and a napkin, balanced artfully on her two knees. She was returning to a skill honed during lonely days in Dijon and weeks spent traveling at sea: she fed herself, and she did it well, delighting in the simple, nourishing act of eating.

Mary Frances quickly realized that she couldn't spend the rest of her life writing one-liners. "It was complete folly for me to be in Hollywood," she said. Her contract, however, was far from done. When she signed she'd agreed to an initial nineteen weeks, followed by yearly time and salary increases: a commitment of seven years.

ON JULY 23, 1942, not even a year after Tim's self-inflicted death, her brother David committed suicide. After returning from Mexico, David had devoted himself to painting, shunning the family tradition of newspaper publishing. His wife, Sarah, was pregnant, and in this regard, at least, life for the two was conventional. But soon it became clear that with World War II, military service would be in David's future. He grew moodier as the conflict heightened, and despite his ambivalence, he enlisted in the army rather than waiting to be drafted.

In the weeks before his suicide, David grew increasingly anxious about the war and his role in it. One day, after chatting and eating walnuts with the ranch's hired man, he climbed into the barn attic and hung himself. He left no note, no will, no explanation, or apology.

The Kennedys tried to remember conversations they'd had with David and any clues that he might have dropped about his plans for the future. "Someone knows the truth," Mary Frances ominously wrote. Perhaps she was thinking of David's close friendship with Tim, wondering if his death had given David any ideas of how to escape from a troubled and painful life.

Mary Frances would call her brother's life a "short sad story." She described David as both charming and intelligent, and wondered about the promising life he had ended. "He might have made a very fine newspaper man," she wrote, "like his father and grandfather. It is possible that he might have become an equally fine social caricaturist . . . his drawings, although steadily more bitter and unhappy, are witty and interesting." But in her more private moments, she agonized about David's internal struggles. A note scrawled in Mary Frances's handwriting found among papers relating to David's death offers possible motivating factors for his suicide: "fear of pain, death, panic; self betrayal; fear of mother's cowardice; ??? war ???" Mary Frances clearly believed that the war was only one of the possible reasons David might have sought to end his life.

His personal papers reveal few clues. David's sketchbooks from Mexico are filled with drawings of men, and there was the uncertainty surrounding his infatuation with Juanito. It is interesting to wonder if fear and self-doubt about his sexuality were a larger force in David's decision. But if Mary Frances or others in the Kennedy family thought this, it went unvoiced.

By JANUARY OF 1943, Mary Frances had returned to work with as much verve as she could manage. She told Larry Powell that she had resigned herself to the dailiness and low-level theatrics of her Hollywood writing job. She was relatively unhappy, regularly sitting at her desk "waiting on the whims of an unpleasant 'producer.'" She wrote that she had "finally reconciled my ethics with my profession, and am working on my own stuff on company time." Instead of laboring quickly on assignments as she had before, she now worked in fits and spurts. The rest of the time she toyed with various projects she hoped might please her publisher, Sam Sloan, who was eager for her to provide a follow-up to *How to Cook a Wolf*. At the end of her letter to Larry, Mary Frances casually mentioned that she might be leaving Hollywood in the next several months to venture east—on what she called a "government job." She described it as being "very nebulous at the moment, but promising."

In March 1943, she wrote Larry again. She told him that she was "sitting close to a volcano, which may suddenly send me on foreign service and a very hush-hush publicity job for the government." She was hoping for the best but "must keep mum about it all. I'll let you know as much as I can, if anything breaks." She repeated a similar tale to her family.

The truth: She was pregnant—a shocking predicament for an unmarried woman in 1943. She hid it carefully, using the foil of secret government work as her cover. In a letter to his cousin, Ted, Rex mentioned that his daughter was "somewhere in the blue writing . . . We don't know where she is stationed because that is a deep secret."

Under the guise of classified government work, Mary Frances retreated to a boardinghouse in nearby Altadena, California. The seclusion was inspiring. She was far enough away from Whittier and Hollywood to be comfortable, but near Dr. Bieler, her old friend and physician, who would deliver the baby when the time came. Day after day, her only duties were relaxing and writing. She began composing brief autobiographical essays that told the story of her life using food as the denominator. She hoped she could braid the essays into a book and admitted to Larry she was hoping to complete the manuscript in only three months.

She wrote during the day and again at night; she had never worked so hard in her life. It was "the first thing I've ever written, really, without Tim's cold judicial ear to listen," she told Larry. "*The Wolf* doesn't count . . . it was mainly recipes." Without Tim's tender but perfectionist ear, she was "scared and bewildered." She worried constantly if the manuscript was any good and never felt entirely confident.

She finished the manuscript in mid-July 1943, shortly after her thirty-fifth birthday. Later she reported that the book had been "conceived and written and typed in ten weeks . . . [but] it's over now, at least my private war with it." Mary Frances airmailed it to New York and crossed her fingers. She called it *The Gastronomical Me*.

She told Larry, one of the rare people with whom she still communicated regularly, that the book was "an odd thing, and may bore the boys in NY. It's autobiographical all right . . . but neither True Confessions nor Leaves From My Kitchen Lovebook. I shudder to think what may happen to it." She told him that there were stories in it that she knew that he would like—recollections of their time in Dijon and the people they had known there. That alone, she thought, made the book worthwhile.

She added that she hoped she would finish with her other, secret project by September and return to Bareacres soon after, perhaps with one of the two children she was planning to adopt. Adoption was "a hell of a discouraging business," she wrote. It couldn't be done in California, both because of the expense and because Mary Frances was unmarried.

The baby was overdue. With Mary Frances uncomfortable and worried that the child would arrive too close to the date she was supposed to vacate her boarding house, Dr. Bieler induced delivery with a strong and savory Japanese tea. On August 15, 1943, Mary Frances Kennedy Fisher gave birth to a daughter whom she named Anne Kennedy Parrish. Dr. Bieler and a nurse attended to the birth of a healthy baby girl with big, round eyes.

As she grew, Anne decided she wanted to be called Anna, which is the name she uses today. But on her birth certificate she is Anne Kennedy Parrish. Her father was listed as Michael Parrish, a fictional serviceman who conveniently had the same last name as Tim.

The made-up name for the baby's father reflects Mary Frances's desire for Anne to have a connection to Tim. And though the baby was wholly hers, when she presented Anne to her family in Whittier a few weeks later, she claimed she was adopted. Rex reported that Mary Frances had taken the baby at birth from a woman in Arizona. She was a "cute little trick and Dote seems happy in having her. Lucky kid."

Overjoyed, Edith cried upon seeing the dark-haired baby, and after seeing her mother's happiness, Mary Frances cried, too. If her parents and siblings wondered about her extended absence and the real origin of baby Anne, they chose to keep their questions to themselves. Instead they opened their arms to their newest family member.

Mary Frances and Anne moved back to Bareacres, where Tim's art studio was converted to a nursery. Mary Frances knew Tim would have approved of the softly colored walls now hung with a small collection of his paintings. Near Anne's crib was a portrait of Mary Frances with a bottle of wine, some apples, and a white flower. It was the only piece that Tim had ever done of her that he felt captured her likeness. The idea of Tim's artwork and her image staring down at baby Anne while she slept made Mary Frances supremely happy.

IN EARLY NOVEMBER 1943, she took her typewriter close to the fire and composed a letter to Larry, one of her oldest and closest friends. "Now and then I can write more freely to you," she told him. "You understand."

"It's a cool clear night, with a young moon," she wrote. "I've brought my typewriter in by the fire, partly because it's nicer that way and partly to be near Anne while she drinks her supper." Her baby daughter was "right in every way. She is a healthy, impish little being with merry dark eyes." After years that were marked with equal amounts of passion and despair, she was happy. "My life seems full and warm and rich again," she wrote. "I was out in the cold for a long time."

The Gastronomical Me had been published to solid reviews. The critic Isabelle Mallet called it a "brew of reminiscence, bright incident and sensuous enjoyment of food . . . with sufficient flavor to delight the gourmet and enough intelligent observations to hold other connoisseurs as well." Yet Mallet found the narrative occasionally rambling and disconnected—an ultimately common complaint.

Clifton Fadiman wondered if it was time for Mary Frances to begin working in a new genre. He found *The Gastronomical Me* "sadder, older, less charming than *Serve It Forth*. It makes more evident than ever the fact that Mrs. Fisher was born to write novels and that it's about time she did. Fadiman's criticism echoed that of Larry Bachmann, a good friend and recent lover, who, after reading *The Gastronomical Me*, told her, "Please try not to write any more about food, if you can help it in a book. And don't write any more about yourself. I am highly dubious and suspicious of people who do—dubious as to their growth as writers."

Rex, however, remarked, "I like this book better than any she has written." Finally, Mary Frances had received the praise that she longed for from her father. Larry Powell also described the book positively, saying it was true to the time: "The restless come and go in it, the money, the luxury."

The memoir seemed to encompass all the dreams Mary Frances had when she first stepped on the *Berengaria* in 1929: the glittering opulence of life in France tempered by childhood innocence and the stark realities of war, illness, and death.

Larry Powell responded quickly to the letter Mary Frances had sent. He wrote from home in Beverly Glen, California, on a rainy November morning. He had read his copy of *The Gastronomical Me* in two days and was astonished by the essays that so beautifully preserved Mary Frances's fondest memories. As she told the story of her life through the settings of meals, large and small, she was also writing about the subtle realities that made being human an intrinsically beautiful and tragic experience.

Larry was overcome with praise. The book, he told her, was "chock-full of life." The writing was rich, sensual, maybe even decadent. "I felt one or two indigestion pains from over-richness," he remarked. He loved Mary Frances's memories of their time together in Dijon, and was happy that she'd portrayed him well—as a brother and confidant.

Yet the book was filled with a strange combination of what he called "cruel candor and tender reticence." She had been kind to him and to most in their Dijon circle. But her pen had become poisonous when it came to others. He felt sorriest for Al, whose influence was oversimplified, and for David's wife, Sarah, who was rendered as a pretty but placid wife. "You Kennedys are a cruel family," he wrote, "turned in on yourselves almost incestuously—and God help the man or woman who marries one of you."

He believed that she had been terribly mean to her first husband in the book—never mentioning Al's career as a writer or the epic poem he drafted in Dijon. It was surprising to Larry, since Mary Frances had such a hand in Al's creative struggle. After all, her departure during the summer of 1931 had made Al crazy with grief. He berated Mary Frances for having made Al a stiff character who appeared rarely, and transparently, in her pages.

Yet Larry understood that Al was eclipsed by Tim; the vividness of Tim's personality muted everything that preceded his arrival. Mary Frances's life with her second husband had been extraordinarily rich and fulfilling. Tim, Larry noted, had "passed beyond the desire to dominate a woman." He had given Mary Frances a "perfect tolerant love," in which she had flourished. It was hard for Larry to believe that she would ever find anyone to match him.

When it came to portraying the heartbreak in her life, Larry believed she had been honest. "I know with what courage and devotion you've faced the most horrible faces life has turned to you and I'm quite humble," he wrote. He was one of the few who had known her through it all: her first and second marriages, the deaths of Tim and David, the birth of her daughter.

Perhaps that was why he felt so intimately acquainted with the stories she told on the pages. "We shared a lot of that life," he told her, "written and unwritten, and what we didn't, you make me feel, warm and immediate." He finished by telling her that it was a "very brave strong book, and I love you for it."

There was one more morsel of praise from Larry tucked into the letter, words that must have resonated with Mary Frances the woman and M.F.K. Fisher the author: "Dear MF . . . ," Larry wrote, "I rejoice in the way you have realized yourself."

After years that were marked with equal doses of passion and despair, Mary Frances had finished writing the story of a life spent discovering herself through the seemingly endless pleasures of food, wine, and travel. If only temporarily, she was sure of her place in the world.

EPILOGUE

*I*N THE LATE spring of 1945, when Mary Frances was nearly thirty-seven years old, she left the West Coast on a whim, traveling to New York City with her two-year-old daughter and nanny. She had become, she later said, "emotional and jittery."

She continued to mourn Tim and David, a grief amplified by the death of President Roosevelt that spring. She had revered the president, and felt that his passing, three weeks before the surrender of Nazi Germany, made the world even more uncertain.

In 1944, she had broken her contract with Paramount, and she had recently weathered the end of a brief but intense relationship with a San Francisco businessman named Harold Price. She felt increased pressure to write, but was motivated now by the need to provide for her small family. Her creative malaise was compounded by the difficulty of focusing on writing with a small child underfoot and no husband to help.

Little seemed stable. She left for Manhattan quickly, in much the same fashion that she had fled to Mexico after Tim died. She told Larry Powell that she was turning her back on "MFKF" for a few months.

Immediately after arriving in New York, Mary Frances introduced herself to a publisher named Donald Friede at a dinner party. The Depression had forced his esteemed firm, Covici-Friede, out of business. But it had published such writers as John Steinbeck, Nathanael West, and Clifford Odets.

Donald was in his early forties, had been married four times, and had a reputation as a gentleman who moved in the finest New York literary and social circles. Mary Frances was immediately drawn to his urbane and erudite personality and to his friends, who included writers, artists, and cartoonists. "He has much the same power Tim had, of making life very real for every one," she said. Donald, a fan of M.F.K. Fisher's ever since he had read *Serve It Forth*, was smitten with the lovely yet remote Mary Frances.

Shortly after the party, Mary Frances called Gloria Stuart, an old friend and actress whom she'd met in California while married to Al, and announced she intended to marry Donald. Gloria—today best remembered for her portrayal of the elderly Rose Calvert in the opening scenes of the epic 1997 film *Titanic*—elegantly voiced her concern. She worried that Mary Frances, a grief stricken single mother who had recently arrived in a big city, was in no shape to begin a new romance. She may have also been concerned that Mary Frances was doing just what she'd done with her prior marriages: escaping an uncomfortable situation with a new love affair and a new location.

Still, the couple married two weeks later. Mary Frances sent Larry a telegram: "I accidentally got married Saturday to Donald Friede." Later Mary Frances remarked that "it seemed very rash, as indeed it was. I felt I was past the great passion of life, and so was he, and that we could build a very good companionship."

But it wasn't that easy, especially for her. Though she loved Donald and described him as a "subtle complex man who is a great challenge to me," she quickly discovered that the inherent difficulties of melding a new marriage with their two careers and her baby were immense. She would acknowledge that she had almost walked out the first week after they were married—but was "too proud and too conscious of all the people who had begged me not to be foolhardy enough to marry you."

In the month after the wedding, relations grew worse. Mary Frances wrote that she "almost walked out a window, but I was still proud, and too conscious of how much further I could hurt people I loved." Her distress stemmed less from regret over the swift marriage than from her startling transition. She had suddenly evolved from a "bereft sorrowful woman all by herself" into being Donald Friede's "new wife in the most brilliant circles in New York."

Donald recognized Mary Frances's talent, and believed that her previous agents, editors, and publishers had done little to win her the reputation and sales she deserved. He quickly decided she should break her existing literary contracts. He signed her with a new publishing house and secured a large advance for her fifth book, a literary history of feasting. The changes were overwhelming, but initially Mary Frances believed that Donald, like Tim, was one of the rare people who inspired her to work with the dedication required of great writing.

Then came another overwhelming change. Facing mounting legal problems that stemmed from a charge of sending pornographic literature through the mail (a case that was later settled), Donald gave up his work in New York. The couple moved to Mary Frances's house in Hemet, hoping to spend a quiet life writing. In March 1946, they welcomed the arrival of her second daughter, Mary Kennedy Friede. Kennedy, as they called her, was born prematurely, and spent the first eight weeks of her life in an incubator. Unable to care immediately for her, Mary Frances suffered from a delayed bout of postpartum depression.

As time passed, it became clear that Donald was, as Mary Frances described it, "completely unfitted to a quiet life of hard work and simplicity." She became drawn and anxious, feeling great creative pressure from Donald who, she believed, had begun to scrutinize her writing habits. Mary Frances was particularly worried about young Anne, whom she worried had been "singed" by what she had "seen and heard and felt" living among battling parents.

Meanwhile, Mary Frances continued to suffer from panic and self-loathing, exacerbated by her failing marriage and Rex's poor health. She seemed particularly susceptible to critiques from these two important men in her life. As she interpreted it, they believed that she was "through, finished, washed up, incapable of sustained effort, and so on and so on." The destructive comments made Mary Frances prone to rage and sadness. Her productivity suffered; she fretted over every word and her work felt joyless.

Her fifth book, *Here Let Us Feast*, was published to good reviews in 1946. The book was a carefully assembled collection of hundreds of years of work by other writers on the topic of feasting and the fundamental need to eat, drink, and celebrate. Next, she began work on a translation of Jean Anthelme Brilliat-Savarin's *The Physiology of Taste*. A French lawyer and politician, Brillat-Savarin had penned a copious book of anecdotes and observations about gastronomy and the pleasures of dining. His sprawling work was published shortly before his death, in 1826. Mary Frances had been introduced to *The Physiology of Taste* when she lived in Dijon. She was deeply invested in the project and hoped it would be regarded as the best translation of the seminal work. But she also hoped that it would be a "summing up, a kind of distillation in a way, of all I have studied and felt about gastronomy in general and B-S's influence on it (and me) in particular."

After submitting the finished manuscript to the publisher, George Macy of The Heritage Press, she remarked that she was sure "no translation has ever been done more . . . thoughtfully or with more love . . . [My] attitude toward it is passionately maternal." After a lengthy dispute with her agent, Mary Pritchett, George Macy, and *Gourmet* magazine, the translation was published in book form in 1949.

After the dispute, Mary Frances signed with a new agent, Henry Volkening, hoping that the alliance would usher in a new phase in her career. She also hoped that *The Physiology of Taste* would mark a graceful farewell to her gastronomical writing. She was bolstered by the idea that the translation might be "the best thing remembered about me, fifty or a hundred years from now." She was ready for other topics.

She had always dabbled in fiction and dreamed up plot lines as a form of escape. While working on other, more serious projects, she had penned a novel titled *Not Now But Now*, which was published in 1947. But the book's tepid sales returned her to food writing. *An Alphabet for Gourmets*, a collection of essays written for *Gourmet*, was published in 1949. It and her other most beloved books, *Serve It Forth*, *Consider the Oyster*, *How to Cook a Wolf*, and *The Gastronomical Me*, were collected in a hefty tome, *The Art of Eating*, in 1954.

AFTER A PERIOD of separation and acrimony, Mary Frances and Donald divorced in 1950. Mary Frances moved to Whittier with Anne and Kennedy, and became Rex's daily caretaker. Edith had passed away after a long illness in 1949, and Rex's health was rapidly diminishing. He needed both the personal and professional help of his daughter, who increasingly helped manage the *Whittier News*.

Mary Frances suffered from what she called "dreadful flashes of panic" brought on by her family duties and the stresses of being the sole family's provider. She knew she was simply experiencing the familiar discontent of any woman of similar age and situation and tried to foster a "dull acceptance of an increasingly limited pattern: the three meals, the marketing, the two trips to the school." Yet she worried constantly and saw a psychologist, George Frumke, regularly.

In Frumke's office, and in the many letters she mailed to him, she worked to examine her ambivalence about M.F.K. Fisher, a literary persona she'd created yet wasn't sure she wanted to nurture. She had begun to realize that the more hastily and carelessly she wrote, the more quickly it seemed to be picked up and paid for. This fact did not, she said, "add to my respect for the present state of The Written Word." It also did not encourage her to devote real effort to her art during a time when she was experiencing a myriad of other stresses.

She wondered if she should "marry M.F.K. Fisher and retire with him-her-it to an ivory tower and turn out yearly masterpieces of unimportant prose?" But she worried that the famed voice would be hard to resurrect: "M.F.K. Fisher has been so thoroughly kicked around and neglected . . . I am quite probably afraid that there's little life left in her."

She still believed writing was essential to her character: "If I became a waitress or even a *vegetable* I would keep on writing, I believe." The challenge was melding her previous successes with the realities of her current existence.

After Rex died, in 1953, Mary Frances moved north to the Napa Valley. It was then dotted with small ranches that raised cattle or grew plums and walnuts. Family farms competed with the first post-Prohibition renegades. Mary Frances settled in the town of St. Helena, because she loved "wine country and the wine people. All I want to do besides help my daughters start out is to write some of the things I have in my head."

SHE WOULD NEVER marry again. In 1943, while pregnant with Anne, she told Larry Powell: "I don't know whether I'd be able to divorce my creative life, or my lover's from our physical one . . . and that of course complicates things. With Al, for instance, it made an inner war for him: he was vain enough to want his wife to appear very intelligent, and yet could not reconcile that wish with his basic desire to keep her on a purely physical relationship with him. With Dillwyn there was no war . . . we met on an unquestioning and equal basis sexually and creatively and as humans. That was mainly because he was the most matured person I've ever met . . . They are rare."

But meanwhile, Mary Frances's love affairs were many and great. In a letter written to her psychiatrist in 1953, she admitted, "About once a year my very old friend L. comes and mauls me about with mild success." L. was Larry Powell, who told Mary Frances in a letter written in 1991: "I suppose I have not loved you as much as I do now, except of course the magical summer of 1949 when love flowered and overflowed more yet more." Their love affair was the result of decades of attraction made real during periods when Mary Frances was isolated and unhappy, and Larry struggled through marital issues with his wife, Fay. At the end of the affair their close friendship always resumed, and toward the end of Mary Frances's life, the two became increasingly devoted. Larry told Norah that he had sixty years of correspondence that showed "We loved each other through it all."

Mary Frances also told Dr. Frumkes that she had had at least one very good sexual experience with a woman she had known for more than twenty years and that she "wouldn't protest if it happened again." Later, she had a more lasting love affair with Marietta Vorhees, a woman fourteen years her senior who was a teacher at St. Helena's high school. Arnold Gingrich, the founder and editor of *Esquire* magazine, was her final long-term companion.

Al Fisher ended his career as an English professor at Smith College in 1967. He married twice more after his divorce from Mary Frances, and enjoyed numerous clandestine love affairs with young women, many of whom were his students. One of his most famous pupils was Sylvia

Plath. The two were never lovers, but they were fond enough of each other's company for Plath to remark in her journal that she enjoyed the companionship of her professor who was "always harping, like senex amans ["old man" in Latin], on his first wife—'The one who wrote the cookbooks.'" He died unexpectedly in 1970, and Mary Frances found herself surprised by how much the news of his death affected her. "I wish he had died loving me, as I still do [love] him in many ways," she wrote. She acknowledged that she was "cruel to him, and he was unforgiving," and seemed sorry that as adults, well past the pains of their divorce, they had not been able to make amends.

Mary Frances's love affairs—some brief, others more lasting, with both men and women—were satisfying. But none was as fulfilling as her love for Tim, which endured for decades past his death. Nearly thirty years after his suicide, Mary Frances wrote, "My subconscious is still in an active grief for Dillwyn, and now and then it sweeps over me so that I am almost knocked to the ground for a few minutes . . . a strange experience and one I do not worry about. In fact, I am probably fortunate, to have known such experience." She was sure that if Tim hadn't died they would still be married.

M.F.K. Fisher died in Glen Ellen, California, at a white stucco home she called Last House, on June 22, 1992. She was eighty-three years old and had survived three husbands, all of her siblings but Norah, and many close friends. At the end of her life she suffered from Parkinson's disease. Yet even as her body slowed and stiffened, her mind remained sharp. She continued her rich correspondence with Larry Powell, and mined her past for stories about her childhood in Whittier, her early married life in Dijon, and current thoughts about the reality of aging.

IN THE INTRODUCTION to the British version of *The Art of Eating*, W. H. Auden said, "I do not know of anyone . . . who writes better prose." His words about M.F.K. Fisher are perhaps the most authentic analysis of her style. Although many people write about food and hunger, there are few who write about it well. Rarer still is a writer who composes prose with the precision and grace of M.F.K. Fisher. Her lines are imbued with poetry and philosophy.

As American interest in food and wine grew, M.F.K. Fisher had many literary successes and experienced a significant rise in fame. Her later writing is collected and well loved, but it is often her early works—*Serve It Forth, Consider the Oyster, How to Cook a Wolf, The Gastronomical Me*, and her translation of *The Physiology of Taste*—that are adored, dog-eared, stained with the deep red imprint of the base of a wineglass, kept on the favored part of the shelf, and returned to again and again.

It was her early work that established food writing as a genre and named M.F.K. Fisher as its queen. But it is the strength of her writing that keeps her from being dethroned. Simply put, there's still no one today who writes about the transcendental experience of eating and drinking better than M.F.K. Fisher. She forever changed how the world thinks, and writes, about food. Without her, our Puritan ancestry might have defined our tastes. But in our current obsessive food culture, ruled by celebrity and gluttony, M.F.K. Fisher is also a voice of restraint. She considered her philosophy about food writing to be simple. As she noted in the introduction to *The Gastronomical Me*: When I write of hunger, I am really writing about love and the hunger for it, and warmth and the love of it and the hunger for it . . . and then the warmth and the richness and fine reality of hunger satisfied . . . and it is all one. I tell about myself, and how I ate bread on a lasting hillside, or drank red wine in a room now blown to bits, and it happens without my willing it that I am telling too about the people with me then, and their other deeper needs for love and happiness."

It was not only talent but experiences that shaped her, that made her pick food, wine, and lovers. She knew this, and she built a career telling tales of her mythical meals in places local and far-flung to a widening and ever-hungry circle of devoted fans.

In her later years, Mary Frances found herself a part of a crowd of culinary legends that included Julia Child and James Beard. Yet she differed distinctly from these luminaries. Child and Beard taught people how to cook; M.F.K. Fisher believed good food was a way to abundantly enjoy life.

She saw her early work widely anthologized. Her current work, which she churned out regularly, fetched premium value. She wrote many more books and countless articles, and editors and authors clamored for her to compose forewords, introductions, or back cover praise for the books of the culinary and literary voices she had influenced. There were numerous awards and accolades.

She reveled in the acclaim. She returned to France to live several times, both with and without her daughters. Regardless of her traveling companions, each trip was filled with a few solitary moments, moments that validated her experience as a woman who traveled, dined, and lived alone. Through those ventures, Mary Frances affirmed that France was truly her spiritual home. "I am more me in France," she wrote. "I'm more awake, more aware . . . Every minute is more of a minute there."

IN APRIL 1971, M.F.K. Fisher moved to Last House, having gently suggested to David Pleydell-Bouverie, a wealthy, sociable Brit, that she'd like to spend her final decades at his sprawling ranch. He agreed to help her design and build a home on his land. It still sits several hundred yards from Highway 12, a narrow road that winds through California wine country, connecting the towns of Sonoma and Glen Ellen. Potential visitors won't find much; the ranch, along with Last House, are part of an expansive nature preserve that is closed to the public.

For the last two decades of her life, Mary Frances ruled from Last House, entertaining legions of friends and fans who made regular pilgrimages to the culinary grande dame. In early autumn, the road is bordered by a golden sea of dried grass. Tiny burrs attach their small tufted hooks to anything soft: denim, cotton, skin. In the distance, dark green hills loom and the sky gleams, its blueness obstructed only by the occasional wisp of cloud.

An antique sign pitched at the foot of her driveway reads BOUVERIE RANCH in skinny, handpainted, white letters. Below it, in smaller script, are the words TRESPASSERS ~ WILL ~ BE ~ VIOLATED. The sign, bordered by a perky row of small black-and-white triangles, is topped by the roughly rendered outline of the Bouverie family crest.

At first glance, the sign is welcoming, the top line reminiscent of a hospitable entrance to a country inn. But beneath it, harder to see, is the stern intention to harm. Just like the sign at the foot of her driveway, M.F.K. Fisher, the woman and literary persona, beckoned and then pushed back gently. She wrote in a way that only she could, her style forged by a sensuous, yet solitary nature, which allowed her to write with aplomb about complex dualities. Eating, for instance, was communal yet private. It was ordinary yet often exceedingly delightful. There were some appetites that even the most magnificent meals couldn't feed.

M.F.K. Fisher's lifelong hungers defined her. Her desire for food, for love, and for attention of any kind, was relentless. Food helped her understand the world: "And with our gastronomical growth will come, inevitably, knowledge and perception of a hundred other things, but mainly of ourselves," she wrote in *How to Cook a Wolf*.

Her work is prized for being evocative, tales so indulgent, they read like fiction. And in some ways, they are. The tantalizing descriptions of unforgettable dinners often hid hardship and misery. But whatever the circumstances, both M.F.K. Fisher and Mary Frances Kennedy lived and ate extravagantly. And well.

ACKNOWLEDGMENTS

*I*FIRST MET THE man who would become my agent, Robert Lescher, at Manhattan's Gramercy Tavern one February afternoon to discuss M.F.K. Fisher and book writing. Sure that he would never take me seriously, I had wooed him: a handwritten note, a collection of essays, a jar of homemade strawberry jam. He called to tell me that he preferred raspberry jam, but not just any raspberry jam—golden raspberry jam. It was the first of many challenges that led, finally, to a book I am most excited, and proud, to share with him.

Others helped too. Kennedy Friede Golden offered gracious friendship, access to private journals and letters, and decades of family photos. Her commitment to this project and to the legacy of her mother, M.F.K. Fisher, has been amazing.

My team at Counterpoint Press was topnotch: Laura Mazer elegantly shepherded the book through every stage of production; Jack Shoemaker was thoughtful, wise, and attentive to my every query. And to publisher Charlie Winton: Thank you for noticing my own extravagant hunger.

Bob Ickes was a superlative book cheerleader and, more important, a fantastic editor. Laura Parker painted a portrait of tangerines that breathtakingly evokes the ripe fruit M.F.K. Fisher toasted on the radiator in Strasbourg.

I am fortunate to have received enthusiastic help from librarians and staff at The Arthur and Elizabeth Schlesinger Library on the History of Women in America, the Mortimer Rare Book Room at Smith College, and the Charles E. Young Research Library at UCLA. Thanks also to Dr. Susan Cayleff, for gracious instruction and mentoring, and to the San Francisco Writer's Grotto for an encouraging writing environment.

Amber Loeffelbein Fries and Sylla McClellan edited early versions of the book, their voices critical yet kind. The Matthay family offered retreats in Pt. Reyes and Paris, spots where many pages were written. Amy Axtell and Beverly Archer Miears offered beds, meals, and conversation in Cambridge, Massachusetts.

I wouldn't be me without Whitney Schubert Gauger, Les Filles, and the Oregon Crew: Our many meals, drinks, and laughs were the real inspiration for this book. And to Sean Tumoana Finney, poet, editor, and epiphany maker: Everything shines brighter thanks to you.

Finally, To my parents, Guy and Mary Zimmerman, and my brother, Patrick: There aren't enough words to hold my love and appreciation.

Thank you, thank you, thank you.

Author's Note

I HAD ALWAYS BELIEVED that there was more to M.F.K. Fisher's life than the stories she told in her autobiographical books and essays. Her writings about food—so ripe and evocative—felt tempered by sadness. Indeed, she reminded me of a beautiful, slightly bruised piece of fruit. This hunch led me, in 2007, to the Schlesinger Library on the History of Women in America, on the campus of Harvard University. The Cambridge winter kept me happily indoors, poring over nearly 150 file boxes. Their contents brimmed with possibility: M.F.K. Fisher's many hundreds of letters, plus personal papers, journals, manuscripts, and other ephemera.

In that first and five subsequent visits to the library, I sought her silences. I believed, for instance, that what Mary Frances didn't say about her first husband, Al Fisher, and their life in Dijon revealed far more than her books did about her chronicling of human hungers.

I was right. As I began writing this book, the Schlesinger library helped me prove, again and again, that Mary Frances's marriage to Alfred Young Fisher was unhappy from the start. That disappointment, coupled with loneliness and overwhelming creative energy, helped birth her literary voice, rich with longing.

My journey didn't end there. I visited the Mortimer Rare Book Room at Smith College, in Northampton, Massachusetts, along with the Charles E. Young Research Library at UCLA, chasing more thorough portraits of Al and Lawrence Clark Powell. What I found proved Al's ambivalence toward his wife—and how Powell filled the void. I also traveled to France and Switzerland, following Mary Frances's path from Paris to Dijon to Strasbourg, and then to Vevey, Switzerland.

During my third visit to the Schlesinger library, in September 2009, I discovered startling information about M.F.K. Fisher's second husband, Tim Parrish, and his terminal illness. I corroborated this data through the expertise of Guy A. Zimmerman, a physician and professor of internal medicine. He helped examine medical files and personal papers, and explain complex medical issues. I also interviewed Gloria Stuart about her recollections of Mary Frances's early love affairs.

Access to other private letters and photos proved crucial to understanding her emotional landscape. These papers—not housed in any library—were a rich and poignant gift from M.F.K. Fisher's daughter, Kennedy Friede.

Below I have noted, by category, the sources that fueled my research, along with a precise accounting of where and how they are referenced throughout *An Extravagant Hunger*.

—A.Z.

BIBLIOGRAPHY AND SOURCES

ARCHIVES

The private papers and photographs of M.F.K. Fisher, July 2010

Mary Frances Kennedy Fisher Papers. Schlesinger Library, Radcliffe Institute, Harvard University. February 2007, February 2009, September 2009, February 2010, May 2010

Al Fisher Archive, Mortimer Rare Book Room, Smith College, Northampton, Massachusetts: March 2010

Lawrence Clark Powell Collection, Charles E. Young Research Library, University of California, Los Angeles, Los Angeles, California: April 2009

BOOKS BY M.F.K. FISHER

An Alphabet for Gourmets

Among Friends

The Art of Eating: Five Gastronomical Works

As They Were

The Boss Dog: A Story

The Cooking of Provincial France

Consider the Oyster

A Considerable Town

A Cordiall Water: A Garland of Odd & Old Receipts to Assuage the Ills of Man & Beast

Dubious Honors

The Gastronomical Me

Here Let Us Feast: A Book of Banquets

How to Cook a Wolf

Last House: Reflections, Dreams, and Observations, 1943-1991

Long Ago in France: The Years in Dijon

Map of Another Town: A Memoir of Provence

M.F.K. Fisher, a Life in Letters: Correspondence, 1929-1991

Not Now But Now

The Physiology of Taste, or Meditations on Transcendental Gastronomy

Serve it Forth

Sister Age

Stay Me Oh Comfort Me: Journals and Stories, 1933-1941

The Story of Wine in California

To Begin Again: Stories and Memoirs, 1908-1929

Two Towns in Provence

With Bold Knife and Fork

BOOKS BY OTHER AUTHORS

Conversations with M.F.K. Fisher, by David Lazar

Poet of the Appetites: The Lives and Loves of M.F.K. Fisher, by Joan Reardon

ADDITIONAL BOOK SOURCES

Fortune and Friendship, by Lawrence Clark Powell

I Just Kept Hoping, by Gloria Stuart

Material Dreams: Southern California Through the 1920s, by Kevin Starr

The Unabridged Journals of Sylvia Plath, by Karen Kukil

Women of the Left Bank, by Shari Benstock

INTERVIEWS

Gloria Stuart, May 2009

Guy A. Zimmerman, M.D., ongoing correspondence regarding Tim Parrish's medical issues

NOTES

CHAPTER 2: THE ART OF KNOWING YOURSELF

40   "one after another": Al Fisher Archive, Smith College

41   "burning look": Al Fisher Archive, Smith College

41   "anywhere at all": *Conversations with M.F.K. Fisher*

42   "off-campus romance": *The Journals of M.F.K. Fisher*

42   it was, instead, "something": *Conversations with M.F.K. Fisher*

43   "freed pigeon": *To Begin Again*

43   "hopeless": private papers and photographs of M.F.K. Fisher

43   he dallied: Al Fisher Archive, Smith College

CHAPTER 3: READY, AT LAST, TO LIVE

46   "sanely and well": *The Journals of M.F.K. Fisher*

46   "myself as a newborn": *The Journals of M.F.K. Fisher*

46   everything she had imagined: *The Gastronomical Me*

49   "The hot chocolate": *The Gastronomical Me*

49   "made Al depart": Schlesinger library

49   "Oz to us": Schlesinger library

50   "gossiped": Schlesinger library

50   "could not bring myself": *Dubious Honors*

51   "ever dreamed of": Schlesinger library

51   "blindfolded": Schlesinger library

CHAPTER 4: A CHARMED GASTRONOMIC CIRCLE

54   "started to grow up": Schlesinger library

54   "veritable palace": Schlesinger library

54   "so amazing": Schlesinger library

55   "avid curiosity": *The Gastronomical Me*

56   "far shores": *The Gastronomical Me*

56   "this French food": Schlesinger library

57   "brittle or salty": Schlesinger library

57   "bright yellow spaghetti": Schlesinger library

58   Drinking was "the best": Schlesinger library

59   "read or write": Schlesinger library

59   "rather dull": Schlesinger library

59   "state of unconsciousness": Schlesinger library

59   "positively hated him": Schlesinger library

59   "I hope it lasts": private papers and photographs of M.F.K. Fisher

60   "specialized loneliness": Al Fisher Archive, Smith College

60   She thought of food: private papers and photographs of M.F.K. Fisher

60   "[c]heap novels": private papers and photographs of M.F.K. Fisher

61   "Perhaps he will": private papers and photographs of M.F.K. Fisher

61   "All my life": private papers and photographs of M.F.K. Fisher

61   "forgotten me": private papers and photographs of M.F.K. Fisher

61   "bliss and mild monotony": Schlesinger library

62   was a virgin: Schlesinger library

62   sexual chemistry: Al Fisher Archive, Smith College

62   act of sex: Schlesinger library

62   refused to sleep with her: Schlesinger library

62   women as objects: Al Fisher Archive, Smith College

63   "perfectly splendid": Schlesinger library

63   "keep up a pretense": Schlesinger library "Lord of Creation": Schlesinger library

64   "Write to me": Schlesinger library

64   "privileged by his sex": Schlesinger library

65   "petted daughter": Al Fisher Archive, Smith College

65   "not behaving": Al Fisher Archive, Smith College

66   "real happiness": *The Journals of M.F.K. Fisher*

66   "hurts like everything": Schlesinger library

67   heated conversation: Schlesinger library

68   She told Edith: Schlesinger library

68:   "really quite nice": Schlesinger library

68   became "morbid": Schlesinger library

69   She dreaded: Schlesinger library

69   "exactly the kind of life": *M.F.K. Fisher: A Life in Letters*

70   "broodish": Schlesinger library

70   In London: Schlesinger library

71   "saw beautiful things": Schlesinger library

71   "a private me": Schlesinger library

72   first wedding anniversary: Schlesinger library

CHAPTER 5: LETTERS AND LONELINESS

74   "shock a flea": Schlesinger library

75   "plan for a poem": Lawrence Clark Powell Collection, UCLA

76   dared to envision: Lawrence Clark Powell Collection, UCLA

76   "preconceived ideas": private papers and photographs of M.F.K. Fisher

76   "well and happy": Lawrence Clark Powell Collection, UCLA

76   "I have to clamor": Schlesinger library

77   "quiet as a wraith": private papers and photographs of M.F.K. Fisher

78   "turn numb": private papers and photographs of M.F.K. Fisher

78   "unreservedly sensual": *The Gastronomical Me*

78   "whorls and swoops": *The Gastronomical Me*

79   "I was too shy": Schlesinger library

79   "smooth round tomatoes": private papers and photographs of M.F.K. Fisher

80   "happily the night was dark": Schlesinger library

80   "We both decided": Schlesinger library

80   "most perfect trip": Schlesinger library

80   "quite completely silly": Schlesinger library

80   "Best love": Lawrence Clark Powell Collection, UCLA

81   "watch me today": Schlesinger library

81   "It's very chic": Schlesinger library

82   "race for the beach": Schlesinger library

82   Mary Frances found the news: Schlesinger library

82   "hurt my feelings": Schlesinger library

82   "So you've decided": Schlesinger library

83   "Why on earth": Schlesinger library

84   "Doesn't it sound perfect?": Schlesinger library

85   "But I can't ignore": Schlesinger library

85   second or third Kennedy: Schlesinger library

86   "inhumanely busy": Schlesinger library

86   "unloosened enough": Schlesinger library

87   reputable boarding school: Schlesinger library

88   even more anxious: Schlesinger library

CHAPTER 6: THE PAIN OF ABSENCE

89   "The great event": Schlesinger library

89   "Is MF really back?": Schlesinger library

90   "feelings of betrayal": *The Journals of M.F.K. Fisher*

90   "studying, drinking, smoking": *Fortune and Friendship*

90   "crazy with grief": Schlesinger library

90   Al described his poem: Lawrence Clark Powell Collection, UCLA

90   "the sailing of my wife": Al Fisher Archive, Smith College

91   "my heart was being torn out": Schlesinger library

91   "my own grief": Schlesinger library

92   Norah was lazy: Schlesinger library

93   "You can't imagine": Schlesinger library

93   "What I saw": *The Gastronomical Me*

94   "We eat just what we like": Schlesinger library

94   "so reduced to vegetables": Schlesinger library

94   "slow voluptuous concentration": Schlesinger library

95   "Al and Lawrence planned books": *The Gastronomical Me*

95   "not wildly enthusiastic": Schlesinger library

95   "I'm quite shameless": Schlesinger library

96   "didn't regret": Schlesinger library

97   "we were in love": *The Gastronomical Me*

97   "This last lap": Schlesinger library

98   "hated to spend time cooking": Schlesinger library

98   "my fur coat": *The Gastronomical Me*

99   "child of luxury": Schlesinger library

99   "I want to thank you": Schlesinger library

100   "It's cold as hell": Schlesinger library

101   "hell of a housekeeper": Schlesinger library

101   "It does seem more reasonable": Schlesinger library

102   "I'm so beaming with comfort": Schlesinger library

102   "Nothing makes me as furious": Schlesinger library

103   "go on forever": Schlesinger library

103   "I want to work": Schlesinger library

103   "while the money lasts": Schlesinger library

104   "It's all my fault": Schlesinger library

106   "withdrawn and interpretive state": *Fortune and Friendship*

106   fearful of what might occur: *M.F.K. Fisher: A Life in Letters*

107   "We hate to leave": Schlesinger library

107   "much less shy": *The Gastronomical Me*

108   "the ship rolled": *The Gastronomical Me*

CHAPTER 7: DEPRESSION

111 "ate, slept, bathed": Schlesinger library

112 sapped the energy: Schlesinger library

113 digging ditches: Schlesinger library

113 Their private life: Schlesinger library

114 want to touch him: Schlesinger library

115 "see the pen writing them": Schlesinger library

116 "like a virus": Schlesinger library

119 "stiff and dulled": Schlesinger library

119 "We're sinking": Schlesinger library

120 "erratically lovely": Schlesinger library

120 personal devastation: Schlesinger library

121 "frowns slightly": Schlesinger library

122 "smelled so good": Schlesinger library

123 "unprepared for adultery": Schlesinger library

124 "Suddenly I told him": *Poet of the Appetites: The Lives and Loves of M.F.K. Fisher*

125 "I've written to Timmy": Schlesinger library

126 "too many books": Schlesinger library

126 "fools to get a child?": Schlesinger library

126 "withstand any torture": Schlesinger library

127 "fairly good body": Schlesinger library

CHAPTER 8: UNSPEAKABLE THOUGHTS

129 "keeping quiet": *The Gastronomical Me*

129 "astonishment and chagrin": Schlesinger library

129 "rest of my life": *The Gastronomical Me*

130 "marshmallow salads": *The Gastronomical Me*

130 "greatly worried": Schlesinger library

131 navy blue: private papers and photographs of M.F. Fisher

131 "cold moonlight": *The Gastronomical Me*

132 "can't figure Dillwyn and me out": private papers and photographs of M.F.K. Fisher

132 "whipped cream": *The Gastronomical Me*

134 springtime afternoon: Schlesinger library

135 "I'm distracted inside": Schlesinger library

136 lit the fireplace: Schlesinger library

136 "in your arms": Schlesinger library

CHAPTER 9: THE EDGE OF RIPENESS

CHAPTER 10: A PENDULUM OF DESIRE

168   But the recommendation: my ongoing correspondence with Guy A. Zimmerman, M.D.

169   "right side of hysteria": Schlesinger library

170   "moving and moaning": Schlesinger library

170   "demands of suffering": Schlesinger library

171   "wounded dragon": Schlesinger library

171   "I really wonder": Schlesinger library

171   "feeling of unfulfillment": Schlesinger library

173   "cruel web of clinics": *The Gastronomical Me*

174   Written in 1940: Schlesinger library

174   sexual pleasure increased: private papers and photographs of M.F.K. Fisher

175   operated again: Schlesinger library

175   "bad piece of pie": Schlesinger library

176   Palm Springs, California: *M.F.K. Fisher: A Life in Letters*

176   "immune to everything": *The Gastronomical Me*

177   "drank and ate": *The Gastronomical Me*

179   "small wracked man": *The Gastronomical Me*

CHAPTER 11: LANDSCAPE OF LOVE AND SORROW

183   Mary Frances had yet to hear: Schlesinger library

183   "the jig will pretty well be up": Schlesinger library

183   "What can I do?": Schlesinger library

184   Tim had talked of suicide: Schlesinger library

184   "No drugs": Schlesinger library

184   "I swear by Christ crucified": Schlesinger library

185   "strange noise": Schlesinger library

185   "I know how to kill T.": Schlesinger library

185   "Maybe I am wrong": Schlesinger library

185   "mad pace": *M.F.K. Fisher: A Life in Letters*

186   "I wish I had not read it": Schlesinger library

187   buy a car: Schlesinger library

188   "good" amputations: Schlesinger library

188   "proved further surgery was useless": Schlesinger library

189   "a quicker death": Schlesinger library

189   "we regret bitterly": Schlesinger library

189   "no cigarettes": Schlesinger library

189   Their instructions: Schlesinger library

CHAPTER 12: THE COLOR OF MOURNING

CHAPTER 13: A PLACE IN THE WORLD

211   "Blackout Lessons": Schlesinger library

211   "We will be stronger": Schlesinger library

212   "strong grief": Schlesinger library

213   "one of very few": private papers and photographs of M.F.K. Fisher

214   A feature about her: Schlesinger library

215   "very good affairs": Schlesinger library

215   "I have often eaten an egg": *Alphabet for Gourmets,* as collected in *The Art of Eating*

215   She came to believe: *Alphabet for Gourmets,* as collected in *The Art of Eating*

216   she had written too fast: *Conversations with M.F.K. Fisher*

216   She usually had a glass or two: *Alphabet for Gourmets,* as collected in *The Art of Eating*

217   "complete folly": Schlesinger library

217   "Someone knows the truth": Schlesinger library

217   "a very fine newspaper man": Schlesinger library

218   A note scrawled: Schlesinger library

218   filled with drawings of men: Schlesinger library

218   "waiting on the whims": *M.F.K. Fisher: A Life in Letters*

218   might be leaving Hollywood: *M.F.K. Fisher: A Life in Letters*

218   "sitting close to a volcano": *M.F.K. Fisher: A Life in Letters*

219   "somewhere in the blue": Schlesinger library

220   "the first thing I've ever written": *M.F.K. Fisher: A Life in Letters*

220   She told Larry: *M.F.K. Fisher: A Life in Letters*

220   "a hell of a discouraging business": *M.F.K. Fisher: A Life in Letters*

220   Dr. Bieler induced delivery: *The Journals of M.F.K. Fisher*

221   Rex reported: Schlesinger library

222   "Now and then": *M.F.K. Fisher: A Life in Letters*

222   "My life seems full": *M.F.K. Fisher: A Life in Letters*

222   "Please try": Schlesinger library

222   "I like this book": Schlesinger library

223   "chockfull of life": Schlesinger library

223   "cruel family": Schlesinger library

224   "passed beyond": Schlesinger library

224   "courage and devotion": Schlesinger library

224   "We shared a lot": Schlesinger library

EPILOGUE

INDEX